Christian Understandings of the
Trinity

Christian

Understandings of the Trinity

The Historical Trajectory

Veli-Matti Kärkkäinen

Fortress Press
Minneapolis

Contents

Abbreviations

ANF   *The Ante-Nicene Fathers: Translations of the Writings of the Fathers Down to a.d. 325.* 9 vols. Edited by Alexander Roberts and James Donaldson, et al. Edinburgh, 1885–1897 (public domain; available at http://www.ccel.org)

NPNF[1]   *A Select Library of the Nicene and Post-Nicene Fathers of the Christian Church.* First Series. 14 vols. Edited by Philip Schaff. Edinburgh, 1886–1880 (public domain; available at http://www.ccel.org)

NPNF[2]   *A Select Library of the Nicene and Post-Nicene Fathers of the Christian Church.* Second Series. 14 vols. Edited by Philip Schaff and Henry Wace. Edinburgh, 1886–1880 (public domain; available at http://www.ccel.org)

All references to and citations from the patristic writings come from these standard sources, unless otherwise indicated. A number of other historical writings are also available at http://www.ccel.org (and will be so noted if referred to in this book).

Introduction

It was no lesser a figure than theologian Karl Barth who set forth the statement that the "doctrine of the Trinity is what basically distinguishes the Christian doctrine of God as Christian, and therefore what already distinguishes the Christian concept of revelation as Christian, in contrast to all other possible doctrines of God or concepts of revelation."[1] If he was right, this means that a primary and foundational task for any serious theologian-to-be or an enlightened layperson would be to gain a basic mastery of the meaning, content, and significance of the doctrine of the Trinity. While there is a host of other doctrines and topics to be grappled with, few would question the primacy of the distinctively *Christian* understanding of God as Father, Son, and Spirit.

If a brief description were needed as a way of introduction for the potential reader regarding the nature and goal of this little book, something like the following statement, borrowed from theologian Stephen Holmes, would be as accurate as any:

> This book is on a big-picture scale, necessarily. Covering in one brief volume two thousand years of debate over what is possibly the central topic of Christian devotion, together with the necessary biblical background, means that at every turn I have obscured details of debates, offered impressionistic sketches of complex positions, and otherwise done violence to scholarly ideals.[2]

1

Even with the "big picture" in mind, without having the luxury of turning over every stone on the long and winding road of the evolving trinitarian doctrine, one has to parse over details and aim at general accuracy. Hence, this account includes rather detailed documentation to serve the needs of the advanced student or the curious.

Furthermore, in order to lay out the landscape of a complex and multilayered terrain, even a basic textbook has to pay attention to the multiplicity of sources and resources. The important advice from the eminent Roman Catholic Jesuit theologian Gerald O'Collins is spot on. He reminds us that should we wish to acquire a comprehensive and dynamic picture of the meaning, significance, and developments of the trinitarian doctrine, "Christian believers have the task of looking at and drawing on three distinct, if interrelated, areas: (1) the historical experience of salvation which the scriptures record and which the teachers in the church have interpreted through the centuries; (2) the testimony of public worship; and (3) the experience of practicing discipleship today."[3]

Regrettably, the limited scope of this short primer does not allow for a full exploration of all of these three types of resources. My main focus will be on the first aspect, namely biblical sources of the doctrine of the Trinity as well as the creedal pronouncements and theological constructions the church's theologians have proposed throughout the centuries. Furthermore, I will be making a concerted effort to delve into some experiences and sources having to do with public and private spiritual life and discipleship, including charismatic experiences and visions.

It goes without saying that because of the nature of this short book as a primer, no constructive task will be attempted here (such an attempt can be found in the second book of my five-volume series, *Trinity and Revelation: A Constructive Christian Theology for the Pluralistic World* [Eerdmans, 2014, Part II]). Nor is it my goal to reconstruct—let alone to challenge the "main-line" scholarly opinion regarding—the historical reading of the trinitarian doctrine.[4] Even for a professional historian, that kind of reconstruction would require special expertise—and I am systematician, after all. Rather, I trust that after so much scholarly ink has been spent on documenting and interpreting trinitarian history, its main contours are well known and reliable enough to be trusted, and communicated to the new generation of theologians and other interested readers.

If there is any little constructive—or perhaps at least novel—element in this primer, it is the space devoted to the charismatic and mystical *experiences* of the Holy Spirit among the people of God. That conscious choice is based on the firm conviction that, with every Christian doctrinal topic, the spiritual experience of the church has to be consulted as an important guide toward a better understanding; and that this is even more the case with this particular theme.

The reader will notice, that throughout the narrative of the development of the doctrine of the Trinity, direct citations from key historical theologians are inserted in the text (and at times, in the footnotes). This is intentional, in order to make it possible for the reader to have firsthand access to the actual writings on which the theological interpretation is based. Even when textbooks such as this one contain detailed, meticulous documentation concerning the historical sources, it is not realistic to expect that the reader has time to delve into those sources during the reading process. Hopefully, the presence of frequent citations from historical figures helps students and other interested persons to both appreciate the theological wisdom of our forebears and inspire them later to dig into this rich spiritual wellspring.

The plan of the book is simple and straightforward. Following the introduction, chapter 1 delves into the biblical background and sources of what became the fully established trinitarian doctrine during the first few hundred years and beyond. While no technical trinitarian doctrine was yet available in the biblical canon, nor even in the New Testament (NT), the deep and wide trinitarian experience of God as Father, Son, and Spirit gave impetus to and called for an intellectual clarification. The second chapter, the longest one, seeks to provide a fairly detailed account of the long and winding road of the development of the *doctrine* of the Trinity in patristic theology, culminating in the authoritative ecumenical Nicene-Constantinopolitan Creed (381) and the many debates and clarifications around it. Since the history of the first three centuries particularly is focused on the clarification of the Father–Son relationship, with much less attention to the role and nature of the Spirit, chapter 3 will continue the patristic and creedal reflections with the accent on pneumatology. Only with the final establishment of the deity and equality of the Holy Spirit in relation to the Son and Father was a full-fledged, distinctively Christian *trinitarian* doctrine made possible.

After the patristic era (roughly speaking, beginning from the sixth century or so), I stand back somewhat from a consideration of historical-theological details, and the "big picture" approach finally takes the upper hand. The millennium-long era of medieval experiences and doctrinal developments both in the Greek-speaking Eastern church and Latin-speaking Western church will be the subject of chapter 4. Chapter 5 touches selectively on some important Reformation and modern developments, reconstructions, and challenges. Chapter 6 opens the windows into the rich and variegated twentieth- and twenty-first-century renaissance of trinitarian reflection, although the many details of that story itself are left to other works (such as my *The Trinity: Global Perspectives* [Westminster John Knox Press, 2007]).

In line with the desire to keep in a dynamic balance the intellectual-doctrinal and spiritual-charismatic approaches as parallel avenues toward theological understanding, comes the precious advice from Gregory of Nazianzus. One of the three famous Cappadocians from the fourth century, Gregory begins his five-part *Theological Orations* with words worth hearing in this introduction to a textbook claiming to present a doctrine of God:

> Not to every one, my friends, does it belong to philosophize about God; not to every one; the Subject is not so cheap and low; and I will add, not before every audience, nor at all times, nor

on all points; but on certain occasions, and before certain persons, and within certain limits. Not to all men, because it is permitted only to those who have been examined, and are passed masters in meditation, and who have been previously purified in soul and body, or at the very least are being purified. For the impure to touch the pure is, we may safely say, not safe, just as it is unsafe to fix weak eyes upon the sun's rays. And what is the permitted occasion? It is when we are free from all external defilement or disturbance, and when that which rules within us is not confused with vexatious or erring images; like persons mixing up good writing with bad, or filth with the sweet odours of unguents. For it is necessary to be truly at leisure to know God; and when we can get a convenient season, to discern the straight road of the things divine. And who are the permitted persons? They to whom the subject is of real concern, and not they who make it a matter of pleasant gossip, like any other thing, after the races, or the theatre, or a concert, or a dinner, or still lower employments. To such men as these, idle jests and pretty contradictions about these subjects are a part of their amusement.[5]

This book owes its existence to the graceful and firm invitation by "The Fortress Historical Trajectories Series" general editor, Professor Denis R. Janz. His enthusiasm, guidance, and mentorship helped shape the content and approach of the book more than I am able to express with these few words of gratitude. In the final phase of the editing of the manuscript, Dr. Janz spent countless hours in helping translate my academic text into a reader-friendly (American) English narrative. Blessed is the author who receives such a superb guidance and assistance! I also owe a big thank you to my Fuller Theological Seminary doctoral student David Muthukumar, of India, who devoted a great number of hours to double-checking the accuracy of all references and notes. Finally, the indexes were compiled by another doctoral student of mine, Viktor Toth.

Notes

1. Karl Barth, *Church Dogmatics*, ed. G. W. Bromiley and T. F. Torrance (Edinburgh: T&T Clark, 1956), I/1:301. Likewise, A. W. Argyle notes that God is not specifically "named" in the New Testament; Argyle, *God in the New Testament* (Philadelphia: J. B. Lippincott, 1965), 9.

2. Stephen R. Holmes, *The Quest for the Trinity: The Doctrine of God in Scripture, History, and Modernity* (Downers Grove, IL: InterVarsity, 2012), xv.

3. Gerald O'Collins, *The Tripersonal God: Understanding and Interpreting the Trinity* (Mahwah, NJ: Paulist, 1999), 1–2.

4. That challenge is set forth vigorously in Holmes, *Quest for the Trinity*. His bold and contested thesis is no less radical than this: "In brief, I argue that the explosion of theological work claiming to recapture the doctrine of the Trinity that we have witnessed in recent decades in fact misunderstands and distorts the traditional doctrine so badly that it is unrecognizable" (xv). While I have benefited from that book's learned historical discussion, for the sake of the current primary there is no need—nor space—to assess its "newness" and whether its challenge to almost all written in recent decades about trinitarian theology is justified or balanced.

5. Gregory of Nazianzus, *Oration 27. The First Theological Oration. A Preliminary Discourse Against the Eunomians*, #3, NPNF[2] 7:285.

1

The Christian Trinity: Biblical Antecedents

No Trinity in the Bible?

For the Christian who inquires into the meaning and sources of the doctrine of the Trinity, it is most natural to "begin from the scriptures and their testimony to the tripersonal God."[1] Where else would one turn to? All Christian traditions agree in principle that the Bible is the highest and most authoritative source of doctrine and faith. That said, it sounds curious at best and perhaps semi-heretical at worst that one of the few commonly shared convictions among both biblical and doctrinal theologians concerning the Trinity is that the doctrine itself cannot be found in the Bible. This statement seems to apply first and foremost to (what Christians name as) the Old Testament (OT). What does this mean? What are the implications for our topic? To point out this scholarly consensus is not to deny the obvious fact that in some real sense, even the OT "contains, in anticipation, categories used to express and elaborate the doctrine of the Trinity."[2] And even more, that therefore "a theology of the Trinity that ignores or plays down the OT can only be radically deficient."[3] It is just to state the obvious, namely that although the doctrine may be able to claim biblical support in light of its *later* creedal and theological development, the Trinity is unknown in the first part of the Scripture; and even in the second part, Father, Son, and Spirit appear somewhat abruptly, and despite their ubiquitous presence everywhere on the NT pages, their interrelations, origin, and roles remain undeveloped.

For precritical Christian exegesis and theology, this state of affairs did not appear to be a problem. Even when early theologians acknowledged the underdeveloped nature of OT faith before the coming of the Messiah, they discerned traces, patterns, and even teachings regarding the Trinity throughout the pages of the OT. Typical "prooftexts" included Genesis 1:26 ("Let *us* make"), which current exegesis regards as an example of plurality of majesty (not unlike the royal pronouncements in the form of "We declare . . ."); the Isaianic threefold "Holy, holy, holy" exclamation (6:1); and the theophanies (divine manifestations) of the "Angel of Yahweh" in Genesis 18 and elsewhere, traditionally interpreted as preincarnation appearances of the second person of the Trinity. Among the church fathers whose way of doing trinitarian theology was deeply and widely founded in Scripture[4] (in contrast to common later prejudice, according to which early creeds were primarily worked out on the basis of "secular" philosophical resources), various other kinds of OT teachings and materials played an important role and often appeared in sophisticated theological debates. Especially important was the Wisdom theme found in the book of Proverbs (particularly in chapter 8) and other writings belonging to the same genre; this will be looked at in some detail in the following section. Many other OT passages played a crucial role in patristic debates and controversies. Just think of Isaiah 53, a passage universally interpreted as messianic and thus related to Jesus the Christ. Similarly, from the book of Psalms a number of christological and trinitarian lessons were drawn, most often from the so-called Royal Psalms; they were not seen to be only about David but also of the heavenly David's son. Also noteworthy is that what at times appears to be a miniscule detail in the inspired text seemed to settle this controversial issue.[5]

Not surprisingly, contemporary scholarship does not agree with these and related approaches. At their best, so it is argued, these kinds of prooftexts may give an indication of the *idea* of plurality in God, but they are hardly sufficient to establish any kind of doctrine of the triune God. Not only that, but questions such as these emerge: Why not a binitarian or quadrilateral view of God? It is also to be noted that the NT does not consider the OT view of God as "underdeveloped," for the simple reason that the God of the NT is also that of the OT. In other words, the "God of Jesus is none other than the God of Jewish faith. . . . He is the God of Abraham, Isaac, and Jacob (Matt 12:26–27), the God whom Israel confesses in the *shema* of Deuteronomy 6:4 (Mark 12:29)."[6] In that light, we need to acknowledge not only that the roots of the NT doctrine of God are to be looked for in the OT, but also that the NT presupposes the teaching about God as explicated in the OT.[7]

For these and related reasons, contemporary theology has taken a different approach to considering the relation of the OT to Trinity. This has meant revisiting and revising some canons of theological scholarship:

> It used to be the conventional wisdom of New Testament scholars that predication of a divine nature to Jesus came about as a result of the impact of Hellenistic culture outside Israel and the ideas that culture had about the Divine. The assumption was that early Jews in tune with their monotheistic language would not use such language of anyone but Yahweh. The oneness of God ruled out speaking of multiple persons in the Godhead.[8]

At the same time, contemporary theology attempts to do full justice to the teachings of the OT on their own Jewish terms, before "baptizing" them into a NT understanding. That said, for a *Christian* reading of the OT—which, after all, constitutes more than half of the canon—there is no need to concede the right to interpret it also in light of the coming of Christ as long as this is done as a second step.

So, what, if any, is the contribution of the OT to the Christian doctrine of God? How does that doctrine fare when placed side by side with the foundational beliefs of the OT? A careful look at this must precede our engagement with the NT.

Old Testament Monotheism

Every inquiry into biblical Christian doctrine of the Trinity should keep in mind at all times the uncompromising monotheism of the faith of Israel, which is the basis of the Christian confession of God as well. Both Christians and Jews join in the famous *Shema*, Israel's "confession of faith": "Hear, O Israel: The Lord our God, the Lord is one" (Deut 6:4). Known under various names, among which the most important is *Yahweh*, going back to the significant self-revelation of God in Exodus 3:14, Israel's God demands unreserved loyalty vis-à-vis the constant tendency of God's people to succumb to the worship of other deities. Any allegiance to other gods was considered nothing less than a blasphemy. In the context of that kind of uncompromising monotheism, any reference to threeness might easily elicit the suspicion of polytheism. No wonder early Christians from the beginning had to defend their faith in Father, Son, and Spirit against charges of tri-theism (belief in three deities).

But what, exactly, is "monotheism" and what is meant by the demand for believing in one God alone? At its core, Israel's monotheism is much less about the "number" of deities and more about absolute devotion and loyalty to one God; "texts such as the *Shema* (Deut 6:4–9) reflect a repeated call to the difficult task of exclusive loyalty to God alone, and God's uniqueness is more soteriological than metaphysical,"[9] that is, it is less about ontological speculations and more about salvation and true faith.

This opens the door to the possibility for some kind of plurality within the one God. Let's ask ourselves: What is there, if anything, in the OT understanding of monotheism that allowed early Christian theology to conceive of God in plural, especially triune terms? How did it come to be that from the very beginning the incipient Christian church came to speak of the one God of the OT, the Yahweh of Israel, in terms of Father, Son, and Spirit? If the sudden appearance of the threefold naming of one God were not so familiar a phenomenon to the Christian reader, we might be in a better place to appreciate its radical nature!

So, what do we mean when speaking of a plurality with regard to the God of the OT? It is an incipient plurality within the one God, expressed in terms of "Wisdom," "Word," and "Spirit." These three seem to serve as (semi-)personified agents of divine activity. And very importantly, the existence of such personified agents was not seen necessarily as a threat to monotheism.

A Plural Possibility: Wisdom–Word–Spirit

In addition to the three mentioned in the heading, namely Wisdom, Word, and Spirit,[10] there are several other semi-personified agents of Yahweh in the OT, such as the "name" of Yahweh, especially in the Deuteronomic theology, which dwells in the temple (Deut 12:5, 11). Another example is the "glory" of God that acts as an agent separately from, yet sent by, Yahweh; the book of Ezekiel is the prime example here.[11] And so forth.

Among these, a highly significant role is played by *hokmah*, Wisdom, which occurs more than three hundred times in the OT (not only in the Wisdom literature). Consider these two formative passages, one from Proverbs and the other one from the apocryphal Wisdom of Solomon, written close to the beginning of the NT times:

> The Lord brought me forth as the first of his works,
> before his deeds of old; I was formed long ages ago, at the very
> beginning, when the world came to be . . . I was there when he set

the heavens in place . . . Then I was constantly at his side. I was filled with delight day after day, rejoicing always in his presence. (Prov 8:22–23, 27, 30, NIV) For wisdom is more mobile than any motion; because of her pureness she pervades and penetrates all things. For she is a breath of the power of God, and a pure emanation of the glory of the Almighty; therefore nothing defiled gains entrance into her. For she is a reflection of eternal light, a spotless mirror of the working of God, and an image of his goodness. Though she is but one, she can do all things, and while remaining in herself, she renews all things; in every generation she passes into holy souls and makes them friends of God, and prophets; for God loves nothing so much as the man who lives with wisdom. (Wis 7:24–28, RSV)[12]

Wisdom's significance lies in that the "[p]ersonified Wisdom or Sophia [in Greek] becomes increasingly related to the divine work of creation, providence, and salvation and grows in dignity and power along with OT sapiential [wisdom] thinking. Within a monotheistic faith, Wisdom takes on functions and attributes of YHWH. . . ."[13]

Wisdom plays a central role particularly in Proverbs (1:20–33; 3:13–24; 4:5–9; and chs. 8 and 9). In the beginning of the book, Wisdom, in the form of a sophisticated Lady, invites people to the source of true wisdom. As mentioned above, this passage was of major importance to patristic exegesis. Not only wisdom and insight come from Wisdom, but also salvation. And according to the famous passage of 8:22–31, Wisdom was "begotten" or "created" "long ago" as God's "first-born."

Echoing the Wisdom of Solomon's profound statements cited above about the unique relation between God and Wisdom—"breath of the power of God, and a pure emanation of the glory of the Almighty . . . a reflection of eternal light"—Sirach,[14] another apocryphal writing, speaks of Sophia (the Greek term for Wisdom) in this way:

In the assembly of the Most High she will open her mouth, and in the presence of his host she will glory: "I came forth from the mouth of the Most High, and covered the earth like a mist. I dwelt in high places, and my throne was in a pillar of cloud. Alone I have made the circuit of the vault of heaven and have walked in the depths of the abyss. In the waves of the sea, in the whole earth, and in every people and nation I have gotten a possession. Among all these I sought a resting place; I sought in whose territory I might lodge.... From eternity, in the beginning, he created me, and for eternity I shall not cease to exist." (24:2–7, 9)

With a little imagination one can see the affinity of these themes with Christ, the "wisdom of God" (1 Cor 1:24). Or, think of the invitation in the Wisdom of Solomon: "Come to me, you who desire me, and eat your fill of my produce.... Those who eat me will hunger for more, and those who drink me will thirst for more" (Wis 24:19, 21). It is fully justified to see here a connection with Jesus's invitations in the Gospels (Matt 11:28–30; John 6:35).[15] The same can be said of the following passage, perhaps the most profound and in many regards astounding passage in the Wisdom of Solomon 7:22–24, a litany of the excellent capacities and virtues of Wisdom. Quite naturally, early Christian theologians saw them embodied in Christ, the preexistent Power and Wisdom and Word (*Logos*) of God (see Col 1:15–17, 19–20; 2:9–10; Heb 1:2–3, among others):

> For in her there is a spirit that is intelligent, holy, unique, manifold, subtle, mobile, clear, unpolluted, distinct, invulnerable, loving the good, keen, irresistible, beneficent, humane, steadfast, sure, free from anxiety, all-powerful, overseeing all, and penetrating through all spirits that are intelligent and pure and most subtle. For wisdom is more mobile than any motion; because of her pureness she pervades and penetrates all things.

Word (*dabar*), another agent of God, appears already in the first creation account (Gen 1:1—2:4a). The psalmist explains that it was through the Word and *ruach* (Spirit) that creation was accomplished (Ps 33:6). Everywhere the Word is able to accomplish its God-given purposes (Isa 55:10–11). Spirit (with about four hundred occurrences in the OT), at times coupled with not only Word but also Wisdom (Deut 34:9; Job 32:8–9; Isa 11:2), appears as the "breath of life" (Gen 1:2), sustaining all life (Ps 104:29–30).

Clearly, these agencies could be taken as an indication of an incipient plurality without a direct threat to belief in one God. Furthermore, very importantly for the purposes of Christian trinitarian thought, we note that they imply not only plurality but also relationality. Take Genesis 1 as an example. The work of the Creator *Elohim* employing the agencies of the Spirit (*ruach*) and Word (divine creative speaking) was rightly taken by Christian interpreters to point to both plurality and relationality in one God.[16] This summary statement by the Catholic Jesuit theologian Gerald O'Collins is accurate:

> The vivid personifications of Wisdom/Word and Spirit, inasmuch as they were *both* identified with God and the divine activity *and* distinguished from God, opened up the way toward recognizing God to be tripersonal. The leap from mere personifications to distinct persons is always, to be sure, a giant one. Nevertheless, without these OT personifications (and the Father/Son language applied to God), the acknowledgment of the Trinity would not have been so well and providentially prepared—by foreshadowings and by an already existing terminology.[17]

These insights get strong support from some leading biblical scholars. Richard Bauckham has argued that, in some real sense, the early Jewish definition of God could include the person of the Son without violating monotheism.[18] What distinguished the Yahwistic faith from polytheistic faiths was the desire not to place Yahweh "at the summit of a hierarchy of divinity" but, rather, to place him in an "absolutely unique category, beyond comparison with anything else."[19] In other words, even the highest angels or heavenly powers so highly appreciated especially in apocalyptic literature, while participating in God's rule over the earth, did not share in God's essence. However, distinctions within one Godhead, such as between God's Spirit and God's Word, were not necessarily understood as compromising the divine unity. Consequently, Bauckham concludes—and this is highly significant for a NT trinitarian outlook—"the Second Temple Jewish understanding of the divine uniqueness . . . does not make distinctions within the divine identity inconceivable."[20]

So, when the NT writers' encounter with the risen Christ and the Holy Spirit forced them to develop a theology that could account for the plurality in unity, they could build on these incipient foundations in the Israelite faith. Wolfhart Pannenberg makes a brilliant comment here: "Christian statements about the Son and Spirit take up questions which had already occupied Jewish thought concerning the essential transcendent reality of the one God and the modes of his manifestation."[21] Yes, they went beyond the OT faith, no doubt, but not against it, and they could hold on to the *Shema* of Israel while talking about Father, Son, and Spirit as one God.[22]

While the NT builds on the foundations laid by the OT, it also is true that it focuses clearly on Jesus, the Son. "In the older testament things are seen from the Father's point of view, whereas the Father is largely viewed from the Son's point of view in the NT."[23] This is the decisive clue to the rise of the trinitarian faith in the OT.

The Trinitarian God of the New Testament

Son of the Father

To the Christian reader it may come as a surprise to read in a typical textbook that "[t]here is no mention of the word 'Trinity' in the New Testament." [24] Really? What are the implications of this? The concerns might be eased if the same reader also gets the following message: "What we do discover from the NT writers, though, is a consistent argument for the filial uniqueness of Jesus Christ in relationship to the Father of the old covenant."[25] So, what we have is this: on the one hand, the *doctrine* of the Trinity cannot be found even in the NT; on the other hand, Jesus's unique relation to the Father calls for an explanation that really takes us beyond the boundaries of the OT. This statement by Stanley J. Grenz focuses the issue:

The initial impetus in the direction of what became the church's teaching about God as triune was spawned by the theological puzzle posed by the early church's confession of the lordship of Jesus and the experience of the indwelling Holy Spirit, both of which developments emerged within the context of the non-negotiable commitment to the one God of the OT that the early believers inherited from Israel.[26]

That development, however, took centuries and was a matter of much debate. In hindsight one may ask: If the NT does not contain a doctrine of the Trinity, how can we then justify the later Christian doctrine?[27] The answer to this question is that, rather than looking for prooftexts or a *doctrine* of the Trinity in the NT, we need to look at the ways the first Christians came to understand salvation history, namely, what the God of Israel was doing through God's Son in the power of the Spirit.

There is no doubt that what became a full-fledged *trinitarian* confession of faith in later creedal tradition began in the NT and earliest Christian tradition as a more-or-less binitarian understanding of God. It was focused on the relationship between the Father and Son. As Stephen Holmes summarizes it succinctly: "The gospels present the relationship between Jesus and the One he calls 'Father' as unique and central" and that "there is a complex relationship of intimacy, union, shared knowledge and action, and subordination."[28] Theologically put: the self-distinction of Jesus from his Father, on the one hand, and their unity, on the other hand, is the foundation of the NT orientations to the Trinity.[29] Or, as O'Collins puts it, there is a "trinitarian face" to the history of Jesus.[30] Just consider the beginnings of the NT Gospels. In the beginning of Luke's Gospel, we are told that the conception of Jesus was an act of God in the power of the Spirit (Luke 1:35). Matthew's way of connecting the coming of Jesus to a trinitarian understanding is to name Jesus as Immanuel, the presence of God, with his people (1:23). The Gospel of John goes back to the OT idea of the Word as God's agent, and names the Word (*Logos*) God (John 1:1). These and similar biblical statements are indications of the fact that the coming of Jesus from the "begin-

16

ning" was understood by the Gospel writers as linked to God and his Spirit, yet distinct from them.

In John's Gospel, the Son–Father relationship plays an important role.[31] During his life, Jesus claimed to have been sent by God (5:37) and having been granted the authority to give life (5:21). To the Son has also been given the authority to execute judgment, similar in this to the Father (5:22). So close is the mutual relationship that whoever does not honor the Son does not honor the Father (5:23). Or, no one can see the Father without the mediatory role of the Son (1:18; 14:6–9).

All of what has been said so far on the basis of the Gospel testimonies has its basis in the critical event that brought the Christian church into existence and made possible the proclamation of the gospel of the one God who now was seen as Father, Son, and Spirit. That is the experience of the earliest followers of the *resurrection* of the crucified Messiah. The significance of that event calls for closer attention.

Resurrection and the Divine Son

According to Pauline theology, before his cross and resurrection, Jesus claimed to have the authority and approval of his Father. And when, as Romans 1:3–4 maintains, Jesus was raised from the dead by his Father, the early Christians interpreted that as divine confirmation. "There was a dramatic change when the crucified Jesus, who had died the death of a criminal cursed by God (cf. Deut 21.23), was experienced by the witnesses to the Easter appearances as the one who had been raised and confirmed by God: this experience became the starting-point for a deepened christological reflection which persistently also shaped the image of God among the early Christians."[32] Without doubt, the resurrection is crucial for the emergence of the conviction of the deity of Jesus, a claim that was of course hotly contested during Jesus's lifetime by his Jewish opponents. No wonder it elicited the Jewish accusation of blasphemy (John 5:18).[33]

Indeed, the resurrection is the defining moment in the rise of the doctrine of the Trinity. A first necessary conclusion on the way to that conclusion was the establishment of the deity of Christ. According to O'Collins,

> First-century Christians proposed a trinitarian interpretation of the events of Good Friday and Easter Sunday. In those events, along with the outpouring of the Spirit, they experienced the unique high point of God's revelatory activity for our salvation. This saving revelation was experienced as threefold. . . . [W]e find at the origin of Christianity a certain sense that the Father, the Son, and the Holy Spirit were revealed as acting in our human history, above all in the events of Good Friday and Easter Sunday and their aftermath.[34]

This is not, of course, to claim—and O'Collins hastens to note it—that any kind of full-fledged trinitarian, or even a christological, doctrine emerged suddenly. It is just to underline the cataclysmic effects of the resurrection event. Even more, resurrection from the dead was interpreted by early Christians to mean that "the Son of God was also at the side of God from all eternity," even though the "church's later view of the full deity of the Son did not have to be related to the idea of preexistence."[35] In other words, what soon came to be known as Christ's preexistence is integrally linked with the raising from the dead. Of course, for a while the concept of the Son's preexistence was fluid, moving between the preexistence of an idea (in the mind of God) and a "real" preexistence.[36]

A decisive impulse for the affirmation of the full deity of the Son, the critical stage in the emerging trinitarian faith, was the applying of the title *Kyrios* to the risen and exalted Son. This is the title "Lord" reserved only for God in the OT (in the Septuagint, the Greek translation of our OT). Indeed, it is astonishing that, as far as we know, "amidst all the variety of primitive Christianity, the worship of Jesus as divine was simply ubiquitous."[37] Just think of these familiar practices and patterns: beginning from the earliest NT witnesses (some letters of Paul), "prayer is offered to the Father 'through Jesus Christ' (Rom

1:8), and to the Father and Jesus together (1 Thess 3:11–13); benedictions can be uttered in either name (Rom 16:20), or in the name of Jesus with no mention of the Father (1 Cor 16:23)."[38] So common is the worship of Jesus as divine that the biblical scholar Larry Hurtado may summarize it thus: "Amidst the diversity of earliest Christianity, belief in Jesus' divine status was amazingly common. The 'heresies' of earliest Christianity largely presuppose the view that Jesus is divine. That is not the issue. The problematic issue, in fact, was whether a genuinely *human* Jesus could be accommodated."[39] Wolfhart Pannenberg concludes:

> The title Kyrios implies the full deity of the Son. In the confession of Thomas in John 20:28 the titles God and Lord are expressly set alongside one another. Yet the Son is not Kyrios in competition with the Father but in honor of the Father (Phil 2:11). The confession of Jesus Christ as the one and only Kyrios in no way weakens the confession of the one God. The former confession is so related to the latter that all things proceed from the one God, the Father, but all are mediated through the one Kyrios (1 Cor 8:6).[40]

To sum up: the foundation for the emerging NT trinitarian faith was laid by the two ideas we have explicated above: the identity between the Yahweh of the OT and the God of Jesus Christ of the NT as well as the distinction, yet unbroken unity, between Jesus and his Father.[41] In order to clarify and deepen the latter statement, let us look further into the distinctively NT view of the fatherhood of God.

The Father of Jesus Christ

Although the idea of the fatherhood of God is not unknown to the OT, it does not occupy the kind of central role it does in the NT.[42] One of the most delightful pictures of fatherhood occurs in Hosea 11 as Yahweh is teaching Israel, his son, to walk (even if the Hebrew word *'ab,* "father," does not appear therein). Only very rarely is the actual term "father" used (Ps 103:13; Prov

3:12; Deut 32:6).[43] Generally speaking, fatherhood in the OT testifies to God's "deep involvement in the story of Israel."[44]

In Jesus's way of addressing his God, the fatherhood theme becomes programmatic and central.[45] Matthew contains thirty references to this theme. The Gospel of John, however, written a few decades later, contains no less than 120![46] At the heart of Jesus's message was the announcement of the nearness of the kingdom of God; this God was none else than the Heavenly Father whose reign was near:[47]

> God shows himself to be Father by caring for his creatures (Matt 6:26; cf. Luke 12:30). He causes his sun to shine and his rain to fall on the bad as well as the good (Matt 5:45). He is a model of the love for enemies which Jesus taught (5:44–45). He is ready to forgive those who turn to him (Luke 15:7, 10, 11ff.), ask for his forgiveness (11:4), and forgive others (Matt 11:25; cf. 6:14–15; 18:23–35). He lets himself be invoked as Father, and like earthly fathers, and even more than they, he grants good things to his children when they ask (Matt 7:11). Thus the prayer to the Father which Jesus taught his disciples combines the prayer for daily bread, the sum of all earthly needs, with the prayer for forgiveness, which is connected with a readiness to forgive (Luke 11:3–4). This prayer also shows that Jesus' proclamation of God's fatherly goodness is related to his eschatological message of the nearness of the divine rule. For the prayer begins with three petitions that are oriented to the coming of the lordship of the Father God.[48]

While Jesus's view of God was not completely new, his mode of address to God was novel because his relationship with God was unique and intimate. Importantly for us, Jesus not only addressed God as his Father, *abba*, but also taught his disciples to address God as "our Father."[49]

From Biunity to Trinity

The Bible speaks of the divine Spirit, the Spirit of God, the Holy Spirit, in terms of symbols, images, metaphors, testimonies, and stories.[50] The basic biblical terms, the OT *ruach* and the NT *pneuma*, carry similar ambiguity: "breath," "air," and "wind." Other metaphors used of the Spirit include fire, dove, and *Paraclete*.

The background of the NT teaching on the Spirit of God is, of course, the OT. As mentioned, the OT[51] contains over four hundred references to *ruach* (and about one hundred references to the "Spirit of *God*"), Gen 1:2; Isa 11:2, among others. From the beginning of the biblical narrative, the Spirit's role in creation, as the principle of life, comes to the fore. The same Spirit of God that participated in creation over the chaotic primal waters (Gen 1:2) is the principle of human life as well (Gen 2:7). This very same divine energy also sustains all life in the cosmos: "When you [Yahweh] send your Spirit [*ruach*], they are created, and you renew the face of the earth" (Ps 104:30). Similarly, when Yahweh "take[s] away their breath [*ruach*], they die and return to the dust" (v. 29). Importantly, the prophetic books make an integral connection between the Spirit of God and the promised Messiah. Indeed, the Messiah is the receiver of the Spirit and the Spirit's power (Isa 11:1–11; 42:1–4; 49:1–6).

Fulfilling the prophetic promise of Joel 2:28–32, on the day of Pentecost a powerful outpouring of the Spirit signaled the birth of the church (Acts 2). The communities of the book of Acts experienced the Spirit's presence and power with visible signs (Acts 4:31; 8:15–19; 10:44–47; and so forth)—so much so that, as a rule, the signs were taken as the evidence of the work of God (Acts 8:12–25, among others).

When it comes to the Gospels' testimonies to the Spirit, it is characterized everywhere by an intimate relationship between the Spirit and Son—and, of course, also between the Spirit and Father. This integral, mutually conditioned relationality between Spirit and Son has given rise to the nomenclature "Spirit Christology." Jesus's birth (Matt 1:18–25; Luke 1:35); his baptism (Matt 3:16; Mark 1:10; Luke 3:22; John 1:33); his testing in the wilderness (Matt 4:1; Mark 1:12; Luke 4:1); his anointing (Luke 4:18–21); his ministry with healings, exorcisms, and other miracles (Matt 12:28; Luke 4:18; 11:20); the eschatological ministry of Jesus as the Baptizer in the Spirit (Matt 3:11)—these are all attributed to the Spirit.[52]

According to the NT testimonies, Jesus was also raised to new life by the power of the Spirit (Rom 1:4), so much so that he "became a life-giving spirit" (1 Cor 15:45). Here we come to the critical stage in moving from a binitarian to a trinitarian understanding of God. It had to do with the growing insistence on the Spirit as the "medium of the communion of Jesus with the Father and the mediator of the participation of believers in Christ."[53] By extension, the same God who raised the Son from the dead by the power of the Spirit is looked upon as the one who will raise believers from the dead (8:11). Indeed, the filial "*abba*" cry of the Spirit in the hearts of believers, echoing the prayer of Jesus in relation to his Father, already testifies to the presence of the life-giving Spirit (8:15–16).

In keeping with this, in the Pauline corpus, a distinctive Spirit Christology comes to the fore, similar to the Gospels.[54] Jesus was raised to new life by the Spirit (Rom 1:4). The Spirit is the Spirit of Christ (Rom 8:9; Gal 4:6; Phil 1:19). Therefore, it is only through the Spirit that the believer is able to confess that "Jesus is Lord" (1 Cor 12:1–3). Indeed, to be "in Christ" and "in the Spirit" are virtually synonymous. Therefore, the Spirit cannot be experienced apart from Christ (1 Cor 12:3). Paul also knows the presence and power of the Spirit in the lives of the Christians and communities, including empowering inspiration (1 Thess 1:5; 1 Cor 2:10–12; 2 Cor 3:15–18) and charismatic endowment and gifting (1 Corinthians 12 and 14). Through the Spirit, the new eschatological age has arrived and the Spirit serves as *arrabon,* a down payment of the coming glory (Eph 1:13–14) and participation in in the kingdom of God (Gal 4:6–7).

Not only is there a close relationship between the Son and Spirit, the same applies also to Father and Spirit, though differently. "In the working of the Spirit[,] God himself is present."[55] This means that the inclusion of believers in the filial relationship between Father and Son is also mediated by the Spirit, similar to the mediation of God's presence by the Spirit in all creation. "The Spirit is thus given to believers, and by receiving the Spirit they have a share in the divine sonship of Jesus."[56]

Clearly, there is a definite shift from binitarianism (Father and Son) to trinitarianism in the NT data. Perhaps we should speak of "explicit binitarianism and implicit trinitarianism."[57] As our survey has clearly evinced so far, binitarian passages about Father and Son abound.[58] Alongside this there emerges a more frequent linking together of all three, Father, Son, and Spirit. Consider, for example, the well-known endings of two NT books:[59]

> Therefore go and make disciples of all nations, baptizing them in the name of the Father and of the Son and of the Holy Spirit. (Matt 28:19)
> May the grace of the Lord Jesus Christ, and the love of God, and the fellowship of the Holy Spirit be with you all. (2 Cor 13:14)

The triadic pattern comes to the fore in various forms, such as in the thematically trinitarian structure of Ephesians 1:3–14 based on the salvation history of Father, Son, and Spirit.[60] Furthermore, already in binitarian passages there is a basic trinitarian consciousness even when the Spirit is not explicitly mentioned.[61] That said, nowhere in the NT are the relations among Father, Son, and Spirit clarified in any systematic manner. Pannenberg summarizes it well:

> The involvement of the Spirit in God's presence in the work of Jesus and in the fellowship of the Son with the Father is the basis of the fact that the Christian understanding of God found its developed and definitive form in the doctrine of the Trinity and not in a biunity of the Father and the Son. . . . The NT statements do not clarify the interrelations of the three but they clearly emphasize the fact that they are interrelated.[62]

So, it is here that the NT leaves us and it is left to postbiblical theology to take up the task of clarifying several open questions and look for a more solid understanding of the interrelations among the three "persons" of the one God. To the investigation of that development we will turn next.

Notes

1. Gerald O'Collins, *The Tripersonal God: Understanding and Interpreting the Trinity* (Mahwah, NJ: Paulist, 1999), 4.

2. Ibid., 11.

3. Ibid. Oddly enough, in light of this statement, a 1999 compilation of essays on the biblical, historical, and contemporary systematic perspectives on the Trinity by leading international scholars does not have any discussion of the role of the OT. Stephen T. Davis, Daniel Kendall, and Gerald O'Collins, eds., *The Trinity: An Interdisciplinary Symposium on the Trinity* (Oxford: Oxford University Press, 1999).

4. For useful comments concerning the OT's use among the church fathers and its relation to contemporary biblical scholarship, see Stephen R. Holmes, *The Quest for the Trinity: The Doctrine of God in Scripture, History, and Modernity* (Downers Grove, IL: InterVarsity, 2012), 34–39.

5. A highly useful survey and discussion of these and other similar OT passages can be found in Holmes, *Quest for the Trinity*, 39–44.

6. Wolfhart Pannenberg, *Systematic Theology*, vol. 1, trans. Geoffrey W. Bromily (Grand Rapids: Eerdmans, 1991), 260.

7. Still useful is the classic study by Arthur W. Wainwright, *The Trinity in the New Testament* (London: SPCK, 1962).

8. Ben Witherington III and Laura M. Ice, *The Shadow of the Almighty: Father, Son, and Spirit in Biblical Perspective* (Grand Rapids: Eerdmans, 2002), 67–68.

9. Holmes, *Quest for the Trinity*, 45–49, at 45. A highly useful scholarly monograph is Nathan MacDonald, *Deuteronomy and the Meaning of 'Monotheism'* (Tübingen: Mohr Siebeck, 2001). An accessible and succinct discussion regarding Yahweh, the one God, and other deities or spiritual beings is John Goldingay, *Old Testament Theology*, vol. 2: *Israel's Faith* (Downers Grove, IL: InterVarsity, 2006), 43–46 particularly.

10. For a detailed discussion of these three, see O'Collins, *Tripersonal God*, 23–34; my exposition here is directly indebted to his. I have also benefited from Robert Letham, *The Holy Trinity: In Scripture, History, Theology, and Worship* (Phillipsburg, NJ: P&R Publishing, 2004), 24–31.

11. See, e.g., Ezekiel 43 with the theme of the return of the glory of God; for useful comments, see Pannenberg, *Systematic Theology*, 1:276–77 particularly.

12. All citations from the apocryphal writings in this chapter come from the RSV.

13. O'Collins, *Tripersonal God*, 24.

14. Or: Wisdom of Jesus Son of Sirach.

15. For finding this passage and the following in the Wisdom of Solomon, I am indebted to O'Collins, *Tripersonal God*, 26.

16. For the further significance of relationality, see Letham, *Holy Trinity*, 19–22.

17. O'Collins, *Tripersonal God*, 34 (italics in the original).

18. Richard Bauckham, *God Crucified: Monotheism and Christology in the New Testament* (Grand Rapids: Eerdmans, 1998): ch. 1 places the discussion of plurality in the Godhead in the context of "early Jewish monotheism," and ch. 2 investigates the emerging "Christological Monotheism in the New Testament"; see also Witherington and Ice, *Shadow of the Almighty*, ch. 3 (which also engages widely Bauckham's main theses). Highly important and similar kind of work has also been done for years by another biblical scholar, Larry Hurtado, who argues that, on that basis, the seemingly seamless move in the early church from the beginning to show devotion to Jesus the Christ as "Lord" (*kyrios*, the name reserved for Yahweh in the Septuagint, the Greek rendering of the Hebrew Torah) was made possible. See especially his massive monograph, *Lord Jesus Christ: Devotion to Jesus in Early Christianity* (Grand Rapids: Eerdmans, 2003).

19. Bauckham, *God Crucified*, 12.

20. Ibid., 22.

21. Pannenberg, *Systematic Theology*, 1:276–77. So also O'Collins, *Tripersonal God*, 89.

22. See Roger E. Olson and Christopher A. Hall, *The Trinity*, Guides to Theology (Grand Rapids: Eerdmans, 2002), 9–10; Pannenberg, *Systematic Theology*, 1:277.

23. Ben Witherington, *The Gospel Code: Novel Claims about Jesus, Mary Magdalene, and Da Vinci* (Downers Grove, IL: InterVarsity, 2004), 156, with reference to Christopher R. Seitz, *Word without End: The Old*

Testament as Abiding Theological Witness (Grand Rapids: Eerdmans, 1998), 258.

24. Olson and Hall, *The Trinity*, 6.

25. Ibid.

26. Stanley J. Grenz, *Rediscovering the Triune God: The Trinity in Contemporary Theology* (Minneapolis: Fortress Press, 2004), 7.

27. Cf. the comment of A. W. Argyle, an exegete of the previous generation: "Broadly speaking, we may say that the God of the New Testament is the God of the Old Testament reinterpreted and more fully revealed in the light of the Person and Work of Jesus Christ." Argyle, *God in the New Testament* (Philadelphia: J. B. Lippincott, 1965), 10.

28. Holmes, *Quest for the Trinity*, 52; for a wider survey, see 51–54.

29. For a careful analysis, see Pannenberg, *Systematic Theology*, 1:263–64. The self-distinction of Jesus from the Father is also a key to the NT's emerging Christology.

30. O'Collins, *Tripersonal God*, 35, in a chapter titled "The History of Jesus and Its Trinitarian Face."

31. The term "son" appears in the NT in various ways, the most important of which is Jesus's self-designation of himself as the "Son of Man," going back to the OT usage (particularly Dan 7:14–15). A helpful discussion in relation to the doctrine of the Trinity can be found in Craig A. Evans, "Jesus' Self-Designation 'The Son of Man' and the Recognition of His Divinity," in Davis, Kendall, and O'Collins, eds., *The Trinity*, 29–47. For other important titles, see Witherington and Ice, *Shadow of the Almighty*, 71–97.

32. Franz Dünzl, *A Brief History of the Doctrine of the Trinity in the Early Church*, trans. John Bowden (London/New York: T&T Clark, 2007), 3.

33. See further, Olson and Hall, *The Trinity*, 8. See also Pannenberg, *Systematic Theology*, 1:264–65.

34. O'Collins, *Tripersonal God*, 4–5.

35. See further Pannenberg, *Systematic Theology*, 1:264–65.

36. Pannenberg, *Systematic Theology*, 1:265. See further Letham, *Holy Trinity*, 48–49; and more widely, Larry W. Hurtado, "Pre-Existence," in *Dictionary of Paul and His Letters*, ed. Gerald F. Hawthorne and Ralph P. Martin (Downers Grove, IL: InterVarsity, 1993), 743–46.

37. Holmes, *Quest for the Trinity*, 54.

38. Ibid.

39. Hurtado, *Lord Jesus Christ*, 650, cited in Holmes, *Quest for the Trinity*, 55.

40. See further Pannenberg, *Systematic Theology*, 1:266.

41. Ibid., 263–64.

42. Witherington and Ice, *Shadow of the Almighty*, 1; for possible reasons behind this scarcity of father imagery in the OT, see further, 4–6. An issue not known among the ancients had to do with the gender debate, so vital and important to our current intuitions. Since that topic can only be briefly treated at the end of this book, suffice it to say this much at this juncture: "In the OT scriptures, God exercises no sexuality and is utterly transcendent. Even if male and sometimes female images are applied to the deity, the sense that God is literally neither male nor female and transcends creaturely representations comes through the official OT prohibition of divine images." O'Collins, *Tripersonal God*, 12.

43. For details, see Witherington and Ice, *Shadow of the Almighty*, 1–16.

44. O'Collins, *Tripersonal God*, 23; see also 12–22.

45. For a brief review of scholarly debates about the "newness" (or lack thereof) in Jesus's introduction of God, see Marianne Meye Thompson, *The Promise of the Father: Jesus and God in the New Testament* (Louisville: Westminster John Knox, 2000), 13–15; for the various meanings of the term "father" in the NT, see 39.

46. Witherington and Ice, *Shadow of the Almighty*, 19. For a detailed study of Gospel passages, see 19–51; and for the rest of the NT, 51–64 (including summative points of the whole NT data). See also chs. 3 and 4 in Meye Thompson, *Promise of the Father*, for a detailed study of Jesus's use of "father" in the Synoptics, ch. 6 in John, and ch. 5 for the rest of the NT epistles.

47. For the integral linking between the kingdom of God and Father in Jesus's ministry and life, especially when it comes to the awaited eschatological coming of God's rule, see George E. Ladd, *A Theology of the New Testament*, rev. ed., ed. Donald A. Hagner (Grand Rapids: Eerdmans, 1993 [1974]), 82–85.

48. Pannenberg, *Systematic Theology*, 1:259.

49. A classic study is Joachim Jeremias, *The Prayers of Jesus*, trans. John Bowden and Christoph Burchard (Philadelphia: Fortress Press, 1967).

While older scholarship—as well as popular teaching even today—maintains that the address *abba* has daddy-like implications based on the language of small children, biblical scholarship reminds us that the term was also used in an intimate relationship between an adult son and father; Witherington and Ice, *Shadow of the Almighty*, 22. For a sympathetic and critical assessment of Jeremias's view of *abba*, see ch. 1 in Meye Thompson, *Promise of the Father*.

50. The main source in this section is George T. Montague, *The Holy Spirit: Growth of a Biblical Tradition* (Peabody, MA: Hendrickson, 1994); for shorter, less technical discussions, see George Montague, "The Fire in the Word: The Holy Spirit in Scripture," in *Advents of the Spirit: An Introduction to the Current Study of Pneumatology*, ed. Bradford E. Hinze and D. Lyle Dabney (Milwaukee: Marquette University Press, 2001), 35–65.

51. A very helpful outline of OT perspectives is offered by E. Kamlah, "Spirit," in *New Dictionary of New Testament Theology*, ed. Colin Brown (Grand Rapids: Zondervan, 1978), 3:690–93.

52. For details, see Veli-Matti Kärkkäinen, *Spirit and Salvation: A Constructive Christian Theology for the Pluralistic World*, vol. 4 (Grand Rapids: Eerdmans, 2016), 35–38; and more widely in my *Christ and Reconciliation: A Constructive Christian Theology for the Pluralistic World*, vol. 1 (Grand Rapids: Eerdmans, 2013), ch. 8.

53. Pannenberg, *Systematic Theology*, 1:266.

54. A massive study on Pauline pneumatological traditions is Gordon Fee, *God's Empowering Presence: The Holy Spirit in the Letters of Paul* (Peabody, MA: Hendrickson, 1994).

55. Pannenberg, *Systematic Theology*, 1:267.

56. Ibid. Thus, it is understandable that the baptismal formula, even though binitarian forms were also in use earlier on, became trinitarian.

57. Letham, *Holy Trinity*, 52 (section-heading title).

58. Rom 1:1; 1 Cor 1:1–3; and so forth.

59. Other passages include Rom 15:30 and 1 Cor 12:4–6, among others.

60. See further O'Collins, *Tripersonal God*, 65–68; Letham, *Holy Trinity*, 63–69.

61. See Peter Toon, *Our Triune God: A Biblical Perspective of the Trinity* (Vancouver, BC: Regent College Publishing, 1996), 117.

62. Pannenberg, *Systematic Theology*, 1:268–69.

2

———

Trinitarian Canons: Emergence and Consolidation

The Theological Tasks

This chapter tells the story of how, in the early Christian centuries, the trinitarian consciousness formed in the NT evolved into a doctrine of the Trinity, which in turn consolidated itself in creeds and theology.[1] We want to pay special attention to discerning the main developments as attempts both to resolve the many problems and to give at least tentative answers to urgent questions. While this is, of course, best done by roughly following chronological order, it also goes without saying that no comprehensive account can be given in a primer such as this one. And at times, the chronological order is replaced by a thematic structure. What may be called "informed selectivity" of the materials is the principle followed here.

The goal of this discussion, in other words, is to set forth a theological reading of the early trinitarian tradition in terms of its main developments, key issues, and critical questions. It is useful to remind ourselves of the truism that we need to know history in order to understand the present. The deeper one goes into the rich tapestry of trinitarian history, the more meaningful it will be to engage contemporary trinitarian theologies in the postmodern global village.

As mentioned in the introduction, my purpose is not to seek to reconstruct or challenge the standard "mainline" scholarly reading of the history of the trinitarian doctrine.[2] Indeed, this survey will pay attention to scholarly divergences. Nevertheless, the current account follows well-known and well-established scholarly insights and instincts in interpreting the basic sources on which the reading of the history is based.

Now, what were the urgent tasks facing the earliest Christian theologies in the postbiblical period? It is helpful to list them here even though many of them have already been alluded to in the biblical section:[3]

1. As long as the Spirit was not differentiated from the Son as a separate hypostatic[4] entity, it was difficult to say if the Spirit was the power or influence of the Father (filling or empowering the Son) or something else less than a person. In other words, how do we distinguish Son and Spirit without separating them in a way that would threaten to truncate the trinitarian doctrine? This distinction was quite unclear in the theologies of the second and third centuries.[5]

2. As long as the distinction between the Son and Spirit was ambiguous and, subsequently, the hypostatic nature of both in the process of being more precisely defined, the relation to *Logos*/Word and Wisdom was confusing. To take an example, what is the relation of the Son to the preexistent Wisdom of Proverbs 8:22–23? Or should we ask, like some early theologians did, what is the relation of the Spirit to Wisdom?

3. While affirming the deity of the Son (and later the deity of the Spirit), early theologians also brought about the

major problem in relation to the monotheism of Jewish-Christian faith.

4. Having gradually affirmed the deity of both Son and Spirit, the major challenge to Christian theology was to negotiate between two extremes: *tritheism*, the belief in Father, Son, and Spirit as "separate gods," on the one hand, and *modalism*, the idea of lack of personal distinctions in the one Godhead, on the other hand. Modalism, which may take more than one form, insists on the unity of the Godhead to the point where the names Father, Son, and Spirit are just that—names. They denote various manifestations or modes of being of the one and same Godhead.[6]

5. Often, resolution of this question was attempted by resorting to subordinationism, the subjecting of the Son and Spirit under the Father. Again, this can happen in more than one way, for example by treating the Father as the "source" (*arche*) of the two. Early heresies, especially Arianism (according to which Christ was a creature rather than an uncreated deity) and various types of monarchianist views (both modalistic and dynamic versions), were efforts to reconcile the seemingly impossible equation between strict monotheism and the idea of three equal divine beings sharing one Godhead.

6. From early on, the Christian East and West developed not only distinctive approaches to spirituality and theology in general but also encountered severe linguistic problems directly related to a key issue in the trinitarian (and christological) doctrine, namely the meaning of *hypostasis* ("person[hood]"). Not only did it take time for both Eastern and Western theologians to begin to understand what the other meant with key concepts, but even more to agree on a common meaning, somewhat independent from purely linguistic and etymological meanings. Any field of inquiry entails an established, often technical terminology; the doctrine of the Trinity is no exception.

Often, however, it takes time for this terminology to be developed in a way that would clarify the discourse.

Let us begin by investigating the very earliest developments on the way to the Councils of Nicea (325) and Constantinople (381), the first definitive ecumenical attempts by the church catholic to come to a shared understanding and basic consensus.

Clarifying the Divine Triad

Son of the Father

As we saw in the preceding chapter, the origin of the trinitarian doctrine lies in the mutual and intimate relationship between the Father and Son as depicted on the pages of the NT. Hence, the Father–Son relationship is the proper place to begin. The very earliest postbiblical Christian thinkers, the so-called Apostolic Fathers (Clement of Rome, Ignatius, Theophilus of Antioch, Hermas, and others), were hardly in a place to offer much clarification, let alone constructive thinking. What they did was to robustly confess strict monotheism and share the deep and wide consciousness of "the conception of a plurality of divine Persons" based on the economy of salvation, namely that "God had made Himself known in the Person of Jesus, the Messiah, raising Him from the dead and offering salvation to men through Him, and that He had poured out His Holy Spirit upon the Church."[7] Although the doctrine of Christ's preexistence prior to the incarnation, an essential trinitarian asset, was still to some extent in the making, it seems like the Apostolic Fathers took the idea for granted. Similarly, they strongly affirmed Christ's role in creation and redemption. But when it came to the more precise formulation as to how to understand Christ's deity, more often than not they were drawn to the "theory that the divine element in Christ was pre-existent spirit" or a "supreme angel" or something similar.[8] The prominent patristic scholar J. N. D. Kelly's conclusion puts the Apostolic Fathers' view of God in perspective: "Of a doctrine of the Trinity in the strict sense there is of course no sign, although the Church's triadic formula left its mark everywhere."[9]

The first developed attempt to clarify the Son–Father relationship, an essential task on the way toward the trinitarian doctrine, came from the so-called Apologists (Justin Martyr, Theophilus of Antioch, Tatian, and others), the late second-century Christian thinkers who sought to offer a robust "apology" (defense of the faith) vis-à-vis rebuttals coming from the Gentile Greco-Roman world.[10] Based on the Johannine Prologue (John 1:1–18)[11]—"In the beginning was the Word [*logos*], and the Word was with God, and the Word was God. . . . The Word became flesh and made his dwelling among us" (vv. 1–2, 14)—and going back to the OT idea of the creative and powerful divine Word (*dabar*), what can be called the *Logos* theology emerged. The choice of the Word as a christological title was particularly appealing to the Apologists, as the idea of the *Logos* played a significant role in the philosophical schools of the antiquity (such as the one related to Heraclitus) and was also known to the leading Jewish philosopher Philo. *Logos* was believed to represent ultimate wisdom and the principle of unity in a world of constant transience.[12]

How did the Apologists employ *Logos* resources in trying to clarify the relationship between Jesus of Nazareth and his Father? The most obvious is, of course, "the theme of the intermediary role of the Son, who is 'another' or 'second' God. As *Logos*, he mediates and is present in all creation."[13] This intermediary agency seemed to fit well with the Apologists' concern to defend the scriptural Jewish monotheism, on the one hand, and the distinction between Father and Son, on the other hand (without in any way compromising their eternal unity). As Kelly puts it succinctly: "[A]s pre-existent, Christ was the Father's thought or mind, and . . . as manifested in creation and revelation, He was its extrapolation or expression."[14] The Son's eternal oneness with the Father (God's Word is always in the life of God) and his appearance in human history was exactly what John the Evangelist seemed to be saying in the passage cited above. The idea of derivation from the Father, in the analogy of human reason and its expression in speech, also seemed to imply the shared substance between Father and Son.[15]

Other metaphors were used, especially those from nature, like the sun and its rays or fire kindling fire. Insisting on the unity of the Godhead—and thus anticipating the question of "consubstantiality" much debated in later theology—the Apologists were careful not to read the idea of separation or difference into the Father–Son relationship. Justin Martyr's explanation tries to pull together all of this when he first reminds his opponents that the Son is not distinct from the Father "in name only like the light of the sun, but is indeed something numerically distinct." Then he notes that the Son was begotten "by His [Father's] power and will, but not by abscission, as if the essence of the Father were divided." This unity in distinction (but not in separation) the Apologist seeks to illustrate with the help of "the case of fires kindled from a fire, which we see to be distinct from it, and yet that from which many can be kindled is by no means made less, but remains the same."[16]

With all the benefits, *Logos* theology also created problems and called for further explanation concerning the Trinity. An obvious liability is subordinationism: that which is derived from the "source" (Son from the Father) is lower than the source. When pressed, this kind of subordinationism may have helped prepare the way for the later Arianist ideas of the different "substance" of deity between Father and Son (to be discussed below). Similarly, the whole question of the "personality" of the *Logos* is left open. And so forth. That said, Kelly's judgment is spot on: "In spite of incoherencies, however, the lineaments of a Trinitarian doctrine are clearly discernible in the Apologists. The Spirit was for them the Spirit of God; like the Word, He shared the divine nature, being (in Athenagora's words) an 'effluence' from the Deity."[17]

The Father–Son relationship continued to challenge patristic theology until Constantinople (381) and beyond, as the ensuing discussion will reveal. In tandem with that question arose the challenge of relating Son and Spirit to each other and, then again, both of them to the Father. Alongside the slow emergence of the doctrine of the Spirit (pneumatology), a pressing task had to do with the need to establish both distinctive roles and identities of Father, Son, and Spirit—without which no authentically *trinitarian* doctrine could be had—and, simultaneously, their unity—without which no authentically *monotheistic* theology could be had.

Distinctiveness and Unity

Although the *doctrine* of the Trinity as we now know it was still in the making, the "rule of faith" (*regula fidei*) was already explicitly trinitarian in structure. Just consider this important statement from Irenaeus ("[t]he theologian who summed up the thought of the second century, and dominated Christian orthodoxy before Origen"[18]):

> The Church, though dispersed throughout the whole world, even to the ends of the earth, has received from the apostles and their disciples this faith: [She believes] in one God, the Father Almighty, Maker of heaven, and earth, and the sea, and all things that are in them; and in one Christ Jesus, the Son of God, who became incarnate for our salvation; and in the Holy Spirit, who proclaimed through the prophets the dispensations of God. . . .[19]

In statements like this, both the distinction between Father, Son, and Spirit and their unity are presupposed even if no explanation is offered as to how to reconcile them. An important, though less than fully satisfactory, stage in the continuing process of clarification of this vital issue had to do with the effort to assign distinct spheres of activities to Father, Son, and Spirit. The oft-cited example comes from Origen. He sought to differentiate the three members of the Godhead according to this scheme: the Father works in all things, the Son only in rational creatures, and the Spirit only in the church.[20] Irenaeus's famous example approaches the matter from a different kind of perspective. For him, the creation of the world is the result of the "two hands of God," Son and Spirit.[21] Or, consider the example of the inspiration of the prophecy of the OT. While of course intuitively related to the work of the Spirit, it could also be linked with that of the Son with reference to *Logos*, the Word and Wisdom. Many other examples could be listed that seek to establish the distinction based on the economy of salvation (widely understood). What are we to say of these attempts? While the distinction of works may function as a way of illustration, it can hardly establish the distinct identities of each trinitarian member.[22] This was grasped quite soon, and attempts to account for the distinct nature of Son and Spirit as well as their relation to the Father took a different route.

An important impulse came from the great Greek thinkers in the Christian East, Athanasius and the three Cappadocians, Gregory of Nyssa, Gregory of Nazianzus (or: Nazianzen), and Basil the Great. Differently from tradition, they sought to highlight the common participation of all trinitarian members in the works in the world. For them, the unity of works is both a condition and consequence of the unity of essence.[23] Although the common participation of Father, Son, and Spirit alone is hardly able to establish the immanent ("intradivine") unity, it points to the importance of considering all God's works as a joint operation. So, even this solution still leaves open the establishment of authentic threeness, particularly with regard to the Spirit.[24]

There were more promising clues provided by earlier theologians, even though in the midst of the existing confusion their value was perhaps not grasped as it should have been. One of the new ways of grounding the distinction among Father, Son, and Spirit makes reference to the inner relations of the Son, Father, and Spirit. This clue could be found in the biblical texts. Just consider the famous Paraclete passages in John 14, regarding which Tertullian rightly noted that therein the Son distinguished both the Father and Spirit from himself.[25] Origen similarly affirmed that Jesus's referring to the Father and the Paraclete as distinct from himself implies the existence of three persons and one shared substance or entity.[26] This, Pannenberg rightly concludes, indicates that the "self-differentiation of the Son from the Father on the one side and the Spirit on the other forms a basis for the thesis that there is a threefold distinction in the deity."[27]

In the same direction points the simple, albeit obviously not yet fully satisfactory, idea of Athanasius, according to which the Father would not be Father without the Son and that therefore the Father never was without the Son.[28] The lasting contribution of Athanasian insight has to do with the principle of relationality as the way to defining the distinction as well as the unity. With that in mind, we should simply overlook its obvious shortcomings, namely that a father may obviously have more than one son, and that obviously the idea is still somewhat subordinationist; yet another liability is its silence about the Spirit.[29] Relationality is the key and main lesson.

An important aspect of the question of the distinctness and unity of divine persons relates to the Spirit–Son relationship, the focus of the following section.

Spirit and Son

As late as until the end of the third century, the nature and role of the Spirit as well as the mutual relationship between the Spirit and Son remained oftentimes confused. The main reason had to do with the simple fact that the NT, of course, fails to define their relations. Another reason is that the OT seems to take Word and Spirit as parallel and virtually interchangeable entities in the service of Yahweh.[30] Just consider the earliest postbiblical writings, such as the second-century *2 Clement*: it is not uncommon to find here a blurring of the distinction between Son and Spirit. Speaking of those who abuse flesh, it says that "such a person will not receive the Spirit, which is Christ" (14:4). Another telling early example of the lack of trinitarian canons is *The Shepherd of Hermas*, a highly influential writing of the second century that struggled to make sense of the Son and Spirit. Indeed, Hermas appears to fall into a number of errors also repeated by later theologians. For example, it is not clear whether Hermas considered the Son to be an angel or more ancient than the angels. Occasionally he blurs the distinction between Son and Spirit, and in one instance seemingly unites them, writing that "the Spirit is the Son of God" (Parable 9.1.78). . . . Although we find support for the unity of God in Hermas' writing, his struggle to define plurality of God was characteristic of his time.[31]

Even among later second-century theologians such as Theophilus of Antioch and Irenaeus, the trinitarian pattern was still in need of clarification in that these important teachers at times spoke of the triad in terms of God, Word, and Wisdom. To add to the confusion, Theophilus equated the Spirit with Word while Irenaeus with Wisdom![32] Happily, quite soon thereafter the equation of the Son with the Word, *Logos*, was established on the basis of Proverbs 8:22–23.[33]

In sum, early patristic theology was unable to resolve the question of the basis for establishing the identities of Son and Spirit, including their mutual distinction and unity. However, eventually there emerged a wide agreement on the deity of both the Son and the Spirit. The defining reason for the affirmation of the deity came from the scriptural passages deemed implicitly trinitarian (discussed in the previous chapter). While contemporary exegesis hardly follows that logic, their value is not to be dismissed in that they hold the conviction that the idea of Trinity is a datum of revelation. Wolfhart Pannenberg—himself an ardent advocate of historical-critical exegesis—adds an important caveat here concerning these allegedly trinitarian passages:

> To modern historico-critical exegesis this procedure seems to be mistaken from some angles. Yet it stands in relation to the history of the exposition of such texts in Jewish thinking. This connection is important. It shows that the Christian view of the Son as a preexistent hypostasis alongside the Father, and similar views concerning the Spirit which developed in the course of the

formation of the doctrine of the Trinity, were not from the very outset opposed to Judaism and its belief in one God.[34]

With the growing affirmation of the deity of Son and Spirit, much work of clarification awaited theologians with regard to the task of not only spelling out their mutual relations but also relation to the Father—and minding at all times the absolute principle of monotheism.

Divine Son and Divine Spirit: Two Gods?

A number of heretical or at least theologically suspicious attempts arose in the search for a solution to the dilemma of affirming the deity of Son and Spirit alongside with the belief in one God. For the purposes of the trinitarian history, the most important ones are monarchianist, subordinationist, and Arian views. Let us focus on the first two in this section and the third in the next one. The continuing struggle between tritheism, belief in three deities, and modalism, the idea that replaces the real distinctions among Father, Son, and Spirit for mere "modes" of being, were the two extremes in this process. "Where tritheism sacrificed the vital identity of Father, Son, and Holy Spirit to their multiplicity, the opposite heresy of modalism took monotheism so rigidly that it sacrificed the multiplicity of the divine persons to their unity."[35]

A tempting—and quite natural—way to negotiate the tension between monotheism and the deity of the Son alongside the Father is the subordination of Son and Spirit to the "higher" status of the Father. Justin Martyr's idea of the Son being "second" and Spirit being "in the third place" in the Godhead is a textbook example.[36] To the same category belongs the above-mentioned Irenaean idea of the Spirit and Son as "two hands" of the Father.[37] The underlying motif behind Irenaean subordinationism was the desire to uphold the uniqueness and transcendence of the Father, the Creator, a concern going back to earlier theology, as noted above.[38] Quite fittingly, then, his view has been named "orthodox subordinationism."[39] This highlights the theological sophistication and candor of Irenaeus: his is a very fine-tuned subordinationism, so to speak. Recall that for him, the Son (as Word) has always been with the Father[40] and is the one who makes the Father known.[41] While taking his clue from the Apologists' *Logos* theology, Irenaeus also develops their view by insisting on the unity between Reason/Intelligence (Father) and Speech/Word (Son).[42] Very importantly, in anticipation of later debates, Irenaeus taught that the Son "did not then begin to exist, being with the Father from the beginning."[43]

Another early theologian, Tertullian,[44] to whom we owe the launching of key concepts such as *trinitas*, *persona*, and *substantia*, similarly struggled with the challenge of subordinationism. He also fought vehemently against Marcion, whose views resembled Gnosticism but at the center of which was the separation between the God of the OT and Father of Jesus Christ. Strongly rejecting any such tendency to compromise the unity of the Godhead,[45] Tertullian also set forth a powerful rebuttal of "monarchianism," a family of heresies whose advocates appropriated elements from the subordinationism of Irenaeus and others, and thereby claimed to defend the "sole sovereignty" (in Greek *mone arche*) of the Father.[46] Simply put: monarchianism questioned as to how Christians could maintain absolute monotheism while believing in "two gods," Jesus Christ and the Spirit, in addition to the Father. The two main subcategories of monarchianism for the purposes of this discussion are "dynamic" and "modalistic" monarchianism.[47] Dynamic monarchianism[48] preserved the sole sovereignty of the Father by promoting the idea that God was dynamically present in Jesus, making Jesus higher than any other human being but not God. In other words, God's power (Greek, *dynamis*) made Jesus *almost* God. Thus, the Father's uniqueness was secured. Modalistic monarchianism[49] defended God's sole sovereignty by seeing the three persons of the Trinity not as self-subsistent "persons" but as "modes" or "names" of the same God. Father, Son, and Spirit do not stand for real distinctions but are merely different ways God presents himself at different times.[50]

As is typical of heresies, they find alleged support from orthodox positions, in this case—alongside the "orthodox" subordinationism of tradition—from *Logos* theology. For them, the idea of the preexistent *Logos* seemed to imply two gods.[51] The monarchistic view not only subordinated the Son to the Father but also blurred the personal distinctions between the two. By extension, Sabellianism (a version of modalism advocated by Sabellius, a third-century theologian) included the Spirit in the scheme. The names "Father," "Son," and "Spirit," are just that, names expressing manifestations in salvation history. In other words, "Father," "Son," and "Spirit" are but *modes* of the one and undifferentiated Godhead, thus the nomenclature "modalism." A heresy by the name *patripassianism* is yet another corollary of the lack of distinctions: God the Father (*pater*) suffered and died in the coming of the Son.[52]

In presenting an orthodox response to these views,[53] Tertullian first noted that preservation of the "monarchy" of God, the main concern of monarchianism, did not necessarily require that God be only one person. In other words, the monarchy of the Father does not necessarily preclude sharing it with an equal and that God is three in one or one in three with real distinctions, yet with no separation. As Justo González explains:

> The "monarchy," that term which is so cherished by Praxeas [one of the leading monarchianists] and his followers, means simply that a government is one, and does not prevent the monarch from having a son or from managing his monarchy as he pleases—what Tertullian calls the divine "economy." Furthermore, if the father thus wishes, the son may share in the monarchy without thereby destroying it. Therefore, the divine monarchy is no reason to deny the distinction between Father and Son.[54]

Tertullian argued forcefully that the threeness of deity as revealed to us in the economy of salvation is in no way incompatible with the unity of the Godhead. To cite Kelly, "he argued that, though three, the Persons were severally manifestations of a single indivisible power, noting that on the analogy of the imperial government one and the same sovereignty could be exercised by coordinate agencies."[55] Furthermore, in line with the Apologists and Christian tradition, Tertullian maintained that the distinction between Father, Son, and Spirit did not imply separation or division. (Technically put, it was a matter of *distinctio* rather than *separatio*.[56]) Illustrations from nature such as the unity of the root and shoot or the source and river, and perhaps more importantly, sun and light, were employed in defense.[57]

In a most carefully drafted seminal statement, anticipating later debates concerning "consubstantiality" (to be discussed below), Tertullian opined that that the Johannine Jesus's saying "I and the Father are one" means that Father and Son are of "one substance";[58] it is a matter of identity of substance rather than numerical unity.[59] By extension, Son and Spirit are of the same substance with Father.[60] Thus, we can speak of God's one "substance" and three distinct yet undivided "persons."[61] Herein, of course, is the genesis of the Latin-speaking Western's church's way of defining the distinctness and unity: "one substance in three persons" (*una substantia, tres personae*). As said, Tertullian is claimed to be the first to apply *persona* and *Trinitas* to the Christian God. "Where *substance* stood for the common fundamental reality shared by Father, Son, and Holy Spirit, Tertullian understood *person* as the principle of operative individuality."[62] Clearly, then, Tertullian helped avoid the modalistic heresy with his insistence on real distinctions in the united Godhead (although, regretfully, he also failed to defeat subordinationism, as mentioned above).

Taking stock of the developments so far, we may conclude that significant advances in early Christian trinitarian theology had been reached in several respects, two of which stand out for the purposes of this discussion. First, the distinction between Spirit and Son was affirmed even though the doctrine of the Spirit was still very much in the making (as will be detailed below). Second, there was a growing consensus on the necessity and possibility of affirming both the deity of the three and belief in one God; this question, while far from being resolved yet, was not so great as to lead necessarily to an impasse. Subordinationism, however, was not yet overcome either in the West or East, even when the monarchianist type of subordinationism was rejected. The fledgling trinitarian doctrine continued struggling with the question of how best to *express* the conviction that the deity of the Son (and Spirit) can be compatible with monotheism. That was the question known in the history of theology as the Arian(ist) controversy.

Arian Controversy and Nicean Response

Origen's Mixed Legacy

Before clarifying what Arianism was and if its role in the history of the trinitarian doctrine is what standard textbook presentations assume, it is useful to take a quick look at the preceding developments. As is routinely—and in my opinion, correctly—mentioned, somewhat mixed contributions coming from the important Eastern father Origen[63] played a role in the rise of Arianism. While he was a brilliant theologian, Origen's primary calling was biblical exposition and commenting. Importantly, gleaning from Irenaeus and others, he helped establish the eternal Trinity in the Godhead with the help of the idea of the eternal begetting of the Son.[64] While Origen's views are open to more than one interpretation,[65] this was a major step on the way to relating Son and Spirit to Father.

As if anticipating later Arianist claims, Origen correctly insisted that there was no time when the *Logos* was not.[66] Indeed, he exerts great intellectual effort to make the point that the Son never had a beginning:

> Wherefore we have always held that God is the Father of his only-begotten Son, who was born indeed of him, and derives from him what he is, but without any beginning, not only such as may be measured by any divisions of time, but even that which the mind alone can contemplate within itself . . . [T]herefore we must believe that Wisdom was generated before any beginning that can be either comprehended or expressed."[67]

45

Consequently, Father and Son share a unity of nature and substance; there is no unlikeness between them.[68] Yet another way to affirm the eternal generation of the Son was to use the expression "light from light," which found its way into the creeds.[69] Or, take the concept of "goodness"; this also confirmed to Origen the equality of Father and Son:

> And therefore also the Saviour Himself rightly says in the Gospel, "There is none good save one only, God the Father," that by such an expression it may be understood that the Son is not of a different goodness, but of that only which exists in the Father, of whom He is rightly termed the image, because He proceeds from no other source but from that primal goodness, lest there might appear to be in the Son a different goodness from that which is in the Father. Nor is there any dissimilarity or difference of goodness in the Son.[70]

This is all good and necessary. At the same time, Origen was not able to overcome fully subordinationism, and his opponents could interpret some of his statements as pointing to the somewhat inferior status and nature of the Son. Just think of this example, as subtle as it may be: "But, as we have already said, the primal goodness is to be understood as residing in God the Father, from whom both the Son is born and the Holy Spirit proceeds, retaining within them, without any doubt, the nature of that goodness which is in the source whence they are derived."[71] A closely related tendency was to speak of gradations in the Godhead, with Father being the "highest" one.[72] This is but part of his enduring subordinationism. Stephen Holmes puts this tendency in the wider framework of Origen's (Middle) Platonist leanings:

> Origen maintains the Platonic hierarchy of being, in which there is an ontological gap between the perfect being of the Father and the partial or limited existence of the creatures; the Son in all his offices bridges this gap, but in so doing is located ontologically below the Father but above the creatures. (The same may be said of the Spirit; tellingly, Origen fairly regularly takes biblical images of the agents of God's rule and applies them to the

Son and Spirit, as for instance the seraphim in Isaiah's temple vision.)[73]

Furthermore, only God/Father is *autotheos*, self-subsistent, without origin.[74] Son and Spirit, on the contrary, are by derivation from the Father. Arians picked up this idea, even though Origen of course rejected their view, according to which there was a time when the Son was not.

Origen's legacy is thus ambiguous, "occasioned by his propensity to think on his feet," as Robert Letham succinctly puts it: "Stress on the subordination of the Son and Spirit would lead to the denial of their deity (by the Arians and the *pneumatomachii*[75]), while the assertion of their deity in that context would foster allegations of tritheism (which Gregory of Nyssa would rebut)."[76] Ironically, then, Origen with all his superb achievements indirectly contributed to Arianism.

Arianism in Perspective

Standard scholarly opinion is that it was during the fourth century that the main decisions regarding the doctrine of the Trinity were hammered out and its basic contours consolidated. As with any general opinion, this one both contains some important truth and, when taken to its extreme, may also become misleading. While there is no doubt about the significance of this historical period, it is also important to remember that much had been prepared in advance and many questions remained in need of further clarification subsequently.[77] Particularly significant here is what was the focus of the previous section, namely the somewhat mixed legacy of Origen in which there was "both a tendency to emphasize the unity of the Son and Father, and a tendency to emphasize the difference." No wonder both leads were followed up by some important leaders and theologians.[78]

Arianism, classically named as one of the "The Four Great Heresies,"[79] sought to offer a solution to the pressing problem of the third and fourth centuries, namely, how to reconcile the unity of God with the deity of Jesus Christ. That much can be safely said of Arianism's agenda. Beyond that, several historical and theological questions and differences of interpretation come to the surface. Fortunately—we may say so!—for an introductory textbook, most of these have to be left out of the discussion; even a casual delving into them would expand this book unduly. Consider this: we have virtually no writings from the main protagonist, namely Arius, a Presbyter in Alexandria. Furthermore, the influence on Arius's views by the relation to his bishop, Alexander of Alexandria, with whom he had a serious conflict of opinions, as well as the influence of complicated ecclesiastical and political circumstances, are still debated among expert historians.[80] Most of what is known under Arianist teaching comes from the rebuttals of Athanasius (of Alexandria), a major defender of Nicean orthodoxy.

What can be assumed safely is that in some way or another Arius inherited the teaching of Origen concerning Father, Son, and Spirit sharing the one divine nature—yet the Father being the source, thus implying in some way or another the inferior role of the Son and Spirit.[81] It seems like Arius pushed the idea of the inferiority of the Son to the point where only the Father is without origin and without birth; the Father is absolutely transcendent. Consequently, so the heretical argument supposedly developed: the Father does not share absolute deity with any creatures, not even with the Son. Furthermore, Arius is attributed with teaching that there was a time when the Son was not, that the Son was made out of nothing, and that the Son had an origin similar to other creatures.[82] O'Collins compares Arianism with an early heresy that also struggled with the challenge of reconciling the deity of the Son with that of the Father:

> Like the modalist monarchians (e.g., Sabellius), Arius and his followers wanted to preserve an absolute "mon-archy" of God, but unlike the Sabellians and other modalist monarchians, they held onto the real difference of identity between the Father and the Son. . . . Where Sabellianism asserted a strict unity of the divine essence without any real distinction of subjects, Arianism distinguished the subjects while denying their unity of essence.[83]

So, can we assume—what the citation above seems to imply—that Arianism was merely a continuation of monarchianist tendencies, and hence, similar to Jewish-monotheistic-driven attempts to safeguard the absoluteness of the Father as God? Opinions vary. There is no doubt that crucial to Arius was the basic premise according to which God the Father is absolutely unique and transcendent, and hence, God's essence (the Greek term *ousia* means both "essence" and "substance") cannot be shared by another or transferred to another, not even the Son. Hence, the distinction between Father and Son was to be understood in Arius's system as one of substance (*ousia*); if Father and Son were of the same substance, there would be two gods. In other words, Arius's logic seems to be something like this: he not only attempted to ensure the divinity of Jesus in regard to other human beings, but he also wished to do so without in any way implying Jesus's equality with the Father.

There is also another way of looking at what ultimately drove Arius. A section of current scholarship opines that behind Arianism might have been something other than primarily Jewish monotheism. What if Arius's teaching stemmed, rather, from the Greek-Hellenistic ideology according to which it is not possible to attribute suffering—let alone death—to gods/divine beings. In other words—although in principle the idea of gods appearing in human form was not the problem (contrary to Jewish intuitions for which it is anathema)—the divine nature had to be saved from any notions of human-like suffering and death. Then, as long as the church continued to speak of the suffering Son of God, something had to be done to the allegedly divine status of the Son. If that conclusion is materially correct, it can also be seen that in many ways Monarchianisms (stemming from the Jewish soil) and Arianism (stemming from the Hellenistic soil) also relate to each other: while the former seeks to defend the uniqueness of God/the Father vis-à-vis any notion of "polytheism," the latter's concern is to defend the idea of the deity free from any notions of suffering and death and, as a result, to make the Son less than divine. Be that as it may, there is no doubt about the seriousness of the Arian challenge to developing orthodoxy. Before looking at the Nicean rebuttal, let us note one important corollary issue in the debate.

To understand the significance of the challenge of Arianism to trinitarian orthodoxy, we have to acknowledge that it was not only about christological[84] and trinitarian debates, but also had everything to do with our salvation. Think about this: if the Son was a creature just as we are, this opens a way for humans to imitate this Savior in conforming their will to the will of the Father as the obedient Son did. Similar to the Son who was adopted into sonship, we can be, too.[85] If so, it looks like both the monarchy of the Father and the role of the Son as merely an "assistant to the Father, operating under orders" could be seen as a major victory for Arianism.[86] Similar to other disputed questions about Arianism, soteriological motifs cannot be examined in any conclusive way within the contours of this brief discussion. What is safe to conclude is that while there is no reason to deny the importance of ontological considerations of deity, the significance of the soteriological agenda probably should not be dismissed. In this respect, Arian claims truly raise grave concerns in the minds of Christians. The biggest, of course, is this: How can a creature-Savior help elevate us into the divine life of God?[87] Only God is able to save; no creature can accomplish this.

The Nicean Rebuttal

What came to be the orthodox position was affirmed at the Council of Nicea and vehemently defended by Athanasius.[88] Alongside him, the three Cappadocians also played an important role in the continuing defense of the matter.[89] Before looking at those rebuttals, let us be mindful of the fact that we can speak of an orthodox consensus only in hindsight. During the time of the debates, the trinitarian canons were, of course, still in the making, and therefore to imply that Arius was attacking a stronghold of orthodoxy with his deviant views is historically not accurate at all. Concerning Nicea, advanced students of theological history also have to be knowledgeable of complicated political influences and motifs behind it, particularly the role of Emperor Constantine and his desire to further the unity of the state.[90] Furthermore, while Athanasius deserves great credit in helping formulate the orthodox position, he was by no means the sole defender of what became the majority view.[91]

The Council of Nicea in 325 (as formulated in the 381 Constantinopolitan Creed[92]) defined Christ's deity in a way that made Christ equal to God the Father. The text says:

> We believe . . . in one Lord Jesus Christ, the Son of God, begotten of the Father [the only begotten, that is, of the essence of the Father, God of God], Light of Light, very God of very God, begotten, not made, being of one substance [*homoousios*] with the Father; by whom all things were made [both in heaven and on earth]; who for us men, and for our salvation, came down and was incarnate and was made man; he suffered, and the third day he rose again, ascended into heaven; from thence he shall come to judge the quick and the dead.

An appendix at the end listed Arian tenets to be rejected:

> But for those who say: "There was a time when he was not;" and "He was not before he was made;" and "He was made out of nothing," or "He is of another substance" or "essence," or "The Son of God is created," or "changeable," or "alterable"—they are condemned by the holy catholic and apostolic Church.[93]

Without going into many christological details,[94] let it suffice to say this much for the sake of the discussion at hand: the expression "begotten . . . of the essence [or: substance] of the Father"—the so-called *homoousios* clause (from Greek "one" and "substance")—established the co-divinity ("consubstantiality") of the Son with the Father (and later, by derivation, of the Spirit). This key term *homoousios*, however, was a debated term in itself, although it served its main purpose at Nicea quite well, namely the defeat of Arians in their uncompromising affirmation of the unity and equality of the Son with the Father. Its liabilities—and hence continuing contested nature—were many: it was not a biblical term; it had a checkered history, having at times been condemned by the (then) orthodox side; and because it could be applied to material substances it could be used as a way to reinforce the once used, but now rejected "material" analogies of deity.[95] Finally, and this really became a major issue: it could be easily used to support modalism. Taken to its extreme, *homoousios* could be interpreted in terms of Father and Son being so much of the same "essence" that there is no real distinction.

Therefore, many preferred the slightly different form *homoiousios*, "of similar substance," which, while it avoids the danger of modalism, also easily leads to virtually endorsing Arius's position of the *almost* same, but not totally equal, status of Father and Son.[96] Hence, the majority (*homoousios*) party doubted if Arianism could be fully combatted with the *homoiousios* phrase.[97] Be that as it may, this gave rise to the so-called Homoian party, whose advocates

> were united by their distaste for the Nicene language of *homoousios*; indeed, they rejected any discussion of divine *ousia* at all; finding the term, with its materialistic overtones, inevitably misleading and unhelpful. They would confess that Father and the Son were 'like' each other, a choice of language that would seem to be a political compromise more than a developed position.[98]

That said, with all the difficulties related to these formulations, there is no denying that "Nicea's main achievement was to place on record once and for all that the being of the Son is identical to the being of the Father, dealing a mortal blow to subordinationism."[99] At the same time, we have to acknowledge that Nicea was hardly able to resolve trinitarian issues, nor was it regarded as a major milestone in its own time. As mentioned, its significance could be ascertained only in hindsight.[100] Indeed, what happened in the aftermath of Nicea and on the way to (and beyond) Constantinople (381) were continuing debates, splits, and at times changing allegiances between "orthodoxy" and heretical positions, not seldom linked with power struggles in the church and society![101]

Advanced students of theology should also be duly informed of the continuing complicated debates of the fourth century related particularly to Eunomius, a major target of the Cappadocians; his views, associated usually with Aetius, are known as "Neo-Arianism."[102] The response to Eunomius will be briefly discussed in the following section.

Athanasius and the Cappadocians

Defeating Arianism

Having already mentioned repeatedly Athanasius[103] and the Cappadocians,[104] it is now useful to take a deeper look at their contributions. It can be said that, in many ways, Athanasius both prepared and built on Nicean foundations in offering a more nuanced reasoning for the rejection of Arianism.[105]

> First, he argued that Arianism undermined the Christian doctrine of God by presupposing that the divine Triad is not eternal and by virtually reintroducing polytheism.[106] Second, it made nonsense of the established liturgical customs of baptizing in the Son's name as well as the Father's, and of addressing prayers to the Son.[107] Third, and perhaps most importantly, it undermined the Christian idea of redemption in Christ, since only if the Mediator was himself divine could people hope to reestablish fellowship with God.[108]

Athanasius's theological response confirms the earlier-mentioned judgment that the fight over Arianism had as much to do with salvation as ontology, following the ancient rule *lex orandi, lex credendi*: the law of prayer is the law of belief. Herein, Athanasius of course turned the Arians' weapons against themselves: were Christ not divine, our salvation would be in jeopardy, as only God is able to save. He also reminded his opponents of the widespread custom in liturgy and prayers to wor-

ship the Son (and Spirit) along with Father, an act to be condemned as blasphemy should the Son's divinity be in question.[109]

Against Arian charges that the Son is a creature, Athanasius
presented the counterargument that since the Father is not a
creature, neither is the Son; whatever is in the Father is in the
Son.[110] This is also the meaning of his famous saying that the
Son is "whole God" (holos theou).[111] "He who looks at the Son,
he says, sees the Father. In turn, the Father's Godhead is in the
Son and is seen in the Son. The Father is in the Son."[112] One
way to express this mutuality for Athanasius is to refer to the
ancient term perichoresis ("mutual indwelling," literally, "danc-
ing around").[113]

Further clarification and deepening of Nicean convictions
came from the Cappadocians. Basil the Great made this important statement:

> For all things that are the Father's are beheld in the Son, and
> all things that are the Son's are the Father's; because the whole
> Son is in the Father and has all the Father in Himself. Thus the
> hypostasis of the Son becomes as it were form and face of the
> knowledge of the Father, and the hypostasis of the Father is
> known in the form of the Son, while the proper quality which
> is contemplated therein remains for the plain distinction of the
> hypostases.[114]

A lasting contribution of Basil, the oldest of the three Cappadocians, was to finally establish the distinction between hypostasis
and ousia (although it has to be admitted that even for himself it took some time!). The former came to denote (something like what we mean by the term) "person," whereas the
latter denotes "essence" (or "substance" in Latin). Related to
this, Basil (along with the other Cappadocians[115]) highlighted
the theological importance of the unknowability and in that
sense mysterious quality of the divine nature—not in terms of
God staying totally "foreign" to us but in terms of the extent
and depth of our knowledge of the divine. As Franz Dünzl summarizes:

In truth the substance [or: essence] of God is in accessible and incomprehensible to all creatures, human beings and even the angels—it is knowable only for the Father, the Son and the Holy Spirit. The assertion of the Neo-Arians around Aetius and Eunomius that they could *grasp the substance* of the Father and the Son and describe it with a *precise* concept represents a great overestimation of themselves and serves only to lead believers astray.[116]

Defeating Eunomianism

Eunomius (along with the like-minded, such as Aetius) and the "Neo-Arian" anti-*homoousios* party continued challenging what became the Nicean orthodoxy. Significantly, both of the Cappadocian brothers, namely Basil the Great[117] and Gregory of Nyssa, wrote important treatises against those heresies.[118] Going to the very heart of the difference of opinion, namely as to whether the Son really is absolutely equal in status and nature to the Father or not, building on his brother Basil's legacy, Gregory sets the record straight. He first describes the position of his opponent, Eunomius, by also borrowing from him:

Let us also investigate this point as well,—what defence he has to offer on those matters on which he was convicted of error by the great Basil, when he banishes the Only-begotten God to the realm of darkness, saying, "As great as is the difference between the generate and the ungenerate, so great is the divergence between Light and Light." For as he has already shown that the difference between the generate and the ungenerate is not merely one of greater or less intensity, but that they are diametrically opposed as regards their meaning; and since he has inferred by logical consequence from his premises that, as the difference between the light of the Father and that of the Son corresponds to ungeneracy and generation, we must necessarily suppose in the Son not a diminution of light, but a complete alienation from light.[119]

Vehemently rejecting Eunomius's argument according to which the "ungenerate" nature of the Father as distinct from the "generate" nature of the Son would result in less than full equality, provided—as every theologian would agree—God's nature is "simple" (without composition), Gregory of Nyssa brilliantly argues that "the term simplicity will in its meaning have no such connection with being ungenerate as that, by reason of its incomposite character, His nature should be termed ungeneracy." Should those two terms be equated, the end result would be "one of two absurd alternatives, either denying the Godhead of the Only-begotten, or attributing ungeneracy to Him also." Why so? Gregory explains: "For if God is simple, and the term simplicity is, according to them, identical with ungenerate, they must either make out the Son to be of composite nature, by which term it is implied that neither is He God, or if they allow His Godhead, and God (as I have said) is simple, then they make Him out at the same time to be ungenerate, if the terms simple and ungenerate are convertible." In other words, each of these terms has its own peculiar meaning.[120]

Part of the defense of the orthodox position is to rebut Eunomius's inference according to which incarnation alone would make Son different in *ousia* from the Father. Responding to the hypothetical objection according to which "because the Light and the Life, and God and the Word, was manifested in flesh, does it follow that the true Light is divergent in any degree from the Light which is in the Father?" Gregory's tight argument is this:

> Nay, it is attested by the Gospel that, even when it had place in darkness, the light remained unapproachable by the contrary element: for "the Light," he says, "shined in darkness, and the darkness comprehended it not." If then the light when it found place in darkness had been changed to its contrary, and overpowered by gloom, this would have been a strong argument in support of the view of those who wish to show how far inferior is this Light in comparison with that contemplated in the Father. But if the Word, even though it be in the flesh, remains the Word, and if the Light, even though it shines in darkness, is no less Light, . . . and if the Life, even though it be in death, remains secure in Itself . . .—if all this be so, how does he show by this

argument variation of the Light to inferiority, when each Light has in equal measure the property of being inconvertible to evil, and unalterable?[121]

Gregory of Nyssa further adds a weighty practical reason against Eunomius's party's refusal to grant full divinity to the Son. He concludes: "For when they are persuaded that He is not truly God, it follows as a matter of course that no other Divine attribute is truly applicable. For if He is truly neither Son nor God, except by an abuse of terms, then the other names which are given to Him in Holy Scripture are a divergence from the truth. For the one thing cannot be predicated of Him with truth."[122]

On another front, the Nyssan bishop also rebutted vehemently the absurd charge—not uncommon during the patristic era—that perhaps Christians are worshiping three gods instead of one God in three "persons." Addressed to Ablatius, a bishop colleague who desired to get some important enlightening on this burning issue, Gregory's treatise named "On 'Not Three Gods'" clarifies in what sense it can be said that Father, Son, and Spirit are both of the same nature and yet not three separate persons. The discussion begins by going back to his earlier well-known trinitarian illustration of "three men" (Peter, James, and John). The dilemma is this: "Peter, James, and John, being in one human nature, are called three men: and there is no absurdity in describing those who are united in nature, if they are more than one, by the plural number of the name derived from their nature."[123] The first reason for that charge not to apply in the case of the Trinity has simply to do with the proper understanding of the meaning of "nature" (as in human nature). Although we call any number of human persons by their proper names, we are not thereby denying that they all share one nature. There cannot be many human natures![124] The second argument by Gregory of Nyssa builds on the principle that "the word 'Godhead' is not significant of nature but of operation." Whereas in the human world what separates persons should be attributed to and is an agency of separate persons rather than one human nature, with regard to God it is the opposite: "But in the case of the Divine nature we do not similarly learn that the Father does anything by Himself in which the Son does not work conjointly, or again that the Son has any special operation apart from the Holy Spirit; but every operation which extends from God to the Creation, and is named according to our variable conceptions of it, has its origin from the Father, and proceeds through the Son, and is perfected in the Holy Spirit."[125] Isn't that simply the formulation of what—somewhat inaccurately historically and theologically—has become to be known as "Augustine's rule," namely that the works of God *ad extra* ("outwardly") are undivided (but that "inwardly" they can be distinguished—or else, modalism follows)?

Furthermore, and very importantly, in terms of a fully *trinitarian* solution, on the basis of everything that has been said so far, it seems justified to link this perichoretic principle by derivation to the Spirit as well. It can be said with full justification that in the Cappadocian theology "[t]o exist as God is to be the Father who begets the Son and breathes forth the Spirit."[126] Therefore, as the late Roman Catholic theologian Catherine Mowry LaCugna explains, for the Cappadocians, trinitarian persons cannot be thought of as disconnected from each other; in other words, "*it is impossible to think of the divine essence in itself or by itself.*"[127] Using the contemporary (to us) terminology: these Greek theologians were thinking along the lines of "communion theology," in which the only way to think of one God is to think of God relationally, as existing as Father, Son, and Spirit.[128] O'Collins's observation is important: "At the heart of God, the Cappadocians saw an interpersonal communion or *koinonia*, with communion as the function of all three divine persons and not simply of the Holy Spirit. For this interpersonal model of the Trinity, God's inner being is relational, with each of the three persons totally related to the other two in 'reciprocal delight'—to borrow an Athanasian expression."[129] Gregory of Nazianzus's argument that the "terms 'Father,' 'Son,' and 'Holy Spirit' are terms of relation" expresses the heart of this orientation. It means that unlike "essence" or "substance," which cannot be shared, relationality is about sharing, communion. [130]

A fitting way to wrap up our consideration of the profound contributions of the three Cappadocians—and also at the same time prepare for the reflections on what can be called the "Neo-Nicean" solution, is to take a more detailed look at the third of them, namely Gregory of Nazianzus. Here the fight against Neo-Arianism, particularly in the form Eunomius presented it, continued.

Gregory of Nazianzus

The friend of Basil and the Nyssan, this Gregory has earned the rare title of "the theologian"—along with St. John of the NT and Symeon "the New Theologian." Around the time of the Council of Constantinople (381), Gregory of Nazianzus preached five sermons known to us as *Theological Orations*.[131] They are generally considered to be a strong support for the mainline Nicean position and so also make an effort to defeat the fairly strong influence of the anti-Nicean (or Neo-Arian and Eunomian) resistance at and around the Council of Constantinople. Having first dealt with Eunomius in the beginning oration, the second one discusses God in general, including our knowledge of God. This sermon supports other Cappadocians' reservations about claiming too much knowledge of God; that is, it follows the path of apophaticism.[132] The third and fourth orations delve in to the theology of the Son, and the last one is on the Spirit—there is thus a decidedly trinitarian order of discussion.

Brushing aside Eunomian and other speculations concerning the lack of equality of the Son—and, importantly, also of the Spirit—in terms of the Father being there "before" the other two, Nazianzus sets forth this argument concerning the way time-related conceptions may (and may not) be related to the triune God:

> They are above all "When." But, if I am to speak with something more of boldness,—when the Father did. And when did the Father come into being. There never was a time when He was

not. And the same thing is true of the Son and the Holy Ghost. Ask me again, and again I will answer you, When was the Son begotten? When the Father was not begotten. And when did the Holy Ghost proceed? When the Son was, not proceeding but, begotten—beyond the sphere of time, and above the grasp of reason; although we cannot set forth that which is above time, if we avoid as we desire any expression which conveys the idea of time. For such expressions as "when" and "before" and "after" and "from the beginning" are not timeless, however much we may force them; unless indeed we were to take the Æon, that interval which is coextensive with the eternal things, and is not divided or measured by any motion, or by the revolution of the sun, as time is measured.[133]

The conclusion from this tight reasoning is:

How then are They not alike unoriginate, if They are coeternal? Because They are from Him, though not after Him. For that which is unoriginate is eternal, but that which is eternal is not necessarily unoriginate, so long as it may be referred to the Father as its origin. Therefore in respect of Cause They are not unoriginate; but it is evident that the Cause is not necessarily prior to its effects, for the sun is not prior to its light. And yet They are in some sense unoriginate, in respect of time, even though you would scare simple minds with your quibbles, for the Sources of Time are not subject to time.[134]

In keeping with this equality of the status of the three divine persons, Gregory of Nazianzus also speaks of the monarchy in a way that is not focused on Father alone but is deeply *trinitarian*:

It is, however, a Monarchy that is not limited to one Person, for it is possible for Unity if at variance with itself to come into a condition of plurality; but one which is made of an equality of Nature and a Union of mind, and an identity of motion, and a convergence of its elements to unity—a thing which is impossible to the created nature—so that though numerically distinct there is no severance of Essence. Therefore Unity having from all eternity arrived by motion at Duality, found its rest in Trinity. This is what we mean by Father and Son and Holy Ghost.[135]

Rightly, Robert Letham avers that here there is "a major advance that offsets any possible tendency to subordinate the Son and the Spirit to the Father."[136] Yet another highly important contribution of Gregory of Nazianzus, already briefly referred to above, has to do with the clarification of what the names "Father" and "Son" (and derivatively, also "Spirit") really mean when applied to the triune Godhead. Noting that his opponents understand the nomenclature Father in terms of either "an essence or of an Action" (both of which lead to logical problems into which we do not need to delve here), Gregory posits his own alternative in terms of "the name of the Relation in which the Father stands to the Son, and the Son to the Father."[137] As concluded above, this is but another way of speaking about communion and relationality.

The final of the five orations is focused, importantly, on the Holy Spirit and further strengthens the authentically trinitarian understanding of the one God; that will be carefully investigated in the following chapter. Suffice it here to draw attention merely to the summary statement, a careful navigation against the charges of tritheism, the errors of Eunomians, and the shadow of modalism:

> To us there is One God, for the Godhead is One, and all that proceedeth from Him is referred to One, though we believe in Three Persons. For one is not more and another less God; nor is One before and another after; nor are They divided in will or parted in power; nor can you find here any of the qualities of divisible things; but the Godhead is, to speak concisely, undivided in separate Persons; and there is one mingling of Light, as it were of three suns joined to each other. When then we look at the Godhead, or the First Cause, or the Monarchia, that which we conceive is One; but when we look at the Persons in Whom the Godhead dwells, and at Those Who timelessly and with equal glory have their Being from the First Cause—there are Three Whom we worship.[138]

The "Neo-Nicean Solution"

Without in any way implying that even the "Neo-Nicean solution," as it is sometimes called, put forth authoritatively in the (Nicene-)Constantinopolitan Creed in 381,[139] would be in any way a final *solution*, it is legitimate to take it as a significant signpost on the way to the final consolidation of orthodoxy. O'Collins summarizes: "It is hard to overestimate the importance of the Nicene-Constantinopolitan Creed; it became the sole baptismal confession of the East and the Eucharistic creed of all Christians. In both the East and West, this was and remains the most significant confession of faith in the tripersonal God."[140] Recalling the earlier, very important clarification between *ousia* and *hypostasis*, as well as the principle of incomprehensibility of the divine nature first developed by Basil and then further developed by his younger brother and the other Gregory, the "Cappadocian Settlement" can be expressed something like this:[141]

> The *hypostasis* of the Father is characterized by being unbegotten and possessing the divine substance of itself. The *hypostasis* of the Son is characterized by being begotten and possessing the same divine substance because that is communicated to it by the Father. Being unbegotten and being begotten are accordingly statements about a particular hypostasis, but not about divine substance which underlies the hypostases. The term "substance" [or: essence] relates to what is common to Father, and Son, what is *general*, whereas the term "hypostasis" denotes what is *particular* to Father and Son, i.e. what makes the Father *Father* and the Son *the Son*. . . . There is only *one* incomprehensible divine substance which is realized in different ways in the *three hypostases* of the Godhead (Greek *mia ousia- treis hypostaseis*): the Father possesses the divine substance *without case* from himself, the Son *by being begotten from the Father* and the Spirit *by proceeding from the Father*.[142]

Above we noticed that in the Christian West, the mainline trinitarian consensus was expressed with the formula: "one substance in three persons" (*una substantia, tres personae*).

Despite a convergent theological intuition between the Latin-speaking and Greek-speaking traditions, terminological confusion was a major challenge among Christians. More often than not, the Greek-speaking Eastern theologians and Latin-speaking Westerners had a hard time understanding the key terms in a similar manner, let alone agreeing on a shared meaning.[143] Indeed, worse than that, even in the same language domain there was uncertainty about the exact meaning of the terms used. The Greek fathers had used *hypostasis* and *ousia* more or less synonymously for a long time.[144] To further add to the confusion, in the Christian West from the time of Tertullian onward, the Greek term *hypostasis* was considered to be the equivalent of the Latin term *substantia* (essence).[145] Therefore, the Eastern suggestion of one *ousia* with three *hypostaseis* for Latin speakers could be interpreted as implying tritheism. Consequently, as has become clear, as long as *hypostasis* and *ousia* were considered to have more or less the same meaning, the *homoousios* statement of Nicea could be understood in a modalist way (i.e., that Father and Son [as well as Spirit by derivation] do not denote real distinctions).[146]

Leaving behind the continuing terminological confusion, the conventional theological wisdom is that "in general, Greek theology [of the Christian East] emphasizes the divine hypostases (persons), whereas Latin theology [of the Christian West] emphasizes the divine nature."[147] In other words, it is claimed that the East begins with the threeness of the Trinity, the West with the oneness or unity.[148] Is that really so? Currently, more and more scholars doubt it.[149] While not entirely without grounds, this standard description of the East and West is also a caricature[150] and may confuse more than it clarifies.

Two points are important to highlight here: first, both Greek and Latin theologians affirmed the oneness and threeness, unity and relationality—albeit often somewhat distinctly due to linguistic, cultural, and contextual reasons. Just consider this: both Athanasius and the Cappadocians, the robust advocates of threeness and relationality, were also strong defenders of the *homoousion* formula of Nicea and later the consubstantiality of the Spirit (in other words, of the unity of God). And, as the discussion below will reveal, Augustine—the alleged initiator of the Western oneness-dominant approach, was also deeply relational and mutual in his trinitarian doctrine. Second, the borderline is not consistent between Latin and Greek speakers with regard to the emphasis or approach taken; rather, more often than not, they overlap.

As noted above, in the Nicene-Constantinopolitan Creed, the early trinitarian canons were hammered out as accurately as they could be at the end of the fourth century. This creed is highly significant ecumenically in that it is confessed even today by both Eastern and Western churches.[151] It affirms the Council of Nicea's incipient doctrine and expands on key issues. Its main omission is the phrase "from the substance (*ousia*) of the Father." The exact reason for the omission is unclear.[152] What is clear, however, is that the theology of the Nicene-Constantinopolitan Creed is fully consubstantial; it includes the *homoousion* phrase ("consubstantial with the Father").

Furthermore, and very importantly, in light of an authentic *trinitarian* (as distinct from a merely binitarian) theology, Constantinople expands significantly the pneumatological section. It says: "And in the Holy Spirit, the Lord and life-giver, who proceeds from the Father, who is worshipped and glorified together with the Father and Son, who spoke by the prophets."[153] The application of the term *kyrios* to the Spirit makes a strong statement of the deity of the Spirit, as does, of course, the inclusion of the Spirit in the worship of the triune God. This is all the more telling when we keep in mind the fact that even at the end of the fourth century many orthodox Christians felt reserved about calling the Spirit "God," notwithstanding the affirmation of the divine status of the Spirit. Unlike the later *filioque* clause, according to which the Spirit proceeds both from the Father and Son, this creed makes the Father the source.[154] What is missing in the Nicene-Constantinopolitan Creed are the explicit statements about the perichoretic relational mutuality that the Cappadocians and

Athanasius advanced. Indeed, there is conspicuously little about relationality there.

In a very helpful way, Letham outlines the "implications of the Trinitarian settlement,"[155] based on Constantinople and the tradition till then, especially that of the Eastern theologians. First, there is the emphasis on the oneness of God as simultaneous with the plurality: "It could be said either that God is one being who exists as three persons (this was to prove the preferred route in the West) or, alternatively, that he is three persons who are simultaneously one undivided being (which tended to be the approach favored in the East)."[156] Second, consubstantiality of all three members is strongly affirmed even when the very term *homoousion* is not applied to the Spirit. "There is only one essence or being of God, which all three persons share completely. Furthermore, each person is God in himself."[157] Third, while not present explicitly in the Nicene-Constantinopolitan Creed itself, there is the growing tradition of *perichoresis* advocated by the Eastern theologians. Later, Eastern theologian John of Damascus would pick up this insight and make it a major theme for the trinitarian theology of the Christian East.[158] Fourth, there is the order of the persons, the divine *taxis*:

> *from the Father through the Son by the Holy Spirit.* These relations can not be reversed—the Son does not beget the Father, nor does the Father proceed from the Holy Spirit. . . . Thus, the Father is the Father of the Son, and the Son is the Son of the Father. The Father begets the Son, and the Son is begotten by Father. This relation is not interchangeable, nor can it be reversed—it is eternal and unchangeable. *Mutatis mutandis*, the Holy Spirit proceeds from the Father . . . while the Father spirates the Spirit. Again this is never reversed.[159]

Having devoted our attention here primarily to Greek-speaking theology's contributions to the developing and consolidating trinitarian faith in the fourth century, it is proper to now take a more focused look at the Latin church's advancements and its relation to that of Eastern Christianity. Thereafter, in a separate chapter (3) we will pick up the story briefly started both in the biblical and the early historical section on the role of the Spirit in the Trinity. So far our focus has been almost entirely on the Son–Father relationship.

Augustine and Latin Theology

Augustine's Western Context

It is important to remember that the Latin theologians also made significant contributions to the trinitarian doctrine. In a litany of rebuttals of all kinds of false doctrines and heretical notions, Ambrose, the Bishop of Milan at the end of the fourth century (and Augustine's mentor), affirmed robustly the content of the orthodox understanding:

> Now this is the declaration of our Faith, that we say that God is One, neither dividing His Son from Him, as do the heathen, nor denying, with the Jews, that He was begotten of the Father before all worlds, and afterwards born of the Virgin; nor yet, like Sabellius, confounding the Father with the Word, and so maintaining that Father and Son are one and the same Person; nor again, as doth Photinus, holding that the Son first came into existence in the Virgin's womb: nor believing, with Arius, in a number of diverse Powers, and so, like the benighted heathen, making out more than one God. For it is written: "Hear, O Israel: the Lord thy God is one God."[160]

As we have already mentioned, the older categorical distinction between the Eastern and Western approaches is to be handled with great care. A telling example is Hilary of Poitiers who, having been exiled in the mid-fourth century, traveled to the East and learned the Greek language very well. He also gained an access to the best writings in Greek and made himself an expert on Eastern debates, particularly on *homoousios* and *homoiousios*. No wonder his *On the Trinity* delves deeply into trinitarian debates among the Greek-speaking theologians.[161] Importantly, he also resists the textbook caricature that, whereas the Eastern church emphasizes apophatic mystical approach to theology, the Latin West one-sidedly opts for the kataphatic (that is, analytic and discursive) method.[162] In his trinitarian study (which, like Augustine, took years to write), Hilary sets the records straight:

> We are well aware that neither the speech of men nor the analogy of human nature can give us a full insight into the things of God. The ineffable cannot submit to the bounds and limits of definition; that which is spiritual is distinct from every class or instance of bodily things. Yet, since our subject is that of heavenly natures, we must employ ordinary natures and ordinary speech as our means of expressing what our mind apprehends; a means no doubt unworthy of the majesty of God, but forced upon us by feebleness of our intellect, which can use only our own circumstances and our own words to convey to others our perceptions and our conclusions.[163]

So, what is the legacy of Augustine's trinitarian thinking?[164] At the moment, it is quite challenging to discern a scholarly consensus in the interpretation of his view of the Trinity.[165] Following the Theodore de Regnon thesis, the older view opines that because of his Neoplatonic leanings, Augustine stressed the unity of the divine essence and had a hard time accounting for threeness. That interpretation would, of course, lead to considering his approach almost diametrically opposed to the Eastern view.[166] This line of thinking in contemporary theology was forcefully represented by the late British systematician Colin Gunton, who argued that Augustine did not correctly understand the tradition, particularly the teaching of the Cappadocians; hence, so his argument went, Augustine ended up viewing the divine substance in a way "behind" relations. For the Cappadocians, so this critic says, on the contrary, relations are ontological rather than logical, as in the Bishop of Hippo's theology. Other charges against Augustine are also listed.[167] Some other scholars have joined this reasoning.[168]

What can be said safely is that the majority of current scholars are hardly convinced that this is a fair reading of Augustine.[169] Two foundational problems are found in the older interpretation of Augustine, the correction of which is past due. First, it is doubtful whether the Cappadocians had as developed a "social doctrine of the Trinity"[170] as is often assumed, and second, it is also doubtful that Augustine really started with the unity of the divine essence rather than with the distinctiveness of persons. Some think Augustine was simply building on the Cappadocians' view: "Augustine begins where the Cappadocians leave off: accepting their answer to the question 'why not three gods?' he proceeds to ask 'three what?'"[171] Current scholarship also debunks the traditional textbook caricature according to which Augustine was virtually incompetent in reading Greek texts and therefore could not even have primary access to the Cappadocians' and others texts (recall also the knowledge of the Eastern tradition for example by Hilary explained above).[172] Happily—again—we may leave the rest of this complicated issue for the experts' continuing debates and new studies.

Augustine *On the Trinity*

The 15-volume treatise[173] *On the Trinity* consists, roughly speaking, of two interrelated sections: the first seven books major in biblical exposition and the rest on (logical) theological considerations, including the well-known but often too strongly highlighted analogies in the created world. This is to say that even though the book is not only a scriptural and theological exposition but also an intellectual exercise par excellence, Augustine did not see the Trinity as a matter of philosophical speculation. Rather, it is a datum of revelation, which in his view Scripture proclaims on almost every page. Inquiry into this supreme doctrine of Christianity illustrates the bishop's foundational theological principle that faith must precede and illumine understanding. The following statement can be taken as a profound summary of the established trinitarian doctrine:

> Therefore let us with steadfast piety believe in one God, the Father, and the Son, and the Holy Spirit; let us at the same time believe that the Son is not [the person] who is the Father, and the

Father is not [the person] who is the Son, and neither the Father nor the Son is [the person] who is the Spirit of both the Father and the Son. Let it not be supposed that in this Trinity there is any separation in respect of time or place, but that these Three are equal and co-eternal, and absolutely of one nature: and that the creatures have been made, not some by the Father, and some by the Son, and some by the Holy Spirit, but that each and all that have been or are now being created subsist in the Trinity as their Creator; and that no one is saved by the Father without the Son and the Holy Spirit, or by the Son without the Father and the Holy Spirit, or by the Holy Spirit without the Father and the Son, but by the Father, the Son, and the Holy Spirit, the only one, true, and truly immortal (that is, absolutely unchangeable) God.[174]

The distinctions of the three persons as well as their uncompromising unity is affirmed in no uncertain terms in this manner, importantly touching also the "begetting" theme, so prevalent in trinitarian debates:

As, therefore, the Father begat, the Son is begotten; so the Father sent, the Son was sent. But in like manner as He who begat and He who was begotten, so both He who sent and He who was sent, are one, since the Father and the Son are one. So also the Holy Spirit is one with them, since these three are one. For as to be born, in respect to the Son, means to be from the Father; so to be sent, in respect to the Son, means to be known to be from the Father. And as to be the gift of God in respect to the Holy Spirit, means to proceed from the Father; so to be sent, is to be known to proceed from the Father. Neither can we say that the Holy Spirit does not also proceed from the Son, for the same Spirit is not without reason said to be the Spirit both of the Father and of the Son.[175]

What has been named as Augustine's rule, namely that the works of the Trinity *ad extra* (outwardly) are undivided whereas the ("inward") eternal relations among Father, Son, and Spirit can and should be distinguished (lest the whole trinitarian distinction be lost), is not his invention but, as noted above, was also affirmed by Greek theologians (clearly formulated by Gregory of Nyssa).[176] Augustine's view of the unity of the works of the Trinity is highly nuanced as it still makes room for the possibility of speaking of unique and irreplaceable roles of each of the trinitarian members in the incarnation. In the beginning of *On the Trinity*, having first repeated the contents of the "Catholic faith" regarding the distinctness of the Three and their uncompromising unity, he relates that theological confession with incarnation, showing that what each of them did is unique to them. In other words, when speaking of the Word becoming flesh, we should distinguish the particular roles of Father, Son, and Spirit:

> Yet not that this Trinity was born of the Virgin Mary, and crucified under Pontius Pilate, and buried, and rose again the third day, and ascended into heaven, but only the Son. Nor, again, that this Trinity descended in the form of a dove upon Jesus when He was baptized; nor that, on the day of Pentecost, after the ascension of the Lord, when "there came a sound from heaven, as of a rushing mighty wind," the same Trinity "sat upon each of them with cloven tongues like as of fire," but only the Holy Spirit. Nor yet that this Trinity said from heaven, "Thou art my Son," whether when He was baptized by John, or when the three disciples were with Him in the mount, or when the voice sounded, saying, "I have both glorified it, and will glorify it again;" but that it was a word of the Father only, spoken to the Son; although the Father, and the Son, and the Holy Spirit, as they are indivisible, so work indivisibly.[177]

This lengthy quotation also highlights one of the abiding interests of Augustine, namely incarnation and its relation to the doctrine of the Trinity. For Augustine, incarnation is a major trinitarian event, and it shapes his view of the Trinity more fully than is often acknowledged by his interpreters; it also helps save his doctrine from overly abstract speculations.[178] The Bishop of Hippo also takes pains in convincing his readers that incarnation is a unique event. For example, in expositing the Gospel story about Jesus's baptism, Augustine argues that while the manifestation of the Spirit in the form of a dove and the Father's voice from above were temporary and symbolic, the incarnation is a permanent assumption of humanity in a real union of two natures.[179]

As much as the Cappadocians and Greek theology should be acknowledged for emphasizing the mutual relationality and hence communion among Father, Son, and Spirit, that central trinitarian principle is in no way a commodity belonging to the East. Even Pannenberg, who otherwise is somewhat critical of the Augustinian legacy, has shown convincingly that "Augustine took over the relational definition of the Trinitarian distinctions which the Cappadocians, following Athanasius, had developed. He made the point that the distinctions of the persons are conditioned by their mutual relations."[180] For Augustine, the relations are eternal.[181] Hence, the Eastern idea of *perichoresis*, mutual interpenetration, is no stranger to his views: "Those three, therefore, both seem to be mutually determined to each other, and are in themselves infinite. But here in corporeal things, one thing alone is not as much as three together, and two are something more than one; but in that highest Trinity one is as much as the three together, nor are two anything more than one."[182]

Although, as said, the analogies Augustine employed to illustrate some trinitarian insights should be put in perspective and not given undue attention, it is also important to see their theological legitimacy. It would be unreasonable to contest his simple principle (based on Rom 1:20): "When therefore we regard the Creator, who is understood by the things that are made we must needs understand the Trinity of whom there appear traces in the creature, as is fitting." The more so when, following this statement, Augustine hastens to add that the "Trinity is the supreme source of all things" and the Three of whom the analogies are used are "infinite."[183] In other words, this is not an attempt to make God in our image, as it were, but, rather, on the basis of the infinite Creator's works to attempt to say something of this supreme God. As is well known, Augustine employs various types of images, from love, lover, and beloved (particularly Book 8 of *On the Trinity*), to mind, mind's knowledge of itself, and the mind's love for itself (Book 9, among others), to memory, understanding, and will (Book 10), and so forth. His logic is compelling: if the human mind knows love in itself, it knows God since God is love.

That said, it is important to note that Augustine did not try to derive the trinitarian distinctions from the divine unity. The psychological analogies that he suggested and developed in his work on the Trinity were meant to illustrate and make more plausible the unity–Trinity relationship.[184] Furthermore, the Bishop of Hippo was aware of the limitations of the images.[185] The potential weakness of his analogy of self-presence, self-knowledge, and self-love—widely used in subsequent tradition—is that it leans toward a "monopersonal, modalistic view of God."[186] This is interesting in that, in principle, Augustine's analogies grow out of an interpersonal, and thus communal and relational, context, especially when it comes to love. Richard of St. Victor in the medieval era picks up the relational aspect of Augustine's emphasis on love and develops it into a communion theology.[187]

Augustine's reflections on the Spirit in the Trinity are highly valuable. He conceives the Spirit as communion (of the Father and the Son),[188] their shared love,[189] and a gift.[190] As mentioned, he also develops his thought on the Trinity with the help of the idea of interpersonal love in terms of filiation and paternity. The Father is Lover, the Son the Beloved, and the Spirit the mutual Love that connects the two. Unlike some critics' opinions, Augustine considers the origin of the Spirit in a nuanced way. The Spirit proceeds "originally" from the Father and also in common from both the Father and Son, as something given by the Father.[191] In other words, Augustine is careful in safeguarding the Father as the primary source of the Spirit.[192] And even when the Son is included in the act of procession of the Spirit, it is not from two sources but, rather, from a single source in order to protect divine unity.[193] That said, there is no doubt that Augustine is an important influence on the gradual consolidation of the *filioque* clause, to be discussed below (that the Spirit proceeds from the Father *and* Son, as opposed to the East's insistence on procession only from the Father).[194]

A leading concern behind Augustine's theological program is the right ordering of love. It can be focused either on things of this earth or God, the highest good. Ultimately, the doctrine of the Trinity is an exposition of this right ordering, as showcased in his *On the Christian Doctrine* (1.5.5),[195] another profound summary of orthodoxy:

> The true objects of enjoyment, then, are the Father and the Son and the Holy Spirit, who are at the same time the Trinity, one Being, supreme above all, and common to all who enjoy Him. . . . The Trinity, one God, of whom are all things, through whom are all things, in whom are all things. Thus the Father and the Son and the Holy Spirit, and each of these by Himself, is God, and at the same time they are all one God; and each of them by Himself is a complete substance, and yet they are all one substance. The Father is not the Son nor the Holy Spirit; the Son is not the Father nor the Holy Spirit; the Holy Spirit is not the Father nor the Son: but the Father is only Father, the Son is only Son, and the Holy Spirit is only Holy Spirit. To all three belong the same eternity, the same unchangeableness, the same majesty, the same power. In the Father is unity, in the Son equality, in the Holy Spirit the harmony of unity and equality; and these three attributes are all one because of the Father, all equal because of the Son, and all harmonious because of the Holy Spirit.

West vs. East?

Now, in light of key ideas of Augustinian teaching, we are in a place to try to address at least tentatively the question of the subheading. For starters, an important distinction must be made between Augustine's own ideas and his legacy as carried on by later (Western) tradition.[196] Looking at Augustine's own writings, "[i]t hardly appears that Augustine had little interest in the distinctions of the persons, or that he was averse to the full import of the Incarnation."[197] Nor is it true that Augustine developed his trinitarian theology abstractly, based on analogies; he did not. He is thoroughly biblical, as a quick look, for example, at the first half of the *De Trinitate* clearly shows (let alone his biblical commentaries). Nor is it right to say that—in contrast to the Cappadocians and Athanasius—Augustine neglected spirituality and salvation.[198] His focus on incarnation alone would counter this charge.

In light of these considerations, a more nuanced and sophisticated way of looking at the differences between the Christian East and West is in order.[199] I think it is best done by trying to discern the key characteristics and unique features in each without trying to artificially reconcile those nor make them more dramatic than they are.[200] Almost everyone agrees that for Eastern theologians the significance of the *hypostatic* distinctions among Father, Son, and Spirit has been a key concern. The East has wanted to speak of the "concrete particularity of Father, Son, and Spirit."[201] Furthermore, as already noted, the East emphasizes the Father as the source of the deity. Son and Spirit proceed from the Father from eternity; that said, our discussion of Augustine's nuanced reflections on the Spirit's proceeding also materially points in that direction.

Whatever the difference between the Christian East and West, each of them has faced its own challenges. For the East, the challenge was the danger of tritheism because of the emphasis on three different *hypostaseis* and subordinationism because of the idea of the Father as the source of divinity. For Westerners, particularly after Augustine's time, modalism has been a danger more so than for the Greek theologians. Moreover, Eastern theological traditions in general and trinitarian ones in particular have been more pneumatologically oriented, whereas in the West Christology has often played the key role. This again brings us to the question of the *filioque*, to be discussed in what follows.

Having said all this, one also has to acknowledge that there are several aspects of Augustine's legacy that in the hands of his Western followers—not seldom against the Master's basic intuitions (when assessed in hindsight)—helped lead to a more marginal role (if not an eclipse, as is sometimes overdramatically charged) of the trinitarian doctrine. First, with all his stress on relationality, there is no denying that Augustine also emphasized not only the divine unity but also the substance and simplicity in a manner that (perhaps erroneously) was taken by some important Westerners as an inspiration for downplaying threeness.[202] Therefore, there is some truth in the insistence that, first, whereas for the Christian East distinctions of persons (*hypostaseis*) are the key to Trinity, for Augustine it is substance, though not to the neglect of relations. Second, Augustine's idea of the Spirit as shared love between Father and Son is a liability both theologically and ecumenically, as "love" can be—and has often been—conceived in nonpersonal ways. Third, as mentioned, Augustine's theology feeds the idea of *filioque*. Finally, while Augustine seemed to handle analogies of the Trinity with care and was aware of their limitations, many of his followers elevated them to a role that easily leads away from concrete biblical salvation history into abstract speculations.

Having now reviewed in some detail the emergence and development of the *doctrine* of the Trinity beginning from the first century of the postbiblical times all the way to the fifth century, before continuing the historical scrutiny to medieval and later periods, an important task awaits us. It has to do with a more focused look at the Spirit, the "third" person of the Trinity. While, of course, the Spirit has not been absent from this discussion, it has not played in any way the kind of central role the Father and the Son have. As typical as that omission may be in standard textbooks and studies, it is not justified. Hence, the next chapter delves into the nature and role of the Spirit in the Trinity.

Notes

1. We need to be mindful that the nearly absolute distinction between Scripture and other writings developed gradually in early Christianity. For useful comments, see Stephen R. Holmes, *The Quest*

for the Trinity: The Doctrine of God in Scripture, History, and Modernity (Downers Grove, IL: InterVarsity, 2012), 58–59.

2. As mentioned, that challenge is set forth vigorously in ibid.

3. This list is taken from Veli-Matti Kärkkäinen, *The Trinity: Global Perspectives* (Louisville: Westminster John Knox, 2007), 20–22, based on sources such as Wolfhart Pannenberg, *Systematic Theology*, vol. 1, trans. Geoffrey W. Bromiley (Grand Rapids: Eerdmans, 1991), 269–71 (particularly); and Gerald O'Collins, *The Tripersonal God: Understanding and Interpreting the Trinity* (Mahwah, NJ: Paulist, 1999), 85–87.

4. From the Greek term *hypostasis*, the basic meaning of which here is "personal" or "something with identity." This term has a checkered history in early Christian theology, as will be noted in what follows.

5. See, further, Maurice Wiles, "Reflections on the Origins of the Doctrine of the Trinity," in *Working Papers in Doctrine* (London: SCM Press, 1976), 10.

6. A classic introduction to these early heresies (plus two others, Apollinarianism and Eutychianism, related mainly to christological debates) is provided by J. W. C. Wand, *The Four Great Heresies* (London: A. R. Mowbray, 1955). While outdated in some respects, the main outline is still reliable and highly accessible to readers with less theological training.

7. J. N. D. Kelly, *Early Christian Doctrines*, rev. ed. (New York: Harper & Row, 1960), 88, 87 respectively.

8. Ibid., 90–95, at 95.

9. Ibid., 95.

10. "The Apologists were the first to try to frame an intellectually satisfying explanation of the relation of Christ to God the Father." Ibid.

11. Highly important biblical support was also found in Proverbs 8, cited in ch. 1, above; for useful comments on Justin's use of it, see, in Holmes, *Quest for the Trinity*, 60–61; for Theophilus of Antioch with regard to the same passage, see 61. Curiously, Iranaeus, another early theologian, linked Wisdom in Proverbs 8 with the Spirit; for details, see 65–66.

12. An accessible, short orientation to the background and meaning of *Logos* can be found in Kelly, *Early Christian Doctrines*, 9–11, 18.

13. O'Collins, *Tripersonal God*, 94 (attributing this particularly to Justin).

Another favorite christological image in Justin, namely, Angel (of the Lord), was also helpful in highlighting the mediatory role of Christ, as in OT theophanies; 88–89, 94.

14. Kelly, *Early Christian Doctrines*, 95.

15. For sources and details, see ibid., 96–97.

16. Justin Martyr, *Dialogue with Trypho, A Jew*, ch. 128, ANF 1:264; for a useful discussion, see O'Collins, *Tripersonal God*, 89. For a detailed discussion of "The Apologists and the Word," see Kelly, *Early Christian Doctrines*, 95–101.

17. Kelly, *Early Christian Doctrines*, 101–4, at 103.

18. Ibid., 104; for a useful account of Ireaneus's fight with Gnosticism (particularly the group by the name Valentinians), see Holmes, *Quest for the Trinity*, 62–65.

19. Irenaeus, *Against Heresies* 1.10.1, ANF 1:330. For comments and other examples, see O'Collins, *Tripersonal God*, 102–3.

20. Origen, *On First Principles* 1.3.5–8, ANF 4:253–56. Also Pannenberg, *Systematic Theology*, 1:271.

21. Irenaeus, *Against Heresies* 4.20.1, ANF 1:487: "It was not angels, therefore, who made us, nor who formed us, neither had angels power to make an image of God, nor any one else, except the Word of the Lord, nor any Power remotely distant from the Father of all things. For God did not stand in need of these [beings], in order to the accomplishing of what He had Himself determined with Himself beforehand should be done, as if He did not possess His own hands. For with Him were always present the Word and Wisdom, the Son and the Spirit, by whom and in whom, freely and spontaneously, He made all things." At times Irenaeus was more analytic in attributing revelation of the Spirit to prophecy, revelation of the Son to incarnation, and revelation of the Father to the eschatological consummation. Irenaeus, *Against Heresies* 4.20.5, ANF 1:488–89. See also Pannenberg, *Systematic Theology*, 1:270–71.

22. For incisive comments, see Pannenberg, *Systematic Theology*, 1:278–79.

23. Ibid., 271 (and literature mentioned therein).

24. Ibid., 278.

25. Tertullian, *Against Praxeas* sect. 9, ANF 3:603–4, quoting John 14:28 and 14:16.

26. Origen, *Homilies on Numbers* 12.1, referenced in Pannenberg, *Systematic Theology*, 1:272 n. 48.

27. Pannenberg, *Systematic Theology*, 1:272.

28. Athanasius, *Four Discourses against the Arians* 1.29, NPNF[2] 4:323. Although he was not the first to employ this device, Athanasius made it a theological theme in trinitarian deliberations; see, further, Pannenberg, *Systematic Theology*, 1:273.

29. In his letters to Serapion, Athanasius made some efforts to transfer the argument from the Father–Son relation to considering the Spirit–Father–Son web of relations; those attempts hardly are convincing since it is very difficult to discern the compelling logic behind it. For details, see Pannenberg, *Systematic Theology*, 1:279.

30. For a detailed investigation, see O'Collins, *Tripersonal God*, 23–34.

31. Roger E. Olson and Christopher A. Hall, *The Trinity*, Guides to Theology (Grand Rapids: Eerdmans, 2002), 18.

32. Theophilus of Antioch, *Theophilus to Autolycus: Book II*, 2.15, in ANF 2:101, among others; Irenaeus, *Against Heresies* 4.20.1, ANF 1:487, among others.

33. See Justin Martyr, *Dialogue with Trypho* 61.1, ANF 1:227–28 and passim; Tertullian, *Against Praxeas* 6–8, ANF 3:601–3, among others. For these and other examples, see Pannenberg, *Systematic Theology*, 1:270.

34. Pannenberg, *Systematic Theology*, 1:275.

35. O'Collins, *Tripersonal God*, 86. See also the helpful discussion in Robert Letham, *The Holy Trinity: In Scripture, History, Theology, and Worship* (Phillipsburg, NJ: P&R Publishing, 2004), 97.

36. Justin Martyr, *The First Apology*, sect. 13, ANF 1:166–67. For helpful comments on this passage and similar in Justin, see O'Collins, *Tripersonal God*, 90–91.

37. Irenaeus, *Against Heresies* 4.20.1, ANF 1:487.

38. For details, see Kelly, *Early Christian Doctrines*, esp. 86–87, 104–5.

39. See Catherine Mowry LaCugna, *God for Us: The Trinity and Christian Life* (San Francisco: HarperSanFrancisco, 1991), 23–24.

40. Irenaeus, *Against Heresies* 2.30.9; 4.20.3, ANF 1:406; 488, respectively.

41. Ibid., 4.20.6, ANF 1:489, among others.

42. See Kelly, *Early Christian Doctrines*, 105.

43. Irenaeus, *Against Heresies*, 3.18.1, *ANF* 1:446. The paragraph says in full: "As it has been clearly demonstrated that the Word, who existed in the beginning with God, by whom all things were made, who was also always present with mankind, was in these last days, according to the time appointed by the Father, united to His own workmanship, inasmuch as He became a man liable to suffering, [it follows] that every objection is set aside of those who say, "If our Lord was born at that time, Christ had therefore no previous existence." For I have shown that the Son of God did not then begin to exist, being with the Father from the beginning; but when He became incarnate, and was made man." In Book 4 he says: "We have shown at length that the Word, that is the Son, was always with the Father." In this same passage, while unfortunately confusing Wisdom and Spirit, Irenaeus extends the idea of consubstantiality to the third member of the Trinity as well: "And that Wisdom, which is the Spirit, was present with Him, anterior to all creation." Ibid., 4.20.3, *ANF* 1:488.

44. A classic study is Benjamin B. Warfield, "Tertullian and the Doctrine of the Trinity," in *Studies in Tertullian and Augustine* (New York: Oxford University Press, 1930), 1–109. As always, a reliable short guide to basic issues is Kelly, *Early Christian Doctrines*, 110–15 (including Hippolytos). Letham, *Holy Trinity*, 97–101, offers a balanced, helpful overall assessment of Tertullian's role in the development of trinitarian traditions. When speaking of the Spirit in the Trinity, a reference will be made to Tertullian's early alliance with Montanism, a pneumatological heresy of the times.

45. Tertullian, *Against Marcion* 1.3, *ANF* 3:272: "If God is not one, then there is no God."

46. Tertullian, *Against Praxeas*, sect. 10, *ANF* 3:604.

47. Indeed, there are more monarchian versions than that. The whole question of monarchianism is complicated and complex both historically and theologically. For the sake of an introductory survey, however, it is right and appropriate to focus on the two "textbook" forms of this heresy.

48. Reliable expositions, with references to original sources, are offered by Kelly, *Early Christian Doctrines*, 115–19; Justo L. González, *A History of Christian Thought*, vol. 1: *From the Beginnings to the Council of Chalcedon* (Nashville: Abingdon, 1970), 146–49, 182–87 (Tertullian's orthodox rebuttal of Praxeas's heretical monarchianism).

49. For details, see Kelly, *Early Christian Doctrines*, 119–23.

50. A less well known (than Tertullian) opponent of modalism, particularly the version represented by Noetus (whose views are materially close to those of Sabellius, another leading modalist), was Hippolytus, who offered a powerful rebuttal in his *Refutation of All Heresies*; for some details, see Holmes, *The Quest for the Trinity*, 68–69.

51. Tertullian, *Against Praxeas*, sect. 13, ANF 3:607–9.

52. Ibid., sect. 2, ANF 3:589.

53. A highly useful discussion of Tertullian's response, particularly as it comes through in his highly influential book *Against Praxeas*, can be found in Holmes, *Quest for the Trinity*, 69–72 particularly.

54. González, *History of Christian Thought*, 1:182–83, particularly with reference to Tertullian, *Against Praxeas* section 3.

55. Kelly, *Early Christian Doctrines*, 113.

56. Tertullian. *Against Praxeas*, sect. 12, ANF 3:606–7.

57. Ibid., sect. 8, ANF 3:602–3.

58. Ibid., sect. 2, ANF 3:598.

59. See ibid., sect. 25, ANF 3:621.

60. Ibid., sect. 3, ANF 3:598–99. Even then, Tertullian's thinking was still tied to the derivationist tendency of the Apologist tradition in that he regarded the Father as the "whole substance," while the Son as derivation from the whole. See further Kelly, *Early Christian Doctrines*, 114–15.

61. Tertullian, *Against Praxeas*, sect. 2, ANF 3:598. Father, Son, and Spirit are three "not in condition, but in degree; not in substance, but in form; not in power, but in aspect; yet of one substance, and of one condition, and of one power, inasmuch as he is one God." Ibid.

62. O'Collins, *Tripersonal God*, 105. The term "substance" rather than "essence" (from Latin *essentia*) was adopted by the Westerners to speak of the undivided unity of the Godhead, corresponding to the Eastern Christians' Greek term *ousia*. We will come later to the terminological obscurities and challenges.

63. For a highly useful discussion of Origen's contributions, see Holmes, *Quest for the Trinity*, 74–80; Letham, *Holy Trinity*, 101–7.

64. Origen, *First Principles* 1.2.4, ANF 4:247.

65. For a helpful discussion of the ambiguity, see Olson and Hall, *The Trinity*, 24–26.

66. Origen, *First Principles* 1.2.9, *ANF* 4:249 (speaking of Wisdom); 2.11, *ANF* 4:251 (similarly of Wisdom); and so forth.

67. Ibid., 1.2.2, *ANF* 4:246.

68. Ibid., 1.2.6, *ANF* 4:247–48.

69. Ibid., 1.2.7, *ANF* 4:248: "According to John, 'God is light.' The only-begotten Son, therefore, is the glory of this light, proceeding inseparably from (God) Himself, as brightness does from light, and illuminating the whole of creation. For, agreeably to what we have already explained as to the manner in which He is the Way, and conducts to the Father; and in which He is the Word, interpreting the secrets of wisdom, and the mysteries of knowledge, making them known to the rational creation; and is also the Truth, and the Life, and the Resurrection,—in the same way ought we to understand also the meaning of His being the brightness: for it is by its splendour that we understand and feel what light itself is."

70. Ibid. 1.2.13, *ANF* 4:251.

71. Ibid.

72. Clearly implied, e.g., in 1.3.5, *ANF* 4:253. For other examples, see Olsen and Hall, *The Trinity*, 25. Pannenberg goes so far as to say that for Origen the son was, in Pannenberg's view, a "creature." Pannenberg, *Systematic Theology*, 1:275. I am not quite sure what he means by that, though.

73. Holmes, *Quest for the Trinity*, 79; at the end of the quotation, reference to Origen, *On First Principles*, 1.3.4 and 4.3.14.

74. Origen, *First Principles* 1.2.13 (*ANF* 4: 251); Origen, *Against Celsus* 5.39, *ANF* 4:561.

75. *Pneumatomachii* (Pneumatomachians), literally "Spirit fighters," were fourth-century heretics who denied the deity of the Holy Spirit.

76. Letham, *Holy Trinity*, 107.

77. Among a number of excellent standard guides to the basic historical and theological discussions and debates (many of them cited in this book), the most prominent place belongs to the massive study of Lewis Ayres, *Nicea and Its Legacy: An Approach to Fourth-Century Trinitarian Theology* (Oxford: Oxford University Press, 2004). An earlier standard text is R. P. C. Hanson, *The Search for the Christian Doctrine of God* (Edinburgh: T&T Clark, 1988). Holmes's *Quest for the Trinity*, chs. 4 and 5, are also now available for a highly informative discussion.

78. Holmes, *Quest for the Trinity*, 83.

79. Wand, *Four Great Heresies*, 38–62, discusses Arianism. A highly regarded contemporary study on various aspects of Arianism is Hanson, *Search for the Christian Doctrine of God.* A reliable guide is also Rowan Williams, *Arius: Heresy and Tradition* (Grand Rapids: Eerdmans, 2002).

80. A highly useful and accessible basic discussion about the Arian views, including the debate with Alexander, the bishop, is ch. 5 in Franz Dünzl, *A Brief History of the Doctrine of the Trinity in the Early Church*, trans. John Bowden (London/New York: T&T Clark, 2007). A highly recommended monograph is Rowan Williams, *Arius: Heresy and Tradition*. For the checkered historiography behind Arius, the alleged architect of Arianism, see *Arianism after Arius: Essays on the Development of the Fourth Century Trinitarian Conflicts*, ed. M. R. Barnes and Daniel H. Williams (Edinburgh: T&T Clark, 1993). As is well known, historians debate whether Arius is to be attributed with the teaching carrying his name or whether Arianism is a more generic heresy defined by Arius's opponents rather than himself. For (alleged) views of Arius, we are totally dependent on his orthodox opponent Athanasius's writings and his quotations from Arius's *Thalia*.

81. For critical differences between Arius and Origen, see the helpful discussion in Letham, *Holy Trinity*, 114–15.

82. Key ideas can be found conveniently in Athanasius, *Against the Arians* NPNF[2] 4:308–9. A helpful summary and explanation of Arian claims can be found in Letham, *Holy Trinity*, 111–14, and in Kelly, *Early Christian Doctrines*, 226–31.

83. O'Collins, *Tripersonal God*, 112.

84. Arius was conspicuously silent about the Spirit.

85. Robert C. Gregg and Dennis E. Groh, in an important study fittingly titled *Early Arianism: A View of Salvation* (Philadelphia: Fortress Press, 1981), sets forth the argument that whatever else Arianism was, it was about salvation (x).

86. Letham, *Holy Trinity*, 112.

87. In the Christian East, salvation is understood in terms of *theosis*, deification, divinization.

88. For a highly useful and accessible discussion of both Nicea and Athanasius, see Holmes, *Quest for the Trinity*, 87–92.

89. An excellent and accurate, richly documented presentation of their views is Olson and Hall, *The Trinity*, 31–40. This section is indebted to it.

90. Apart from consulting standard church histories, a highly useful short and accessible theological account can be found in ch. 6 of Dünzl, *Brief History*.

91. Athanasius and Arius, as far as we know, did not have a personal encounter, Arius probably having died before Athanasius, as a young man, started opposing his views. For an interesting study, see C. Kannengiesser, *Arius and Athanasius: Two Alexandrian Theologians* (Aldershot, UK: Variorum, 1991).

92. The creedal text referred to as the Nicene Creed is from the Council of Constantinople in 381, which gave this statement its final formulation. Hence, it is often called the Nicene-Constantinopolitan Creed. For a detailed comparison between the Nicean "statement" and Constantinopolitan Creed, see ch. 6 in O'Collins, *Tripersonal God*.

93. Philip Schaff, ed., *The Creeds of Christendom*, 6th ed. (Grand Rapids: Baker, 1990 [1931]), 1:28–29, available at http://www.ccel.org/ccel/schaff/creeds1.html. For a definitive, detailed treatment of Nicea's theology of Christ (and Trinity), see Kelly, *Early Christian Doctrines*, 231–37.

94. For which, see my *Christology: A Global Introduction*, rev. 2d ed. (Grand Rapids: Eerdmans, 2016), 51–54 particularly.

95. See O'Collins, *Tripersonal God*, 119; Holmes, *Quest for the Trinity*, 88 particularly.

96. For details and sources, see O'Collins, *Tripersonal God*, ch. 6. For a careful discussion of these terms (*homoousios, homoiousios*), their background, and various nuances, see Kelly, *Early Christian Doctrines*, 233–37.

97. For a brief account of the modalistic rejections of Photinus of Sirmium and others, see Holmes, *Quest for the Trinity*, 93–94.

98. Holmes, *Quest for the Trinity*, 93.

99. Letham, *Holy Trinity*, 117.

100. While it clarified the relation of the Son to Father in a foundational way, it also brought about Anti-Nicene parties; for an accessible account, see Kelly, *Early Christian Doctrines*, 247–51; and Letham, *Holy Trinity*, 122–26.

101. For an accessible theological account (mindful of sociopolitical and ecclesiastical factors) of some of the basic debates and turns, consult Dünzl, *Brief History*, chs. 7–10. An important figure behind some of the key *homoousios* debates was Marcellus of Ancyra with his deep modalistic leanings. In addition to ibid., for a brief helpful consideration, see Holmes, *Quest for the Trinity*, 85–90 particularly; and for a monographic presentation, see Sara Parvis, *Marcellus of Ancyra and the Last Years of the Arian Controversy 325-345* (Oxford: Oxford University Press, 2006).

102. For a highly useful discussion, see Holmes, *Quest for the Trinity*, ch. 5; other names used include Eunomians—and, coined by Ayres (*Nicea and its Legacy*), "Heterousians" (see 144–49 particularly).

103. For a careful and accessible discussion of Athanasius's trinitarian theology, see Letham, *Holy Trinity*, 127–45.

104. For a careful and accessible discussion of the Cappadocians' trinitarian theology, see Letham, *Holy Trinity*, 146–66; Kelly, *Early Christian Doctrines*, 263–69.

105. Kelly, *Early Christian Doctrines*, 233. The following three references to Athanasius are provided by Kelly in the cited text.

106. E.g., Athanasius, *Against the Arians* 1.17f.; 1.20; 3.15f., $NPNF^2$ 4:316ff.; 318; 402ff.

107. Ibid., 2.41f., $NPNF^2$ 4:370ff.

108. Ibid., 2.67; 2.70, $NPNF^2$ 4:384–85; 386–87.

109. For a detailed discussion of Athanasius and his pro-Nicene defense, see Kelly, *Early Christian Doctrines*, 240–47; 284–89.

110. Athanasius, *On Luke 10:22 (Matthew 11:27)*, sects. 4–6, $NPNF^2$ 4:89–90.

111. Athanasius, *Against the Arians* 3.6, $NPNF^2$ 4:396–97.

112. Letham, *Holy Trinity*, 137.

113. According to ibid., 178: "Although the precise word *perichoresis* was not used for some time yet, the truth it signifies was already widely accepted."

114. Basil of Caesarea, *Letters* 38.8, $NPNF^2$ 8:141. (It is not certain if Basil or Gregory of Nyssa is the author; in any case, this quotation nicely reflects the view of the Cappadocians.)

115. See, e.g., Gregory of Nazianzus, *Oration 28. The Second Theological Oration*, #4, $NPNF^2$ 7:289: "It is difficult to conceive God but to define

Him in words is an impossibility, as one of the Greek teachers of Divinity taught, not unskilfully (sic), as it appears to me; with the intention that he might be thought to have apprehended Him; in that he says it is a hard thing to do; and yet may escape being convicted of ignorance because of the impossibility of giving expression to the apprehension. But in my opinion it is impossible to express Him, and yet more impossible to conceive Him."

116. Dünzl, *Brief History*, 106–7.

117. Saint Basil of Caesarea, *Against Eunomius*, trans. M. DelCogliano and A. Radde-Gallwitz, *The Fathers of the Church*, vol. 122 (Washington, DC: Catholic University of America Press, 2011).

118. Gregory of Nyssa wrote two treatises, namely *Against Eunomius* and *Answer to Eunomius' Second Book*. (This follows the standard categorization of Gregory's writings dealing with Eunomius in *NPNF*[2] 5, somewhat differently from the original Greek textual edition.)

119. Gregory of Nyssa, *Against Eunomius*, bk. 12, ch. 2, *NPNF*[2] 5:242 (and so throughout).

120. Gregory of Nyssa, *Answer to Eunomius' Second Book*, *NPNF*[2] 5:252–53; for useful comments, see also Holmes, *Quest for the Trinity*, 104–5.

121. Gregory of Nyssa, *Against Eunomius*, 12.3, *NPNF*[2] 5:244.

122. Gregory of Nyssa, *Answer to Eunomius' Second Book*, *NPNF*[2] 5:255–56.

123. Gregory of Nyssa, *On "Not Three Gods,"* *NPNF*[2] 5:331–33.

124. Ibid.

125. Ibid., 334.

126. LaCugna, *God for Us*, 69.

127. Ibid., 70 (emphases in the original).

128. See Gregory of Nazianzus, *Oration 31. The Fifth Theological Oration. On the Holy Spirit*, #14, *NPNF*[2] 7:322.

129. O'Collins, *Tripersonal God*, 131–32.

130. González, *History of Christian Thought*, 1:321–22, at 321, with reference particularly to Gregory of Nazianzus, *Theological Orations* 16.

131. For a useful and insightful reading, see Letham, *Holy Trinity*, 157–64; Holmes, *Quest for the Trinity*, 111–16.

132. See Gregory of Nazianzus, *The Second Theological Oration*, #4, *NPNF*[2] 7:309–19.

133. Gregory of Nazianzus, *Oration 29. The Third Theological Oration. On the Son*, #3, *NPNF*[2] 7:301–2.

134. Ibid.

135. Ibid., #2, in *NPNF*[2] 7:301.

136. Letham, *Holy Trinity*, 159.

137. Gregory of Nazianzus, *On the Son*, #16, *NPNF*[2] 7:307. As typical of the Apostolic Fathers, the meaning and significance of the divine names plays an important role in the reasoning. Consider Gregory's musings on the name Son in *Oration 30: The Fourth Theological Oration, Which is the Second Concerning the Son*, #20, *NPNF*[2] 7:316: "In my opinion He is called Son because He is identical with the Father in Essence; and not only for this reason, but also because He is Of Him. And He is called Only-Begotten, not because He is the only Son and of the Father alone, and only a Son; but also because the manner of His Sonship is peculiar to Himself and not shared by bodies. And He is called the Word, because He is related to the Father as Word to Mind; not only on account of His passionless Generation, but also because of the Union, and of His declaratory function. Perhaps too this relation might be compared to that between the Definition and the Thing defined. . . . For, it says, he that hath mental perception of the Son (for this is the meaning of Hath Seen) hath also perceived the Father;—and the Son is a concise demonstration and easy setting forth of the Father's Nature." Thereafter, the text continues with similar kinds of comments on a number of other names.

138. Gregory of Nazianzus, *On the Holy Spirit*, #14, *NPNF*[2] 7:322; for useful comments, see Holmes, *Quest for the Trinity*, 115–16.

139. As with Nicea, the official convocation by the emperor (then Theodosius) of the Council in Constantinople was motivated more by political aspirations for the unity in the society than by religious and theological disputes (for which any standard scholarly church history text can be consulted). Furthermore, we do not have records from the Council itself; we only know of its proceedings in the documents of Chalcedon 451. That said, there is no doubt that Constantinople further helped the majority Nicean orthodox party to continue defeating opposing interpretations and so clarify its own position as well. For a reliable discussion of the Creed, see J. N. D. Kelly, *Early Christian Creeds*, 3d ed. (Harlow, UK: Longman, 1972), 296–331; highly useful for the beginning student is ch. 6 in O'Collins, *Tripersonal God*,

with a careful look at how the creed of Constantinople is related to the statement of Nicea (325).

140. O'Collins, *Tripersonal God*, 114–15; p. 115 shows in detail which parts of the Creed were in the Nicean statement and which were added at Constantinople.

141. The term "Cappadocian Settlement" is, of course, only a scholarly construct, a conclusion from the emerging theology of the Cappadocians, and as such needs to be handled with care. For words of warning, see Joseph T. Lienhard, S.J., "Ousia and Hypostasis: The Cappadocian Settlement and the Theology of 'One *Hypostasis*,'" in *The Trinity: An Interdisciplinary Symposium on Trinity*, ed. Stephen T. Davis, Daniel Kendall, S.J., and Gerald O'Collins, S.J. (Oxford: Oxford University Press, 1999), 99–103.

142. Dünzl, *Brief History*, 107 (emphases in the original).

143. See, further, Hanson, *Search for the Christian Doctrine of God*, 181: "people holding different views were using the same words as those who opposed them, but, unawares, giving them different meanings from those applied to them by their opponents." And even more: "Tertullian may well have supplied the West with its Trinitarian vocabulary; he certainly did not supply the East with its Trinitarian theology," 184. I am indebted to Letham, *Holy Trinity*, 118–20, for finding these two references in Hanson's monumental work.

144. For the history of the term *hypostasis*, see O'Collins, *Tripersonal God*, 117–18.

145. Even Augustine hesitated calling the persons hypostases because *hypostasis* and *substantia* were considered to be synonyms. Augustine, *On the Trinity* 7.5–6, NPNF[1] 3:111–14.

146. See, further, O'Collins, *Tripersonal God*, 118. Basil the Great framed the contours in a pointed way: "as he who fails to confess the community of the essence or substance falls into polytheism, so he who refuses to grant the distinction of the *hypostases* is carried away into [the error of] . . . Sabellius." Basil of Caesarea, *Letters* 210.5, NPNF[2] 8:251. Other terms in need of clarification were those describing the idea of birth and coming into existence as long as they were applied to trinitarian members: *genetos/agenetos* (created/"uncreated," that which has never existed before but rather is eternal) and *gennetos/agennetos* (begotten, generated/unbegotten, ingenerate). In the earliest Christian theology before Origen there was little distinction between the idea of being created and being generated. Orthodox doctrine had it

that the Son was *gennetos non genetos*, begotten of the Father but not created, while Arians taught that the Son is *genetos*. For a detailed discussion, see George L. Prestige, *God in Patristic Thought* (London, ON: W. Heinemann, 1936), 37–54.

147. Catherine Mowry LaCugna, "The Trinitarian Mystery of God," in *Systematic Theology: Roman Catholic Perspectives*, vol. 1, ed. Francis Schüssler Fiorenza and John P. Galvin (Minneapolis: Fortress Press, 1991), 170. LaCugna calls the Eastern view emanationist in terms of descending order from Father to Son to Spirit and finally to the world, whereas the Western view can be depicted as a circle enclosing all trinitarian members in which the whole Trinity relates to the world. Ibid., 170–71.

148. The classic work contrasting Eastern and Western views is Théodore de Régnon, *Études de théologie positive sur la sainte Trinité*, 3 vols. (Paris: Retaux, 1892–1898).

149. For a passionate critique, see, e.g., Holmes, *Quest for the Trinity*, 129–30 and passim.

150. O'Collins, *Tripersonal God*, 140.

151. For a comprehensive historical and theological account of Constantinople, a good source is Kelly, *Early Christian Creeds*, ch. 10.

152. See, further, Hanson, *Search for the Christian Doctrine of God*, 817–18.

153. Here and the rest of this chapter, the Nicene-Constantinopolitan Creed as translated in Hanson, *Search for the Christian Doctrine of God*, 815.

154. O'Collins makes the important point that the approach of Constantinople as well as of Nicea is "genetic," meaning that the divinity streams from the Father to the Son and to the Spirit rather than with the idea of one divine substance that would subsist in three persons. The Father is the source of the unity. O'Collins, *Tripersonal God*, 122. In this regard, Letham's statement that in the Nicene-Constantinopolitan Creed "[t]here is nothing . . . to suggest that the Son or the Holy Spirit derives his deity from the Father" is not well taken. Letham, *Holy Trinity*, 177.

155. Subheading for the section in Letham, *Holy Trinity*, 175–81. This paragraph is almost verbatim from my *Trinity*, 41.

156. Letham, *Holy Trinity*, 176.

157. Ibid., 177.

158. See, further, in ibid., 178–79.

159. Ibid., 179–80 (italics in the original).

160. Ambrose, *Exposition of the Christian Faith* 1.1.6, NPNF^2 10:202. Another key Latin thinker of the fourth century is Hilary of Poitiers, whose *The Trinity* is a landmark Western contribution. Hilary of Poitiers, *The Trinity*, in *Fathers of the Church*, vol. 25, trans. Stephen McKenna (Washington, DC: Catholic University of America Press, 2002).

161. For a useful and lucid exposition of Hilary's contributions, including a brief consideration of what happened since Tertullian and his own times, see Holmes, *Quest for the Trinity*, 122–29.

162. The same can be said of Augustine. Just consider these two statements: "If you understand, it is not God" and "We can more easily say what he is not than what he is." Both sayings (one from Sermon 117.5 and the other one from Exposition of Ps. 85.12) are reproduced in E. J. Fortman, ed., *Theology of God: Commentary* (New York: Bruce, 1968), 120.

163. Hilary of Poitiers, *De Trinitate (On the Trinity)*, bk. 4, #2, NPNF^2 9:71. The location of this passage might be intentional, though, in the sense that it is here where Hilary focuses his attention on the Eastern debates, whereas the shorter first part of the book is more on the general (Western) debates. Be that as it may, the statement itself is noteworthy.

164. "It is impossible to do contemporary Trinitarian theology and not have a judgment on Augustine." Michel René Barnes, "Rereading Augustine's Theology of the Trinity," in Davis, Kendall, and O'Collins, eds., *The Trinity*, 145.

165. Augustine's trinitarian theology was developed in many of his writings. The main sources besides the fifteen-volume *On the Trinity* are *The City of God*, *Confessions*, *Tractates on the Gospel of John*, *Letter 169* to Bishop Evodius, *Letter 11* to Nebridius, *On the Spirit and the Letter*, *On the Soul and Its Origins*, and *Sermons on Selected Lessons of the New Testament*. Olson and Hall (*The Trinity*, 46n97) contains a comprehensive listing. That said, there is no doubt that the center is *On the Trinity*, composed in the beginning of the fifth century (which, not untypically of the times, was labored over a lengthy period of time, almost two decades). For recent readings of *On the Trinity*, see Holmes, *Quest for the Trinity*, 129–39; ch. 15 in Ayres, *Nicea and Its Legacy*. For a massive monographic study of all-things Augustinian, see Ayres, *Augustine and the Trinity* (Cambridge: Cambridge University Press, 2011).

166. See, e.g., Prestige, *God in Patristic Thought*, 237.

167. See particularly Colin Gunton, *The Promise of Trinitarian Theology*, 2d ed. (Edinburgh: T&T Clark, 1997), ch. 3, titled "Augustine, The Trinity and the Theological Crisis of the West."

168. See, e.g., Thomas Marsh, *The Triune God: A Biblical, Historical, and Theological Study* (Mystic, CT: Twenty-Third Publications, 1994), 131–35 and passim.

169. In addition to the general opposition to the older thesis among recent scholars such as Ayres and Holmes, perhaps the most vocal critic of particularly the alleged Neoplatonic influence on Augustine is Barnes, "Rereading Augustine's Theology of the Trinity." A careful, cautious interpretation, quite critical of the old consensus, is also offered by Basil Studer, *Trinity and Incarnation: The Faith of the Early Church*, trans. Matthias Westerhoff, ed. Andrew Louth (Collegeville, MN: Liturgical, 1993), ch. 14.

170. Consult Holmes, *Quest for the Trinity*, to get the details.

171. Philip Cary, "Historical Perspectives on Trinitarian Doctrine," *Religious and Theological Studies Fellowship Bulletin* (November-December 1995), 7n6, also found in the PDF version, used here, http://templetonhonorscollege.com/wp-content/uploads/2014/04/History-of-Trinity-by-Dr.-Phil-Cary.pdf (12). A helpful summary of views pro and con can be found in Olson and Hall, *The Trinity*, 44–45; Holmes, *Quest for the Trinity*, 129–30. Most ironically, though often forgotten, the older view (going back allegedly to de Regnon) was not meant to disparage Augustine at the expense of the Cappadocians but exactly the opposite; that is, Augustine's approach was taken as superior (130).

172. See, e.g., Holmes, *Quest for the Trinity*, 130–31.

173. When speaking of fifteen "books," it is not to be taken in the sense of contemporary "book," as in this case (similar to many ancient sources) that nomenclature is equivalent roughly to a (long) chapter. Furthermore, as said, due to the (at times extremely) long process of preparing treatises at the time, the finished work seldom manifests the kind of coherent and logical development typical of modern/contemporary books and monographs.

174. Augustine, *Letter* 169 (ch. 2, #5) [To Evodius], in NPNF[1] 1:540. For the consubstantiality of the Son with the Father, see, e.g., Augustine, *On the Trinity* 1.6.9, NPNF[1] 3:21–22; and for the Spirit with the Father

and Son, see, e.g., ibid., 1.6.13, *NPNF*[1] 3:23–24; 7.3.6, *NPNF*[1] 3:108–9. An excellent exposition of Augustine's trinitarian views with meticulous documentation is Kelly, *Early Christian Doctrines*, 271–79.

175. Augustine, *On the Trinity* 4.20.29, *NPNF*[1] 3:85.

176. For an informed essay (including the English translation of #2 in Augustine's *Letter* 12, which is not available in standard English editions, see Lewis Ayres, "'Remember That You Are Catholic' (Serm. 52.2): Augustine on the Unity of the Triune God," *Journal of Early Christian Studies* 8 (2000): 39–82; I am indebted to Holmes, *Quest for the Trinity*, 132, for finding this source.

177. Augustine, *On the Trinity* 1.4.7, *NPNF*[1] 3:20. Augustine is deeply aware of the potential tension between the teaching on the unity and peculiar role of each of the Three (and even the later doctrine of *attribution* of specific works to each of the Three, such as that Father is the Creator, and Son the Redeemer, and Spirit the Sanctifier may not totally resolve it). Consider this passage, following the previous quotation: "Some persons, however, find a difficulty in this faith . . . especially when it is said that the Trinity works indivisibly in everything that God works, and yet that a certain voice of the Father spoke, which is not the voice of the Son; and that none except the Son was born in the flesh, and suffered, and rose again, and ascended into heaven; and that none except the Holy Spirit came in the form of a dove. They wish to understand how the Trinity uttered that voice which was only of the Father; and how the same Trinity created that flesh in which the Son only was born of the Virgin; and how the very same Trinity itself wrought that form of a dove, in which the Holy Spirit only appeared. Yet, otherwise, the Trinity does not work indivisibly, but the Father does some things, the Son other things, and the Holy Spirit yet others: or else, if they do some things together, some severally, then the Trinity is not indivisible. It is a difficulty, too, to them, in what manner the Holy Spirit is in the Trinity, whom neither the Father nor the Son, nor both, have begotten, although He is the Spirit both of the Father and of the Son." Ibid., 1.5.8., *NPNF*[1] 3:21.

178. See, further, Studer, *Trinity and Incarnation*, 168–85 especially.

179. Augustine, *Letters* 169.2.5–9, *NPNF*[1] 1:540–41.

180. Pannenberg, *Systematic Theology*, 1:284.

181. Ibid.

182. Augustine, in *On the Trinity*, 6.10.12, *NPNF*[1] 3:103.

183. Ibid.

184. Pannenberg, *Systematic Theology*, 1:284; see also 287: "Augustine's psychological analogies should not be used to derive the trinity from the unity but to simply illustrate the Trinity in whom one already believes."

185. Augustine, *On the Trinity* 15.23.43, NPNF[1] 3:222 is titled "The Infirmity of the Human Mind."

186. O'Collins, *Tripersonal God*, 137.

187. So also ibid., 135.

188. Augustine, *On the Trinity* 5.11.12, NPNF[1] 3:93; 15.27.50, NPNF[1] 3:226–27.

189. Ibid., 15.17.27, NPNF[1] 3:215; Augustine, *[Homilies] Tractates on the Gospel of St. John* 105.7.3, NPNF[1] 7:396.

190. Augustine, *On the Trinity* 5.12.13, NPNF[1] 3:93–94; 5.15.16, NPNF[1] 3:95.

191. Ibid., 15.26.47, NPNF[1] 3:225. Note this healthy warning: "Wherefore let him who can understand the generation of the Son from the Father without time, understand also the procession of the Holy Spirit from both without time."

192. See ibid., 4.20.29, NPNF[1] 3:84–85.

193. Ibid., 5.14.15, NPNF[1] 3:95: "[I]t must be admitted that the Father and the Son are a Beginning of the Holy Spirit, not two Beginnings; but as the Father and Son are one God, and one Creator, and one Lord relatively to the creature, so are they one Beginning relatively to the Holy Spirit. But the Father, the Son, and the Holy Spirit is one Beginning in respect to the creature, as also one Creator and one God."

194. For thoughtful reflections, see O'Collins, *Tripersonal God*, 138–41.

195. Augustine, *On the Christian Doctrine* 1.5.5, NPNF[1] 2:524.

196. For a balanced judgment, see Letham, *Holy Trinity*, 198–200.

197. Ibid., 195.

198. This is one of the theses of LaCugna's *God for Us*, 81–104.

199. Overstatements abound and those need to be corrected: "We must acknowledge that the doctrine of the trinity in the East is an integral part of its total theological understanding. The same cannot be said for the Western formulation stemming chiefly from Augustine. Here, the doctrine is an unneeded appendage to theology." John B. Cobb Jr., "The Relativization of the Trinity," in *Trinity in Process: A Relational*

Theology of God, ed. Joseph A. Bracken and Marjorie Hewitt Suchocki (New York: Continuum, 1997), 5.

200. Letham's *The Holy Trinity* includes a quite helpful chart of the key features of both East and West, even when it tends to be quite categorical (250–51).

201. Stanley J. Grenz, *Rediscovering the Triune God: The Trinity in Contemporary Theology* (Minneapolis: Fortress Press, 2004), 8.

202. Augustine, *On the Trinity*, 5.2.3, *NPNF*[1] 3:88: "[God] is, however, without doubt, a substance, or, if it be better so to call it, an essence, which the Greeks call οὐσία. For as wisdom is so called from the being wise, and knowledge from knowing; so from being *Esse* comes that which we call essence. And who is there that is, more than He who said to His servant Moses, "I am that I am;" . . . But other things that are called essences or substances admit of accidents, whereby a change, whether great or small, is produced in them. But there can be no accident of this kind in respect to God; and therefore He who is God is the only unchangeable substance or essence, to whom certainly being itself, whence comes the name of essence, most especially and most truly belongs. For that which is changed does not retain its own being; and that which can be changed, although it be not actually changed, is able not to be that which it had been; and hence that which not only is not changed, but also cannot at all be changed, alone falls most truly, without difficulty or hesitation, under the category of being."

3

The Holy Spirit: Divine and Equal?

Early Spirit Experience and Theology

Pneumatology Left Behind

As mentioned above, it is typical of trinitarian discussions and particularly histories to focus so much on the Father–Son relationship that the consideration of the doctrine of the Spirit (pneumatology) may be left on the margins. While understandable, that tendency is also theologically suspect, for the simple reason that without a proper and solid place for the Spirit, there can be no integrally *tri*-nitarian account of God. Hence, the purpose of this chapter is twofold. First, it will highlight the unique nature of the Holy Spirit alongside the Father and Son, including the grave difficulties the church had in trying to figure out what exactly the Spirit's nature and role is. Second, the ultimate goal is trinitarian, namely to follow the path in Christian theology that finally led to a trinitarian rather than binitarian confession.

Why did it take so long time for Christian theology to come up with a precise and accurate account of the doctrine of the Holy Spirit?[1] The basic reason is that the Spirit was first *experienced* in Christian life and community and only in a second movement reflected upon in terms of theological categories: "Long before the Spirit was a theme of doctrine, He was a fact in the experience of the community."[2] Furthermore, questions related to the Trinity and Christology occupied the best minds of the church during the first centuries, leaving less energy to focus on the Spirit.[3] There was also a biblical precedent here with regard to the way salvation history and its understanding have emerged. No less a trinitarian genius than Gregory of Nazianzus, in his *Fifth Oration*, which focused on a careful consideration of pneumatological errors, pronounced these oft-cited words:

> The Old Testament proclaimed the Father openly, and the Son more obscurely. The New manifested the Son, and suggested the Deity of the Spirit. Now the Spirit Himself dwells among us, and supplies us with a clearer demonstration of Himself. For it was not safe, when the Godhead of the Father was not yet acknowledged, plainly to proclaim the Son; nor when that of the Son was not yet received to burden us further (if I may use so bold an expression) with the Holy Ghost; lest perhaps people might, like men loaded with food beyond their strength, and presenting eyes as yet too weak to bear it to the sun's light, risk the loss even of that which was within the reach of their powers; but that by gradual additions . . . the Light of the Trinity might shine upon the more illuminated.

Not only that, but Gregory even goes father and argues that "[f]or this reason it was, I think, that He *gradually* came to dwell in the Disciples, measuring Himself out to them according to their capacity to receive Him, at the beginning of the Gospel, after the Passion, after the Ascension, making perfect their powers, being breathed upon them, and appearing in fiery tongues. And indeed it is by little and little that He is declared by Jesus, as you will learn for yourself if you will read more carefully."[4]

Related to this, it seems to many to be more difficult to try to say something doctrinal about the Spirit than about the Father and Son, since by definition the Spirit is more subtle and less concrete a phenomenon.[5] Not only that, but there seems to be a biblical precedent according to which the Holy Spirit never draws attention to herself but, rather, turns our attention to the Son and through the Son to the Father. For these kinds of reasons, it is justified to speak of the Spirit as the "Unknown Third"—as long as that statement is not taken in any sense implying an inferior status in the Godhead.[6]

There are other possible reasons for the slow doctrinal development of pneumatology. One of them might have to do with what was implied above in the discussion of Augustine's doctrine of the Trinity, namely that—differently from the Bishop of Hippo himself—later (Western) tradition at times mistook the naming of the Spirit as the "bond" of love between the Father and Son for a generic description of the Spirit, some kind of nonpersonal conception. To put it somewhat bluntly: "love" or "bond" doesn't have to be as "personal" as Father and Son.

The Eastern Orthodox Church untiringly points to a particular reason behind the lack of proper attention to the Holy Spirit. It has everything to do with the _filioque_ clause, which was added to the Nicene-Constantinopolitan Creed (381). This clause, which means literally "and from the Son," suggests the double derivation of the Spirit from both Father and Son (rather than from the Father alone, as the original creedal form said). This, in turn, might have led to the subordination of the Spirit to Christ—in other words, the placement of pneumatology under Christology.

On top of these and related biblical-theological factors contributing to the "oblivion" of the Spirit in theology, there is also another reason, more practical in nature. What I mean is this: over and over again throughout history, various types of charismatic revival movements emerged, beginning from the second-century Montanism (to be briefly discussed below). As much as the church might have appreciated their enthusiasm and vigor, more often than not they were also felt as a threat to the peace, organization, and unity of the Christian community. Particularly concerning to bishops, theologians, and other leaders was those movements' frequent appeal to the spiritual authority allegedly received directly from the Holy Spirit; for many spiritualists that meant an excuse to bypass the "earthly" ecclesiastical authorities—or, in some cases, even the written word of God. No wonder a need was felt to control the Spirit.

Biblical and Early Church Experience

Our first chapter presented a brief introduction to the nature and work of the Spirit in the biblical materials. Without a repetition of that overview, as a way of introduction to the historical developments of pneumatology during the patristic era a few summary reflections are in order here. The reason is that both the legitimate differences among various Christian traditions and the heretical diversions from orthodoxy regarding the doctrine of the Spirit claim to be based on Scripture. Hence, for a proper understanding of the growth and development of pneumatological traditions, the biblical background and context is indispensable.[7]

First, there is the need to acknowledge and celebrate the diversity and plurality of biblical testimonies to the Spirit. While there is no denying some common themes, such as the Spirit's role in creation, inspiration, salvation, empowerment, and in relation to Christ, there is an almost bewildering diversity of symbols, narratives, testimonies, experiences, and descriptions of the Spirit. Indeed, no attempt can be found among the biblical writers to reduce or limit the sphere or the ministry of the Spirit. Just consider this: the work of the Spirit has a gentle and subtle facet as well as the rushing wind or stormy side. Furthermore, there is the silent, hidden side as well as the audible, visible, and tangible aspect. Or think of the salvific, soteriological ministry of the Spirit among the people of God as well as the gifting and empowering energies; and so forth.

In light of the diversity and plurality of testimonies to the Divine Spirit in the canon, it is highly interesting theologically that in the last part of the NT, the so-called Catholic Epistles, there is a shift from the charismatic and dynamic ministry of the Spirit toward more "institutionalized" forms such as the inspiration of Scripture and gifting to the ministry ("ordination"). Such a shift also happened soon after the first centuries when church structures, established ministries such as the episcopacy, and the Christian canon were formed. This development is intriguing in light of the later developments of pneumatology and church life. According to the British NT scholar James D. G. Dunn, two ecclesiological "streams" have flowed alongside each other in the postbiblical era, one charismatic and enthusiastic, the other more conventional and traditional. The former might have been the "mainstream" during the first postbiblical century, while the latter, the more established one, soon took the upper hand.[8]

From the early writings and histories we know that during the first centuries, the NT type of fresh and somewhat spontaneous charismatic experience with spiritual gifts and visions continued in the church. The premier late Roman Catholic pneumatologist Yves Congar mentions as an illustrative example Clement of Rome, who said that the apostles "set out, filled with the assurance of the Holy Spirit, to proclaim the good news of the coming of the kingdom of heaven." Toward the end of the first century, Clement was also obliged to give rules for the church at Corinth as to the right use of charisms, implying that spiritual gifts were active at that time. The French expert on the doctrine of the Spirit lists other early witnesses to the widespread charismatic experience, namely Justin Martyr. As rational and intellectual as that leading Apologist was, he also claimed that prophecy and charismatic gifts still existed; in fact, it was believed that the charisms should accompany the church until the end.[9]

Furthermore, according to Congar, there was no opposition yet between the growth of tradition (doctrinal development) and charisms, such as visions and warnings from the Spirit. Cyprian is reported to have said of the Council of Carthage (252) that it had made decisions "under the inspiration of the Holy Spirit and according to the warnings given by the Lord in many visions." Cyprian himself is claimed to have had had various kinds of visions from the Spirit.[10] In sum, both in the biblical canon and in the ensuing early centuries, diversity and plurality were the hallmarks of the experiences of the Spirit as well as doctrinal formulations. To these historical developments we turn next.

Not surprisingly, in light of the christological and trinitarian heresies and debates already discussed, much of the early development of pneumatology emerged out of painful encounters with and rebuttals of heretical views. It is illustrative that as late as in the second half of the fourth century, after Nicea and at the time of Chalcedon, Gregory of Nazianzus still felt overwhelmed by rebuttals, errors, and heresies concerning the Spirit. In his vigorous and colorful manner, the Cappadocian complains in his preface to the discussion of the Spirit:

> Now the subject of the Holy Spirit presents a special difficulty, not only because when these men have become weary in their disputations concerning the Son, they struggle with greater heat against the Spirit . . . , but further because we ourselves also, being worn out by the multitude of their questions, are in something of the same condition with men who have lost their appetite; who having taken a dislike to some particular kind of food, shrink from all food; so we in like manner have an aversion from all discussions.

The Cappadocian further complains that some "are angry with us on the ground that we are bringing in a strange or interpolated God, viz.:—the Holy Ghost."[11] No wonder, particularly during the earlier centuries of Christian history, that it seemed at times to be easier for the church leaders to say what they did not believe rather than to state positively the orthodox position.

Before delving into these quite complex doctrinal issues that build on the earlier christological and trinitarian clarifications, it is appropriate to reflect briefly on the experience of the Spirit in early communities and the "economic" rather than (strictly speaking) theological-doctrinal level. After all, the way to the pneumatological *doctrine* went through the Spirit *experience*.

Spirit Experience and Reflection

In order to get a feel of the earliest postbiblical pneumatologies and experiences of the Spirit, it is instructive to look at some defining theological topics and themes related to the ministry of the Spirit.[12] In the anonymous second-century *First Epistle to the Corinthians*,[13] we can find a number of references to the inspiration of the Scriptures by the Spirit, which are "the true utterances of the Holy Spirit."[14] Not surprisingly, it was often claimed that the Holy Spirit was instrumental in the preaching and establishment of the first Christian communities.[15] Alongside the doctrine of the Scripture, early theologians established links between the Spirit and the church. According to Ignatius, the Bishop of Antioch, the church at large, including the episcopacy whose task it is to preserve the unity of the community, functions under the leadership of the Spirit.[16]

As mentioned above, prophetic, mystical, and charismatic spiritual experiences were quite common during the era of the Apostolic Fathers and beyond. A telling example is *The Shepherd of Hermas*,[17] a mid-second-century document, which narrates transportations and visions in the Spirit. As a result, there arose the need to create criteria for the discernment of the Spirit. Similarly, *The Shepherd of Hermas* encourages Christians to "[t]ry the man who has the Divine Spirit by his life," whether he possess the qualities of a sanctified person and behaves appropriately or not. At the same time, it points out the need not to grieve the Spirit; that may happen, for example, because of doubt.[18]

The most serious early pneumatological challenge with both ecclesiastical and doctrinal implications had to do with the second-century Montanist movement. It arose around 160–170 ce in the area of modern Turkey. Notwithstanding various, even contradictory, assessments of Montanism, the overall evaluation is that it arose from a false spirit and held an erroneous pneumatology. It was blamed for undermining the authority of the apostles and church hierarchy as well as for its evil lifestyles.[19] Hippolytus, the Bishop of Rome, criticized Montanus and the two accompanying women Priscilla and Maximilla, for creating "novelties," heretical views concerning the Paraclete, the Holy Spirit, and Trinity (with reference to Noetus, the Modalist).[20] Hippolytus was also concerned about the rapid spread of this Montanist heresy.[21]

It is significant that no less an orthodox authority than Tertullian was, in one part of his life, intimately related to Montanism. While leaving behind the movement, he is claimed to have written a treatise on ecstasy originally consisting of six books, to which a seventh was added, refuting the charges of Apollonius, the major critic of Montanus. Unfortunately, this writing, *De Ecstasi*, has not survived. Note also that Tertullian's important work *On Baptism* is a major pneumatological treasure as well.[22] As the following passage indicates, there is a deep pneumatological-trinitarian aspect to the sacrament of baptism:

> Not that *in* the waters we obtain the Holy Spirit; but in the water, under (the witness of) the angel, we are cleansed, and prepared *for* the Holy Spirit. In this case also a type has preceded; for thus was John beforehand the Lord's forerunner, "preparing His ways." Thus, too, does the angel, the witness of baptism, "make the paths straight" for the Holy Spirit, who is about to come upon us, by the washing away of sins, which faith, sealed in (the name of) the Father, and the Son, and the Holy Spirit, obtains. For if "in *the mouth of* three witnesses every word shall stand:"—while, through the benediction, we have the same (three) as witnesses of our faith whom we have as sureties of our salvation too—how

much more does the number of the divine names suffice for the assurance of our hope likewise! Moreover, after the pledging both of the attestation of faith and the promise of salvation under "three witnesses," there is added, of necessity, mention of the Church; inasmuch as, wherever there are three, (that is, the Father, the Son, and the Holy Spirit,) there is the Church, which is a body of three.[23]

A contemporary writing titled *The Passion of the Holy Martyrs Perpetua and Felicitas* is routinely attached to Tertullian. It is a kind of hagiography that offers a fascinating description of an eschatologically loaded charismatic spirituality similar to that of Montanism. Although historically the claim for Tertullian's authorship can hardly be established,[24] the linking with such a great doctrinal authority is significant.

The widespread Spirit experience pushed Christian theologians to reflect more carefully on the doctrine of the Holy Spirit. Without repeating the few occasional notes on pneumatology in the previous chapter, let us follow the path of the development beginning from the earliest church fathers.

Pneumatological Clarification

As mentioned above, the earliest Christian teachers in the postbiblical era were the Apostolic Fathers. Rather limited in their constructive work, they made every effort to ensure a faithful transmission of the apostolic tradition. Hence, there was no desire for any kind of sophisticated doctrinal pronouncements about the Spirit. The Apostolic Fathers, rather, wanted to stay close to their spiritual experiences and the NT testimonies on the economic level (that is, concerned with the Spirit's role in salvation). Illustrative of the lack of sophistication in terminology is the often vague and undefined usage of the term "Spirit," which led at times to a confusion between the Son (Word) and Spirit.[25] As long as the Spirit was not differentiated from the Son as a separate "person," it was difficult to say if the Spirit was the power or influence of the Father (filling or empowering the Son) or something else less than a person.

The reasons for the pneumatological confusion until at least the third Christian century are many (in addition to those mentioned above): the focus on the Spirit's activity in the order of salvation at the economic rather than theological level; the lack of NT clarity about the relations between trinitarian members; and the apparent parallelism in the OT between Word and Spirit.[26] Consider the second-century writing *2 Clement*, in which the proper distinction between Son and Spirit is confused in sayings such as the following: "Such a one then shall not partake of the spirit, which is Christ."[27] Clearly, there is an equation here between the second and third persons of the Trinity. Other examples are not hard to find. Not surprisingly, the early documents mentioned above such as *The Shepherd of Hermas* are guilty of blurring the distinction between Son and Spirit; at times, it even conflates the two by stating that the "Spirit is the Son of God."[28] Astonishingly, even the famous Apologist Justin Martyr opined that "[i]t is wrong, therefore, to understand the Spirit and the power of God as anything else than the Word, who is also the first-born of God."[29] His colleague Athenagoras presented a view of the Spirit strongly emanationist—"an effluence of God, flowing from Him, and returning back again like a beam of the sun"[30]—that had a hard time accounting for the full personality of the Spirit. And so forth.

The trinitarian canons were, of course, not yet fixed even in later second-century theologians such as Theophilus of Antioch and Irenaeus. Both of them define the threeness in terms of God, Word, and Wisdom! When explaining what happened on the fourth day of creation, Theophilus states: "[T]he three days which were before the luminaries, are types of the Trinity, of God, and His Word, and His wisdom. And the fourth is the type of man, who needs light, that so there may be God, the Word, wisdom, man."[31] And Irenaeus:

> I have also largely demonstrated, that the Word, namely the Son, was always with the Father; and that Wisdom also, which is the Spirit, was present with Him, anterior to all creation, He declares by Solomon: "God by Wisdom founded the earth, and by under-

standing hath He established the heaven. By His knowledge the depths burst forth, and the clouds dropped down the dew." And again: "The Lord created me the beginning of His ways in His work: He set me up from everlasting, in the beginning, before He made the earth, before He established the depths, and before the fountains of waters gushed forth; before the mountains were made strong, and before all the hills, He brought me forth."[32]

In other words, Theophilus equated the Spirit with the Word, while Irenaeus equated it with Wisdom! Because of the lack of confession of the full deity of the Spirit, there were times when the Spirit was clearly ranked as the third in status. Justin Martyr's reflection on the theme of "Christians Serve God Rationally" in his *First Apology* illustrates this clearly:

> Our teacher of these things is Jesus Christ, who also was born for this purpose, and was crucified under Pontius Pilate, procurator of Judæa, in the times of Tiberius Cæsar; and that we reasonably worship Him, having learned that He is the Son of the true God Himself, and holding Him in the second place, and the prophetic Spirit in the third, we will prove. For they proclaim our madness to consist in this, that we give to a crucified man a place second to the unchangeable and eternal God, the Creator of all; for they do not discern the mystery that is herein, to which, as we make it plain to you, we pray you to give heed.[33]

Slowly and gradually, there emerged a wide and deep consensus of the equality of the rank of the Spirit in the Divine Triad. That said, it took until the time of Augustine for theologians to freely and without reservation name the Spirit as God (notwithstanding the widespread conception of the Spirit as divine no less than the Father and Son).

Toward Full Deity

The Spirit's Ministry

In this section, focusing on the third century, we will proceed beginning from the Spirit's ministry and spiritual experiences before moving to theology and doctrine. Although there were important trinitarian contours developed during this period of time, that did not mean neglecting the role of spiritual experience as a guide to deeper understanding. Again, we have to remind ourselves of the ancient rule *lex orandi, lex credendi*; the basis for doctrinal insights was always the "economy" of the Spirit.

Rich testimonies and teachings can be found in the third-century Apostolic Fathers concerning the Spirit's work in the church, ministry, and sacraments. Let us begin with the ecclesiological sphere. A fitting "bridge-person" in this regard is Irenaeus, who passed away somewhere around the turn of the third century. In keeping with the NT and subsequent intuitions, the Bishop of Lyons considered the church and ecclesiology at large as a special place for the Spirit's ministry and energies. Even his "definition" of the Christian community is pneumatologically loaded. The following longer programmatic citation from the third book of his *Against Heresies* reveals both pneumatological and trinitarian foundation of the church and her ministry. Having mentioned that "there is no other God" than the one who has created everything, he continues:

> [T]he preaching of the Church is everywhere consistent, and continues in an even course, and receives testimony from the prophets, the apostles, and all the disciples . . . through the entire dispensation of God. . . . [O]ur faith; which, having been received from the Church, we do preserve, and which always, by the Spirit of God, renewing its youth, as if it were some precious deposit in an excellent vessel, causes the vessel itself containing it to renew its youth also. For this gift of God has been entrusted to the Church, as breath was to the first created man, for this purpose, that all the members receiving it may be vivified; and the [means of] communion with Christ has been distributed throughout it, that is, the Holy Spirit, the earnest of incorruption, the means of confirming our faith, and the ladder of ascent to God. "For in the Church," it is said, "God hath set apostles, prophets, teachers," and all the other means through which the Spirit works; of which all those are not partakers who do not join themselves to the Church, but defraud themselves of life through their per-

verse opinions and infamous behaviour. For where the Church is, there is the Spirit of God; and where the Spirit of God is, there is the Church, and every kind of grace; but the Spirit is truth. Those, therefore, who do not partake of Him, are neither nourished into life from the mother's breasts, nor do they enjoy that most limpid fountain which issues from the body of Christ; but they dig for themselves broken cisterns out of earthly trenches, and drink putrid water out of the mire, fleeing from the faith of the Church lest they be convicted; and rejecting the Spirit, that they may not be instructed.[34]

For Irenaeus's pupil, Hippolytus, the presbyter in Rome, the Holy Spirit guaranteed the faithful transmission of Christian tradition in the service of which the episcopal office also functioned. The Spirit helped refute heretical notions, which were many at the time.[35] Not only were ministry and episcopacy pneumatologically grounded, so also were the sacraments. Tertullian's *On Baptism* is a profound exposition of the way the Spirit lingers over the baptismal waters similarly to the way the Spirit of God hovered over the primal waters.[36] Speaking of the meaning of anointing the baptismal candidate with oil, a standard custom at the time, he provides an amazing pneumatological-trinitarian explanation:

After this, when we have issued from the font, we are thoroughly anointed with a blessed unction,—(a practice derived) from the old discipline, wherein on entering the priesthood, *men* were wont to be anointed with oil from a horn, ever since Aaron was anointed by Moses. Whence Aaron is called "Christ," from the "chrism," which is "the unction;" which, when made spiritual, furnished an appropriate name to the Lord, because He was "anointed" with the Spirit by God the Father; as *written* in the Acts: "For truly they were gathered together in this city against Thy Holy Son whom Thou hast anointed." Thus, too, in *our* case, the unction runs carnally, (*i.e.* on the body,) but profits spiritually; in the same way as the *act* of baptism itself too is carnal, in that we are plunged in water, *but* the *effect* spiritual, in that we are freed from sins.[37]

In keeping with this, in the laying of the hand on the baptized person, an "invoking and inviting the Holy Spirit through benediction"[38] took place.

Several other third-century teachers of the church can be mentioned here as advocates of the Spirit-driven trinitarian language with regard to the church and sacraments. The first major ecclesiologist, Cyprian, highlighted the Spirit's ministry in baptism with regard to our sanctification and purification.[39] Clement of Alexandria, often called the first Alexandrian theologian, saw "illumination, and perfection, and washing" as results of the Spirit's work in water baptism.[40] Similarly, several third-century theologians also spoke of the sacrament of the Eucharist in pneumatological terms. Clement's allegorical explanation of the salvific meaning of Christ's blood in the Eucharist is set in the context of a robust Spirit Christology:

> And the blood of the Lord is twofold. For there is the blood of His flesh, by which we are redeemed from corruption; and the spiritual, that by which we are anointed. And to drink the blood of Jesus, is to become partaker of the Lord's immortality; the Spirit being the energetic principle of the Word, as blood is of flesh. Accordingly, as wine is blended with water, so is the Spirit with man. And the one, the mixture of wine and water, nourishes to faith; while the other, the Spirit, conducts to immortality. And the mixture of both—of the water and of the Word—is called Eucharist, renowned and glorious grace; and they who by faith partake of it are sanctified both in body and soul.[41]

The unity of the church—a key concern for early theologians as illustrated wonderfully in Cyprian's *On the Unity of the Church*—has its basis in the unity among the trinitarian members and has a distinctively pneumatological basis with reference to the gentle, dove-like nature of the Spirit. Cyprian explains these principles carefully in turn:

> He can no longer have God for his Father, who has not the Church for his mother. . . . He who breaks the peace and the concord of Christ, does so in opposition to Christ; he who gathereth elsewhere than in the Church, scatters the Church of Christ. The Lord

says, "I and the Father are one;" and again it is written of the Father, and of the Son, and of the Holy Spirit, "And these three are one."[42]

Therefore also the Holy Spirit came as a dove, a simple and joyous creature, not bitter with gall, not cruel in its bite, not violent with the rending of its claws, loving human dwellings, knowing the association of one home; when they have young, bringing forth their young together; when they fly abroad, remaining in their flights by the side of one another, spending their life in mutual intercourse, acknowledging the concord of peace with the kiss of the beak, in all things fulfilling the law of unanimity. This is the simplicity that ought to be known in the Church, this is the charity that ought to be attained, that so the love of the brotherhood may imitate the doves, that their gentleness and meekness may be like the lambs and sheep.[43]

Continuing Confusion and Struggle

On the way towards the establishment of the full deity of the Spirit in the (Nicene-) Constantinopolitan Creed (381), the third-century fathers made significant contributions, notwithstanding the fact that even the ablest fathers such as Origen also continued to encounter tremendous difficulties. A telling example has to with his confusing idea of the derivation of the Spirit from the *Logos*. Under the heading, "How the Word Is the Maker of All Things, and Even the Holy Spirit Was Made Through Him," this great theologian explains in much detail why this highly counterintuitive idea of the created nature of the Holy Spirit has to be true:

Thus, if all things were made *through* the Logos . . . we have to enquire if the Holy Spirit also was made through Him. It appears to me that those who hold the Holy Spirit to be created, and who also admit that "all things were made through Him," must necessarily assume that the Holy Spirit was made through the Logos, the Logos accordingly being older than He. And he who shrinks from allowing the Holy Spirit to have been made through Christ must, if he admits the truth of the statements of this Gospel, assume the Spirit to be uncreated. There is a third resource besides these two (that of allowing the Spirit to have been made by the Word, and that of regarding it as uncreated), namely, to assert that the Holy Spirit has no essence of His own beyond the Father and the Son. But on further thought one may perhaps see reason to consider that the Son is second beside the Father, He being the same as the Father, while manifestly a distinction is drawn between the Spirit and the Son. . . .

On the basis of this logical reasoning, Origen then comes to the conclusion that "there are three hypostases, the Father and the Son and the Holy Spirit; and at the same time we believe nothing to be uncreated but the Father." At the same time, Origen has already established that, as a result of all things having been made by the *Logos*, "the Holy Spirit is the most excellent and the first in order of all that was made by the Father through Christ." Regarding this, he draws a strange conclusion that "this, perhaps, is the reason why the Spirit is not said to be God's own Son." The final conclusion is this: "The Only-begotten only is by nature and from the beginning a Son, and the Holy Spirit seems to have need of the Son, to minister to Him His essence, so as to enable Him not only to exist, but to be wise and reasonable and just, and all that we must think of Him as being. All this He has by participation of the character of Christ, of which we have spoken above."[44] This litany is, of course, a showcase of unorthodox and highly suspicious statements in light of the later creedal establishment of the full deity of the Spirit in the Trinity. That said, these kinds of examples help us better understand the utmost difficulty of the task at the time.

The subordination of the Spirit to the Father—and at times even to the Son, as already referred to above—was a general idea among the Fathers. Irenaeus's idea of the Word and Spirit as the "two hands" of God bringing about creation has already been referred to several times.[45] Examples of the Spirit's placement under not only the Father but also the Son—in other words, at a "third" level—are not difficult to find either. Let us consider Tertullian's use of the metaphors of the Trinity drawn from nature. The following illustration, which starts with the statement regarding the Son–Spirit relation, that in itself is theologically as suspicious as it may be helpful pedagogically, clearly reveals subordinationism. While it first argues carefully for the indistinguishable, though subordinationist, relation of the Son to the Father, thereafter it relegates the Spirit in an even more inferior status (in order to make it easier for the reader to discern these two levels of subordinationism in this unusually long citation, I have divided it into two parts, although the original text does not):

> But the Word was formed by the Spirit, and (if I may so express myself) the Spirit is the body of the Word. The Word, therefore, is both always in the Father, as He says, "I am in the Father;" and is always with God, according to what is written, "And the Word was with God;" and never separate from the Father, or other than the Father, since "I and the Father are one." This will be the prolation, taught by the truth, the guardian of the Unity, wherein we declare that the Son is a prolation from the Father, without being separated from Him. For God sent forth the Word, as the Paraclete also declares, just as the root puts forth the tree, and the fountain the river, and the sun the ray. For these are προβολαί, *or emanations*, of the substances from which they proceed. I should not hesitate, indeed, to call the tree the son or offspring of the root, and the river of the fountain, and the ray of the sun; because every original source is a parent, and everything which issues from the origin is an offspring. Much more is (this true of) the Word of God, who has actually received as His own peculiar designation the name of *Son*. But still the tree is not severed from the root, nor the river from the fountain, nor the ray from the sun; nor, indeed, is the Word separated from God. Following, therefore, the form of these analogies, I confess that I call God and His Word—the Father and His Son—*two*. For the root and the tree are distinctly two things, but correlatively joined; the fountain and the river are also two forms, but indivisible; so likewise the sun and the ray are two forms, but coherent ones. Everything which proceeds from something else must needs be second to that from which it proceeds, without being on that account separated.
> Where, however, there is a second, there must be two; and where there is a third, there must be three. Now the Spirit indeed is third from God and the Son; just as the fruit of the tree is third from the root, or as the stream out of the river is third from the fountain, or as the apex of the ray is third from the sun. Nothing,

however, is alien from that original source whence it derives its own properties. In like manner the Trinity, flowing down from the Father through intertwined and connected steps, does not at all disturb the *Monarchy*, whilst it at the same time guards the state of the *Economy*.[46]

Furthermore, at times the stress on the integral relationship between the Spirit and the Word in Tertullian borders on the blurring of the hypostatic distinction between the two. Taking his cue from Psalm 33:6, which speaks of the creation of the heavens and earth by the Word and Spirit, Tertullian surmises that "the Spirit (or Divine Nature) . . . was in the Word" and then continues: "Do you then . . . grant that the Word is a certain substance, constructed by the Spirit and the communication of Wisdom? Certainly I do."[47] Or, to go back to the statement cited above: "But the Word was formed by the Spirit, and (if I may so express myself) the Spirit is the body of the Word."[48]

Efforts to Be Definitive

Notwithstanding difficulties in the development of the doctrine, there is no doubt that for Tertullian and others the Trinity is the unique and defining doctrine of Christianity (it also distinguishes Christian faith from Judaism[49]). These teachers of the church did everything in their power to work out an authentic trinitarian formulation. As we saw above, Tertullian vehemently attacked modalists and other heretics who were not willing to side with the emerging orthodox position. Notwithstanding his subordinationist orientation, Tertullian was successful in properly distinguishing the third person of the Trinity without any idea of separation. This is clearly evident in the following chapter heading in his *Against Praxeas*, "The Paraclete, or Holy Ghost . . . is Distinct from the Father and the Son as to Their Personal Existence . . . [and at the same time] One and Inseparable from Them as to Their Divine Nature." Importantly, the North African teacher bases the distinction among Father, Son, and Spirit on the inner relations of the Son, Father, and Spirit.[50] Taking note of number of passages about the Spirit in John's Gospel, Tertullian concludes clearly "distinguishing the Father and the Son, with the properties of each," adding that

> Then there is the Paraclete or *Comforter*, also, which He promises to pray for to the Father, and to send from heaven after He had ascended to the Father. *He is called* "another Comforter," indeed; but in what way He is *another* we have already shown "He shall receive of mine," says Christ, just as *Christ* Himself received of the Father's. Thus the connection of the Father in the Son, and of the Son in the Paraclete, produces three coherent Persons, *who are yet distinct* One from Another. These Three are one *essence*, not one *Person*, as it is said, "I and my Father are One," in respect of unity of substance not singularity of number.[51]

From the biblical statements about the Holy Spirit and his work, Origen and others found a more solid basis for the emerging affirmation of the divinity of the Spirit.[52] For Origen, the fact that it was impossible to think of regeneration or deification apart from the full cooperation of the Father, Son, and Spirit pushed the doctrinal reflections toward the idea of the full equality of the three.[53]

Similarly, the dual role of the Son and Spirit comes to the fore in salvation. Irenaeus formulates his soteriology in terms of the Eastern concept of *theosis*, deification: in the last days, the Son "was made a man among men, that He might join the end to the beginning, that is, man to God . . . in order that man, having embraced the Spirit of God, might pass into the glory of the Father."[54] Irenaeus displays a healthy balance between christological and pneumatological understandings of salvation:

> Since the Lord thus has redeemed us through His own blood, giving His soul for our souls, and His flesh for our flesh, and has also poured out the Spirit of the Father for the union and communion of God and man, imparting indeed God to men by means of the Spirit, and, on the other hand, attaching man to God by His own incarnation, and bestowing upon us at His coming immor-

tality durably and truly, by means of communion with God—all the doctrines of the heretics fall to ruin.[55]

Importantly, Tertullian materially anticipated the later Arian *homoousios* debates when, on the basis of the Johannine Jesus's saying, "I and the Father are one," he taught that that Father and Son are of "one substance." The details of his somewhat cumbersome and meticulous argument are that

> the three *Persons*—the Father, the Son, and the Holy Ghost . . . [are]: three, however, not in condition, but in degree; not in substance, but in form; not in power, but in aspect; yet of one substance, and of one condition, and of one power, inasmuch as He is one God, from whom these degrees and forms and aspects are reckoned, under the name of the Father, and of the Son, and of the Holy Ghost.[56]

The affirmation of the Father, Son, and Spirit sharing the same "substance" effectively leads to the full establishment of the deity of the Spirit. Among the Greek Fathers, Origen finally came to this idea—after much vacillation, as reported above—when he affirmed that "nothing in the Trinity can be called greater or less, since the fountain of divinity alone contains all things by His word and reason, and by the Spirit of His mouth sanctifies all things."[57]

The final clarification as to how to establish definitely the full deity of the Spirit and Spirit's role in the Trinity was left to the Greek-speaking theologians, the Cappadocians and Athanasius.

Decisive Contributions from the East

Pneumatological Heretics

The fourth-century Greek-speaking theologians who made lasting contribution to pneumatology came mainly from Alexandria and the Cappadocia; Alexandria was the major center of theological reflection in the Christian East, along with

Antioch.[58] Setting their views against pneumatological heretical opinions such as those of the *Tropicii* (Tropici), a group that was not willing to give the same divine status to the Spirit as to the Son, Athanasius wrote his *Letters to Serapion on the Holy Spirit* (355–60). Athanasius's method was straightforward: the first part investigated scriptural passages used by the opponents in their denial of the Spirit's divinity (1.1–14). The second part (1.15–33) then refuted the main arguments of the *Tropicii*, one of which was that the Spirit is a "son" (or "brother") of the Son (1.15).

The Cappadocians' main target was another version of pneumatological heresies, routinely called the *Pneumatomachoi*, the "fighters of the Spirit." They undermined the Nicean orthodoxy and thus echoed Arian misgivings about the equality of the Son with the Father. Basil the Great's *On the Holy Spirit* (376) had as its main target these heretics. Wrong views regarding the Spirit were the cause for naming the opponents "transgressors."[59] Having been trained in rhetoric and logic, Basil offers a highly sophisticated and detailed rebuttal of the arguments set forth by the *Pneumatomachoi*, analyzing the pronouns used, both at the beginning (2.4—5.12) and the end of the treatise (25.58—27.68).[60] He also lists attributes of the Spirit that belong to deity, such as preexistence.[61] The consideration of the Spirit's nature and role is set in the wider context of establishing a fully trinitarian doctrine of God; hence, mixed with Spirit–Son and Spirit–Father relations, the status of the Son in relation to the Father is also dealt with extensively.[62]

St. Basil's brother Gregory, the Bishop of Nyssa, penned his *On the Holy Trinity of the Godhead of the Holy Spirit to Eustathius* and *On the Holy Spirit against the Followers of Macedonius* (381), in which he unabashedly defends the equality of the Spirit in the Trinity against Macedonius, a sectarian leader, deposed from the See of Constantinople in 360 ce. With Arian and Eunomian tendencies, Macedonius compromised the Spirit's divinity and full equality with the Father. Against those heresies, Gregory mounts evidence hard to dismiss:

> [T]he Holy Spirit is . . . because of qualities that are essentially holy, that which the Father, essentially Holy, is; and such as the Only-begotten is, such is the Holy Spirit; then, again, He is so by virtue of life-giving, of imperishability, of unvariableness, of everlastingness, of justice, of wisdom, of rectitude, of sovereignty, of goodness, of power, of capacity to give all good things, and above them all life itself, and by being everywhere, being present in each, filling the earth, residing in the heavens, shed abroad upon supernatural Powers, filling all things.[63]

Yet another Cappadocian Father, Gregory of Nazianzus, devoted the fifth sermon in his *The Theological Orations* to the Holy Spirit. A one-time bishop and temporary presider of the Council of Constantinople, he joined the struggle to clarify the doctrine of the Spirit vis-à-vis heretical views of Arians, Eunomians, and others.[64] As with his colleagues, the ancient rule *lex orandi, lex credendi* was a key tool in defending the deity of the Spirit: "For if He is not to be worshipped, how can He deify me by Baptism? But if He is to be worshipped, surely He is an Object of adoration, and if an Object of adoration He must be God."[65]

Although equal in the Trinity, concerning the particular role of the each of the Three, there is a kind of "rule of knowledge," opined Basil. That is, the Spirit is the first "contact" point for us with the Trinity. From the Spirit, through the Christ, we finally ascend to the knowledge of the Father: "Thus the way of the knowledge of God lies from One Spirit through the One Son to the One Father, and conversely the natural Goodness and the inherent Holiness and the royal Dignity extend from the Father through the Only-begotten to the Spirit."[66]

The Scriptures on Deity and Equality

It bears repeating: for all the Apostolic Fathers the scriptural teaching laid the basis for the establishment of the trinitarian doctrine. Not for nothing did they labor on the details of the scriptural texts. They did not want to establish any opinion concerning the Spirit without biblical warrant. Says Cyril of Jerusalem:

> For concerning the divine and holy mysteries of the Faith, not even a casual statement must be delivered without the Holy Scriptures; nor must we be drawn aside by mere plausibility and artifices of speech. Even to me, who tell thee these things, give not absolute credence, unless thou receive the proof of the things which I announce from the Divine Scriptures. For this salvation which we believe depends not on ingenious reasoning, but on demonstration of the Holy Scriptures.[67]

That said, alongside the constant consultation of scriptural resources, the Greek theologians also had a highest regard of the developing Christian tradition, particularly the teaching of the Fathers.[68] That teaching was believed to be in keeping with the Bible.

The scriptural teaching about the deity of the Spirit seemed unambiguous and uncontested for Basil.[69] Boldly and unabashedly, he went so far as to affirm the preexistence of the Spirit: "He existed; He pre-existed; He co-existed with the Father and the Son before the ages." In keeping with this high status, Basil continues, divine works such as miracles, forgiveness of sins, resurrection, and even the original creative work of the world could be assigned to the same Spirit![70]

A key resource in Scripture employed by many of the Apostolic Fathers relates to the naming of the Spirit (and the Son, as discussed in the previous chapter). A telling example comes from St. Basil's *On the Holy Spirit*. A long litany of divine names, nomenclatures, and descriptions taken from the biblical testimonies helped establish the deity of the Spirit: "He is called Spirit, as 'God is a Spirit,' and 'the breath of our nostrils, the anointed of the Lord.' He is called holy, as the Father is holy, and the Son is holy, for to the creature holiness was brought in from without, but to the Spirit holiness is the fulfillment of nature, and it is for this reason that He is described not as being sanctified, but as sanctifying." Then he continues:

He is called good, as the Father is good, and He who was begotten of the Good is good, and to the Spirit His goodness is essence. He is called upright, as "the Lord is upright," in that He is Himself truth, and is Himself Righteousness, having no divergence nor leaning to one side or to the other, on account of the immutability of His substance. He is called Paraclete, like the Only begotten, as He Himself says, "I will ask the Father, and He will give you another comforter." Thus names are borne by the Spirit in common with the Father and the Son, and He gets these titles from His natural and close relationship. From what other source could they be derived? Again He is called royal, Spirit of truth, and Spirit of wisdom. "The Spirit of God," it is said "hath made me," and God filled Bezaleel with "the divine Spirit of wisdom and understanding and knowledge. Such names as these are super-eminent and mighty, but they do not transcend His glory.[71]

The last sentence of the citation ("Such names as these are super-eminent and mighty, but they do not transcend His glory") relates to one of Basil's lasting contributions to the trinitarian doctrine and practice, namely the introduction of a new doxological formula, contested by many of his opponents: "Glory to the Father with the Son together with the Holy Spirit."[72] Basil contended that it was appropriate to glorify the Spirit along with the Father and Son. While he acknowledged that this phrase was considered a novelty and against the tradition, Basil still believed it was in keeping with biblical teaching and tradition.

Reflecting biblical teaching, both in the Gospels and Pauline literature, the integral link between the Spirit and Christ was a leading theme: "when we are given to drink of the Spirit, we drink Christ" (with appeal to 1 Cor 10:4).[73] The cooperation in creation and resurrection similarly speaks of the close link between the Son and Spirit.[74] This Spirit Christology is an important theme in Eastern pneumatology at large. Basil's brother, Gregory of Nyssa, explains this in a most dramatic way:

For as between the body's surface and the liquid of the oil nothing intervening can be detected, either in reason or in perception, so inseparable is the union of the Spirit with the Son; and the result is that whosoever is to touch the Son by faith must needs first encounter the oil in the very act of touching; there is not a part of Him devoid of the Holy Spirit. Therefore belief in the Lordship of the Son arises in those who entertain it, by means of the Holy Ghost; on all sides the Holy Ghost is met by those who by faith approach the Son. If, then, the Son is essentially a King, and the Holy Spirit is that dignity of Kingship which anoints the Son, what deprivation of this Kingship, in its essence and comparing it with itself, can be imagined?[75]

The Breakthrough

Everywhere, the fourth-century Greek Fathers affirmed boldly the equality of the Spirit with the Son.[76] The teaching manual *Catechetical Lectures* by Cyril, the Archbishop of Jerusalem, urged Christians to regard the Spirit in the same way as the Father and Son. Instructing the baptismal candidates "On the Ten Points of Doctrine," including Father, Son, virgin birth, and judgment, he summarizes:

> Believe thou also in the Holy Ghost, and hold the same opinion concerning Him, which thou hast *received to hold* concerning the Father and the Son, and follow not those who teach blasphemous things of Him. . . . "Who with the Father and the Son together is honoured with the glory of the Godhead: of Whom also *thrones, and dominions, principalities, and powers* have need. For there is One God, the Father of Christ; and One Lord Jesus Christ, the Only-begotten Son of the Only God; and One Holy Ghost, the sanctifier and deifier of all, Who spake in the Law and in the Prophets, in the Old and in the NT.[77]

Importantly, the latter part of the citation materially affirms what, at the 381 Constantinopolitan Council, became the core of the article on the Holy Spirit.[78]

For his part, Athanasius insisted that the Spirit is in Christ as the Son is in the Father,[79] and he also insisted on the indivisibility of the Trinity as another proof of the equal status of the Spirit.[80] As with Christology, it is of utmost importance for Athanasius to reject any position which argues that the

Spirit was a creature in any sense of the word. The same principle applies to the whole Trinity. If there ever was time when the Father was not—meaning he was not eternal because there then was a beginning—then the Son would not be eternal either, and by derivation the Spirit. The Cappadocians highlighted the same point. Basil's testimony to Spirit's preexistence was affirmed above. Gregory of Nazianzus concurred and put together a most important statement concerning the need to truly establish the co-equality of the Spirit, without which no solid doctrine of the Trinity was possible:

> If ever there was a time when the Father was not, then there was a time when the Son was not. If ever there was a time when the Son was not, then there was a time when the Spirit was not. If the One was from the beginning, then the Three were so too. If you throw down the One, I am bold to assert that you do not set up the other Two. For what profit is there in an imperfect Godhead? Or rather, what Godhead can there be if It is not perfect? And how can that be perfect which lacks something of perfection? And surely there is something lacking if it hath not the Holy, and how would it have this if it were without the Spirit? For either holiness is something different from Him, and if so let some one tell me what it is conceived to be; or if it is the same, how is it not from the beginning, as if it were better for God to be at one time imperfect and apart from the Spirit? If He is not from the beginning, He is in the same rank with myself, even though a little before me; for we are both parted from Godhead by time. If He is in the same rank with myself, how can He make me God, or join me with Godhead?[81]

Gregory's summative statement about the oneness of the Godhead and full equality of the Spirit among the three is worth citing in full:

> To us there is One God, for the Godhead is One, and all that proceedeth from Him is referred to One, though we believe in Three Persons. For one is not more and another less God; nor is One before and another after; nor are They divided in will or parted in power; nor can you find here any of the qualities of divisible things; but the Godhead is, to speak concisely, undivided in

separate Persons; and there is one mingling of Light, as it were of three suns joined to each other. When then we look at the Godhead, or the First Cause, or the Monarchia, that which we conceive is One; but when we look at the Persons in Whom the Godhead dwells, and at Those Who timelessly and with equal glory have their Being from the First Cause—there are Three Whom we worship.[82]

With these and related statements, the notion of the *Tropicii* that the Spirit would be nothing more than a highly elevated creature—a heretical notion akin to the Arian heresy in Christology—is brushed away.[83] Kelly summarizes succinctly the Greek theologians' profound contribution to trinitarian orthodoxy (using Athanasius as the template): Athanasius's teaching

is that the Spirit is fully divine, consubstantial with the Father and the Son. . . . [T]he Spirit "belongs to and is one with the Godhead Which is the Triad." . . . [T]he Spirit comes from God, bestows sanctification and life, and is immutable, omnipresent and unique. . . . [T]he Triad is eternal, homogenous and indivisible, and . . . since the Spirit is a member of it He must therefore be consubstantial with Father and Son. . . . He belongs in essence to the Son exactly as the Son does to the Father.[84]

Similar to their predecessors, the Eastern Fathers also saw indications of the Trinity and the Spirit in the created order, both in the human being—"The threefold Names are sown in a threefold way, in the spirit and in the soul and in the body, as in the mystery"[85]—and in nature: "Lo, there is a similitude between the sun and the Father, the radiance and the Son, the heat and the Holy Ghost; and though it be one, a trinity is beheld in it!"[86]

As much as the Cappadocians labored in defense of the deity and equality of the Spirit, in the final analysis they never came to call the Spirit "God," since the Bible does not do so. The closest one gets in my reading of the Cappadocians is Gregory of Nazianzus's positive affirmation of the rhetorical question posed by himself: "What then? Is the Spirit God? Most certainly. Well then, is He Consubstantial? Yes, if He is God."[87]

Materially, the same is affirmed in Basil's calling the Spirit "Lord," based on the biblical teaching.[88] He also said "that the Holy Spirit partakes of the fullness of divinity."[89]

With all their sophistication and intellectual capacities, the Eastern Fathers were always keen on the spiritual and soteriological implications of the orthodox doctrine. Following the *lex orandi, lex credendi* principle, we found above Athanasius opining in his defense of the deity of the Son that only God is able to save; this was said in opposition to both Arian and Eunomian claims to the contrary. Had we less than a god as the Savior, our salvation would be in jeopardy; the alleged savior would then be in need of salvation himself. This same economic logic also relates to pneumatology. Everywhere in the writings of the Eastern Fathers, the Holy Spirit is connected with the salvific vision of *theosis*, deification. The Spirit's status had to be fully divine in order for us to be able to be linked with the life of the triune God. Clearly, union between the human being and God brought about by the Holy Spirit is yet another indication of the divinity of the Spirit. Basil's litany of the salvific works of the Spirit is illustrative:

> [T]he Holy Ghost, having His subsistence of God, the fount of holiness, power that gives life, grace that maketh perfect, through Whom man is adopted, and the mortal made immortal, conjoined with Father and Son in all things in glory and eternity, in power and kingdom, in sovereignty and godhead; as is testified by the tradition of the baptism of salvation.[90]
>
> Through the Holy Spirit comes our restoration to paradise, our ascension into the kingdom of heaven, our return to the adoption of sons, our liberty to call God our Father, our being made partakers of the grace of Christ, our being called children of light, our sharing in eternal glory, and, in a word, our being brought into a state of all "fulness of blessing," both in this world and in the world to come, of all the good gifts that are in store for us, by promise hereof, through faith, beholding the reflection of their grace as though they were already present, we await the full enjoyment.[91]

Having now delved in some detail into the rich trinitarian treasure of the Greek-speaking Fathers, let us highlight in the following the insights and doctrinal advancements of later Latin-speaking teachers. Thereafter, to wrap up this chapter, a review of the creedal material is in order.

The Later Latin Fathers

The Spirit in the Bible

No less than their Eastern counterparts, Latin theologians also built the trinitarian and pneumatological statements on a scriptural foundation. The former lawyer and governor, the Bishop of Milan (who took that position only eight days after his baptism), St. Ambrose found pneumatological-trinitarian lessons in the allegorical exposition of the OT. This is evident in his three-volume *Of the Holy Spirit*, which, indeed, is nothing else than a biblical exposition. The first two volumes concentrate on the OT. Symbols such as water and river illustrate the nature and work of the Spirit.[92] In the OT stories of offerings, Ambrose found Jesus and the Holy Spirit spoken of, including baptism with the Spirit and fire.[93] Similarly, Gideon, the charismatic judge, was seen as yielding lessons about the Holy Spirit.[94]

Biblical teaching was invoked in the establishment of the deity of the Spirit. At times, a minute detail in the biblical text sufficed to prove the deity, such as the mention of "eternal" with regard to the Spirit in Hebrews 9:14[95] or the fact that if in the Bible the Father and Son are called Spirit, then—by force of logic—it is obvious that the Spirit is divine as well![96] Yet another evidence of the Spirit's deity was found in the biblical statement that Christ (whose deity had been firmly established by this time) lives in us through the Spirit of God, which implies the similarity of nature among all three trinitarian members.[97] Similarly, the Great Commission's command to baptize in the name of the Father, Son, and Spirit leads to the conviction of the shared divine nature.[98]

Ambrose also found a way to affirming the Spirit's deity based on her nature as incorporeal and immutable (similar to the Father and Son) as distinct from corporeal and changing human beings.[99] Related, Ambrose reasoned that the forgiveness of sins is an evidence of the Spirit's deity since that is a task also performed by Father and Son.[100] The conclusion thus was inevitable: "When we hear the name *Father*, is not sonship involved in that Name? The Holy Ghost is mentioned by name; must He not exist? We can no more separate fatherhood from the Father or sonship from the Son than we can deny the existence in the Holy Ghost of that gift which we receive."[101]

St. Augustine's trinitarian doctrine, including some key pneumatological teachings, was already considered in some detail above. Let us deepen it a bit here. Among the many names he knows for the third person of the Trinity, the following three are significant for our purposes here, namely, *Holy Spirit*, *Spirit as Love*, and *Spirit as Gift*. All these he found in the biblical teaching. The Bishop of Hippo reminds us of the fact that while both the Father and Son are called "holy" and "spirit" in the Bible—indeed, "the Trinity can be called also the Holy Spirit"—what makes the third person unique is that the "Holy Spirit is a certain unutterable communion of the Father and the Son."[102] In other words, "He is the Spirit of the Father and Son, as the substantial and consubstantial love of both."[103] This reasoning also refers to the nature of the Spirit as the bond of love, a favorite designation of Augustine. Again, while acknowledging the fact that any of the members of the Trinity could be called love, on the basis of biblical passages such as 1 John 4:7–19, and Romans 5:5, he comes to the conclusion that the Spirit particularly can be called Love, the bond of love uniting Father and Son, and derivatively, uniting the triune God and human beings.[104] The third biblical designation dear to Augustine is "gift." Passages such as Acts 2:38 specifically name the Spirit as "gift,"[105] while other NT allusions such as John 7:37[106] and particularly Romans 5:5[107] refer to the reception in the human heart of the Spirit.

The NT statements such as "God is Spirit" (John 4:24) and "For the Lord is Spirit, and where the Spirit of the Lord is, there is liberty" (2 Cor 3:17) helped clarify the twofold reference of the term "Spirit": on the one hand, it speaks of God's nature as "invisible and incomprehensible," and on the other hand, as the Gift of God given to the believer, in other words, as the name of the third person of the Trinity.[108]

Final Consolidation

Not only in the East but also in the Christian West, the opponents' claim for the creaturely nature of the Holy Spirit persisted. Ambrose vehemently rejected that heretical notion.[109] Similar to his forebears, Ambrose also had to tackle a common version of that claim, namely that according to the biblical teaching everything was created through the Word, Son (John 1:3). With regard to "The words, 'All things were made by Him,'" this is not a proof that the Holy Spirit is included amongst all things, since He was not made," the Bishop of Milan simply dismissed the suggestion as nonbiblical (as John never mentions the Spirit among the made things) and nonsensical (as the Spirit is divine along with Father and Son). Here is his conclusion:

> But it is equal irreverence to detract from the dignity of the Father, or the Son, or the Holy Spirit. For he believes not in the Father who does not believe in the Son, nor does he believe in the Son of God who does not believe in the Spirit, nor can faith stand without the rule of truth. For he who has begun to deny the oneness of power in the Father and the Son and the Holy Spirit certainly cannot prove his divided faith in points where there is no division. So, then, since complete piety is to believe rightly, so complete impiety is to believe wrongly.[110]

On the basis of both biblical teaching and theological argumentation, Ambrose fully affirmed the orthodox position of the Greek Fathers: "The Spirit is the Lord and Power; and in this is not inferior to the Father and the Son."[111] Related: "The statement of the Apostle, that all things are of the Father by the Son, does not separate the Spirit from Their company, since what is referred to one Person is also attributed to each," to cite the (beginning of) the epigraph to chapter 3 in the first part of Ambrose's *On the Holy Spirit*.[112] And to further accentuate the high status of the Spirit, Ambrose reminded us: "The great dignity of the Holy Spirit is proved by the absence of forgiveness for the sin against Him. How it is that such sin cannot be forgiven, and how the Spirit is one."[113]

Effectively, this is to say that the Holy Spirit is God. While the Eastern Fathers, as explained above, did not dare to call the Spirit God even when they fully affirmed the Spirit's divinity, Ambrose's most famous mentee, Augustine, dared to do so. For him, the Holy Spirit was "Very God, Equal with the Father and the Son."[114] The following statements from the Bishop of Hippo come as close as any in formulating the official opinion of the Western church. They invoke the teaching of both the Bible and tradition and set forth the doctrine of the Spirit in the framework of the Trinity:

> All those Catholic expounders of the divine Scriptures, both Old and New, whom I have been able to read, who have written before me concerning the Trinity, Who is God, have purposed to teach, according to the Scriptures, this doctrine, that the Father, and the Son, and the Holy Spirit intimate a divine unity of one and the same substance in an indivisible equality; and therefore that they are not three Gods, but one God: although the Father hath begotten the Son, and so He who is the Father is not the Son; and the Son is begotten by the Father, and so He who is the Son is not the Father; and the Holy Spirit is neither the Father nor the Son, but only the Spirit of the Father and of the Son, Himself also co-equal with the Father and the Son, and pertaining to the unity of the Trinity.[115]
>
> Therefore let us with steadfast piety believe in one God, the Father, and the Son, and the Holy Spirit; let us at the same time believe that the Son is not [the person] who is the Father, and the Father is not [the person] who is the Son, and neither the Father nor the Son is [the person] who is the Spirit of both the Father and the Son. Let it not be supposed that in this Trinity there is

any separation in respect of time or place, but that these Three are equal and co-eternal, and absolutely of one nature: and that the creatures have been made, not some by the Father, and some by the Son, and some by the Holy Spirit, but that each and all that have been or are now being created subsist in the Trinity as their Creator; and that no one is saved by the Father without the Son and the Holy Spirit, or by the Son without the Father and the Holy Spirit, or by the Holy Spirit without the Father and the Son, but by the Father, the Son, and the Holy Spirit, the only one, true, and truly immortal (that is, absolutely unchangeable) God.[116]

Again, we see that it is inaccurate to claim that whereas the Cappadocians begin with threeness (relationality) and then move to oneness, the Latin tradition acts contrariwise. On the contrary, it is easy to see that both the "unity-orientation" and "threeness-orientation" are present in both. The mutual relationality of the Spirit and Christ comes to the fore already in the annunciation and conception of Jesus in the Virgin Mary.[117] Mutuality is also manifested in that the Spirit is not only sent by Jesus but that Jesus, similarly, was sent by the Spirit: "the Spirit was upon Christ; and . . . as He sent the Spirit, so the Spirit sent the Son of God. For the Son of God says: 'The Spirit of the Lord is upon Me, because He hath anointed Me, He hath sent Me to preach the Gospel to the poor, to proclaim liberty to the captives, and sight to the blind.'"[118] Ambrose's way of connecting the inner-trinitarian *perichoresis* ("mutual indwelling") in relation to the Spirit's work in the hearts of the human person is illustrative of relationality:

[F]or as the Father is in the Son, and the Son in the Father, so, too, "the love of God is shed abroad in our hearts by the Holy Spirit, Who hath been given us." And as he who is blessed in Christ is blessed in the Name of the Father, and of the Son, and of the Holy Spirit, because the Name is one and the Power one; so, too, when any divine operation, whether of the Father, or of the Son, or of the Holy Spirit, is treated of, it is not referred only to the Holy Spirit, but also to the Father and the Son, and not only to the Father, but also to the Son and the Spirit.[119]

The Holy Spirit in the Creeds

The clarification of the status and role of the Spirit in the Trinity and thus establishment of a truly authentic doctrine of the Trinity took place gradually and through much theological and spiritual reflection.[120] Consider this: whereas at the Council of Nicea in 325, the statement on the third person of the Trinity is very short, "And [we believe] in the Holy Ghost,"[121] in the Creed of Constantinople I (381) the consubstantiality of the Spirit was officially confirmed: "And [we believe] in the Holy Ghost, the Lord and Giver-of-Life, who proceedeth from the Father, who with the Father and the Son together is worshipped and glorified, who spake by the prophets."[122]

The Constantinopolitan Creed contains a number of important affirmations about the Holy Spirit.[123] First, the equal status of the Spirit was officially confirmed in that the Holy Spirit is to be "worshiped and glorified together with the Father and the Son." Related to this is the mention of the proceeding of the Spirit from the Father, reminding us of the trinitarian structure of the creed and confession of faith in the Spirit; here I am following the original text of the creed rather than the early amended text that also makes the derivation of the Spirit from the Son.

Second, the nomenclature "Giver-of-Life" makes an integral connection with the doctrine of salvation. This is in keeping with the central role of the Spirit in *ordo salutis*, the "order of salvation" in the Western tradition and in the doctrine of deification in the East. Third, the soteriological connection is brought home also in the nomenclature *Holy* Ghost, in other words, the Spirit's sanctifying work in the life of the believers. As discussed above, the quality of the holiness of the Spirit was seen both in the Christian East and West as an indication of the deity, as only God is able to be the source and fountain of holiness. Fourth, in keeping with later theological developments, the connection between the inspiration of prophetic Scripture and the Holy Spirit was established at Chalcedon. This statement follows the NT understanding of the written word of God, embodied in the Word-become-flesh, as "breathed in" by the Holy Spirit (2 Tim 3:16). Not coincidentally, the NT at times also seems to call all of Scripture a "prophetic" word, which was believed to be made such by the Holy Spirit (2 Pet 1:20–21, among others).

Fifth, considering more widely the whole context of the third article of the creed, in which the pneumatological statement is located, calls for two important remarks. It mentions the ecclesial-liturgical context for the confession of faith in the Holy Spirit: the Spirit will be lifted up and celebrated at the church's worship. The ecclesiological connection is further enhanced by the statement about belief in the one, holy, apostolic, and catholic church and the communion of saints immediately following the confession of belief in the Spirit. Soteriological and ecclesiological themes are always interrelated in Christian life and theology.

Having now considered quite carefully the final consolidation of the doctrine of the Trinity, first with the focus on the Father–Son relationship (the previous chapter) and then the Spirit's role in the Trinity (the current chapter) during the patristic era, it is time for us to move to medieval and subsequent eras. In doing so, we will first highlight the defining postpatristic summarizer of Greek theology's consensus, namely John of Damascus, and then the towering systematic figure of the Latin tradition, Thomas Aquinas.

Notes

1. This section draws directly from Veli-Matti Kärkkäinen, "Introduction," in *The Holy Spirit: A Guide to Christian Theology* (Louisville: Westminster John Knox, 2012), 1–3.

2. Eduard Schweizer, "pneuma," in *Theological Dictionary of the New Testament*, ed. Gerhard Kittel and Gerhard Friedrich, trans. Geoffrey W. Bromiley, 10 vols. (Grand Rapids: Eerdmans, 1964–1976), 6:396.

3. See, further, Franz Dünzl, *A Brief History of the Doctrine of the Trinity in*

     the Early Church, trans. John Bowden (London/New York: T&T Clark, 2007), 117–18; ch. 12 is a succinct guide to the development of the doctrine of the Spirit during the patristic era.

4. Both citations are from Gregory of Nazianzus, *Oration 31. The Fifth Theological Oration. On the Holy Spirit*, #26, NPNF² 7:326.

5. This is also the reasoning of Origen, *On First Principles*, 1.3.1, ANF 4:252: "For although no one is able to speak with certainty of God the Father, it is nevertheless possible for some knowledge of Him to be gained by means of the visible creation and the natural feelings of the human mind; and it is possible, moreover, for such knowledge to be confined from the sacred Scriptures. But with respect to the Son of God, although no one knoweth the Son save the Father, yet it is from sacred Scripture also that the human mind is taught how to think of the Son; and that not only from the New, but also from the Old Testament, by means of those things which, although done by the saints, are figuratively referred to Christ, and from which both His divine nature, and that human nature which was assumed by Him, may be discovered."

6. See Vladimir Lossky, *The Mystical Theology of the Eastern Orthodox Church* (New York: St. Vladimir's Seminary Press, 1976), 168.

7. The rest of this section draws directly from Kärkkäinen, *Holy Spirit*, 8–9.

8. See, e.g., James D. G. Dunn, *Unity and Diversity in the New Testament: An Inquiry into the Character of Earliest Christianity* (London: SCM Press/ Philadelphia: Trinity Press International, 1991), ch. 9.

9. Yves Congar, *I Believe in the Holy Spirit*, trans. David Smith, three volumes in one (New York: Herder, 1997), 1:65.

10. Ibid., 1:65–68.

11. Gregory of Nazianzus, *On the Holy Spirit*, #2, 3, NPNF² 7:318.

12. This section draws directly from Kärkkäinen, *Holy Spirit*, 12–14.

13. The so-called Two Epistles of Clement, *First Epistle to the Corinthians* and *Second Epistle of Clement*, are not so named because of knowledge of authorship but because of an early association with Clement of Rome, believed to be the third bishop of Rome after the apostles.

14. Clement of Rome, *First Epistle to the Corinthians* 45, ANF 1:17; see also, e.g., *First Epistle to the Corinthians* 8, ANF 1:7.

15. Ibid., 42, ANF 1:16.

16. Ignatius, *Epistle to the Philadelphians* 7, ANF 1:83–84.

17. Called also *The Pastor of Hermas.*

18. *The Pastor [Shepherd] of Hermas* 2.11, ANF 2:27.

19. For a brief, reliable source, see William Tabbernee, "'Will the Real Paraclete Please Speak Forth!': The Catholic-Montanist Conflict over Pneumatology," in *Advents of the Spirit: An Introduction to the Current Study of Pneumatology*, ed. Bradford E. Hinze and D. Lyle Dabney (Milwaukee: Marquette University Press, 2001), 97–118.

20. Hippolytus, *The Refutation of All Heresies* 8.12, ANF 5:123–24.

21. Ibid., 10.21–22, ANF 5:147–48.

22. For Tertullian's relation to Montanism and its potential influence on his theology, see Kilian McDonnell, "Communion Ecclesiology and Baptism in the Spirit: Tertullian and the Early Church," *Theological Studies* 49 (1988): 671–93.

23. Tertullian, *On Baptism*, ch. 6, ANF 3:672. http://www.ccel.org/ccel/schaff/anf03.vi.iii.vi.html.

24. Tertullian's *A Treatise on the Soul* (par. 45), mentions the names of Perpetua and Felicitas, who suffered martyrdom in the reign of Septimius Severus about the year 202 ce.

25. I am reminded of the remark by Wolfhart Pannenberg: "The N[ew] T[estament] statements do not clarify the interrelations of the three but they clearly emphasize the fact that they are interrelated." *Systematic Theology*, vol. 1, trans. Geoffrey W. Bromiley (Grand Rapids: Eerdmans, 1991), 269.

26. For details, consult Gerald O'Collins, *The Tripersonal God: Understanding and Interpreting the Trinity* (Mahwah, NJ: Paulist, 1999), 23–34.

27. *The Second Epistle of Clement*, 14, ANF 7:521. For such examples in Justin Martyr, see J. N. D. Kelly, *Early Christian Creeds*, 3d ed. (Harlow, UK: Longman, 1972), 148.

28. The Shepherd of Hermas, *Similitude* 9.1, ANF 2:44.

29. Justin Martyr, *First Apology*, 33, ANF 1:174.

30. Athenagoras, *A Plea for the Christians* 10, ANF 2:133.

31. Theophilus of Antioch, *Theophilus to Autolycus: Book II*, 15, ANF 2:101.

32. Irenaeus, *Against Heresies* 4.20.3, ANF 1:488.

33. Justin Martyr, *First Apology*, 13, ANF 1:166–67.

34. Irenaeus, *Against Heresies* 3.24.1, *ANF* 1:458. http://www.ccel.org/ccel/schaff/anf01.ix.iv.xxv.html.

35. Hippolytus, *The Refutation of All Heresies* 1, Preface, *ANF* 5:10: "But none will refute these, save the Holy Spirit bequeathed unto the Church, which the Apostles, having in the first instance received, have transmitted to those who have rightly believed."

36. Tertullian begins the fourth chapter, titled "The Primeval Hovering of the Spirit of God Over the Waters Typical of Baptism. The Universal Element of Water Thus Made a Channel of Sanctification. Resemblance Between the Outward Sign and the Inward Grace," in this way: "But it will suffice to have *thus* called at the outset those points in which withal is recognised that primary principle of baptism,—which was even then fore-noted by the very attitude *assumed* for a type of baptism,—that the Spirit of God, who hovered over (the waters) from the beginning, would continue to linger over the waters of the baptized" Tertullian, *On Baptism* 4, in *ANF* 3:670.

37. Ibid., 7, *ANF* 3:672.

38. Ibid., 8, *ANF* 3:672.

39. Cyprian, *On the Dress of Virgins* 23, *ANF* 5:436: "All indeed who attain to the divine gift and inheritance by the sanctification of baptism, therein put off the old man by the grace of the saving laver, and, renewed by the Holy Spirit from the filth of the old contagion, are purged by a second nativity."

40. Clement of Alexandria, *The Instructor* 1.6, *ANF* 2:215: "But He is perfected by the washing—of baptism—alone, and is sanctified by the descent of the Spirit? Such is the case. The same also takes place in our case, whose exemplar Christ became. Being baptized, we are illuminated; illuminated, we become sons; being made sons, we are made perfect; being made perfect, we are made immortal. 'I,' says He, 'have said that ye are gods, and all sons of the Highest.' This work is variously called grace, and illumination, and perfection, and washing: washing, by which we cleanse away our sins; grace, by which the penalties accruing to transgressions are remitted; and illumination, by which that holy light of salvation is beheld, that is, by which we see God clearly." (This work is also known by the title *Paedagogus*, a fitting name for a manual for Christian formation for those who have left behind paganism.)

41. Ibid., 2.2, *ANF* 2:242.

42. Cyprian, *On the Unity of the Church* 6, *ANF* 5:423.

43. Ibid., 9, *ANF* 5:424; in addition to the dove, a biblical symbol of the Spirit, Cyprian also refers in this passage to the gentleness and meekness of lambs and sheep as well.

44. This and the preceding citations are from Origen, *Commentary on John* 2.6, *ANF* 9:328–29.

45. Irenaeus, *Against Heresies* 4.20.1, *ANF* 1:487.

46. Tertullian, *Against Praxeas* 8, *ANF* 3:603.

47. Ibid., 7, *ANF* 3:602. Here he also states: "Nor need we dwell any longer on this point, as if it were not the very Word Himself, who is spoken of under the name both of Wisdom and of Reason, and of the entire Divine Soul and Spirit."

48. Ibid., 8, *ANF* 3:603.

49. Ibid., 31, *ANF* 3:627: the chapter is titled ". . . The Doctrine of the Blessed Trinity Constitutes the Great Difference Between Judaism and Christianity."

50. See ibid., 9, *ANF* 3:603–4, quoting John 14:28 and 14:16.

51. Ibid., 25, *ANF* 3:621.

52. See, e.g., Origen, *On First Principles* 1.3.2, *ANF* 4:252. Having cited a number of familiar biblical passages referring to the Holy Spirit, he concludes: "From all which we learn that the person of the Holy Spirit was of such authority and dignity, that saving baptism was not complete except by the authority of the most excellent Trinity of them all, i.e., by the naming of Father, Son, and Holy Spirit, and by joining to the unbegotten God the Father, and to His only-begotten Son, the name also of the Holy Spirit. Who, then, is not amazed at the exceeding majesty of the Holy Spirit, when he hears that he who speaks a word against the Son of man may hope for forgiveness; but that he who is guilty of blasphemy against the Holy Spirit has not forgiveness, either in the present world or in that which is to come!"

53. Ibid., 1.3.5, *ANF* 4:253: "I am of opinion, then, that the working of the Father and of the Son takes place as well in saints as in sinners, in rational beings and in dumb animals; nay, even in those things which are without life, and in all things universally which exist; but that the operation of the Holy Spirit does not take place at all in those things which are without life, or in those which, although living, are yet dumb; nay, is not found even in those who are endued indeed with

reason, but are engaged in evil courses, and not at all converted to a better life. In those persons alone do I think that the operation of the Holy Spirit takes place, who are already turning to a better life, and walking along the way which leads to Jesus Christ, i.e., who are engaged in the performance of good actions, and who abide in God."

54. Irenaeus, *Against Heresies* 4.20.4, ANF 1:488.

55. Ibid., 5.1.1, ANF 1:527.

56. Tertullian, *Against Praxeas* 2, ANF 3:598.

57. Origen, *On First Principles*, 1.3.7, ANF 4:255. While this statement is in keeping with the later orthodox tradition, the background to this statement, ironically, can be found in Origen's speculation about the different spheres of operation of the trinitarian persons: the Father's in creation, the Son's in salvation, and the Spirit's in inanimate creation; this idea was supposed to guard the unity of the Trinity. Neither idea (namely, different spheres of operation and defense of unity on this basis) can be sustained in light of creedal traditions.

58. Eastern Christian traditions, of course, include others than those mentioned above, such as the East Syrian (Assyrian) Church and several non-Chalcedonian churches, Armenian, Coptic, Ethiopian, and Jacobite (West Syrian) churches. This section draws directly from Kärkkäinen, *Holy Spirit*, 18–22.

59. Basil, *On the Holy Spirit* 11.27, NPNF[2] 8:17–18.

60. A delightful example of Basil's attention to the details—in this case of grammar and logic—is ch. II of his *On the Holy Spirit*: "The origin of the heretics' close observation of syllables."

61. Ibid., 19.49, NPNF[2] 8:30–31.

62. Ibid., 6.13–7.17, NPNF[2] 8:8–11.

63. Gregory of Nyssa, *On the Holy Spirit against the Followers of Macedonius*, NPNF[2] 5:323.

64. A telling example is this long listing of titles, descriptions, and nomenclatures for the Holy Spirit: "the Spirit of God, the Spirit of Christ, the Mind of Christ, the Spirit of The Lord, and Himself The Lord, the Spirit of Adoption, of Truth, of Liberty; the Spirit of Wisdom, of Understanding, of Counsel, of Might, of Knowledge." Gregory Nazianzus, *On the Holy Spirit*, #29, NPNF[2] 7.327. Other similar examples from Gregory include *Oration* 41 *On Pentecost* 11, NPNF[2] 7:382 and *Oration* 41 *On Pentecost* 14, NPNF[2] 7:384.

65. Gregory Nazianzus, *On the Holy Spirit*, #28, NPNF[2] 7:327.

66. Basil, *On the Holy Spirit*, 18.47, NPNF[2] 8:29.

67. Cyril, *Catechetical Lectures* 4.17, NPNF[2] 7:23.

68. Ibid., 16.11, NPNF[2] 7:117; Basil lists a number of his predecessors whom he finds supporting his teaching such as Irenaeus, Clement of Rome, Origen, and many more (*On the Holy Spirit* 29.71–74, NPNF[2] 8:45–47).

69. Ibid. Over and over again Basil brushed aside arguments of his opponents and argued strongly, "Against those who say that it is not right to rank the Holy Spirit with the Father and the Son" (the title for ch. 10 in *On the Holy Spirit*), and "Against those who say that the Holy Ghost is not to be numbered with, but numbered under, the Father and the Son" (ch. 17).

70. Ibid., 19.49, NPNF[2] 8:30–31: "And His operations, what are they? For majesty ineffable, and for numbers innumerable. How shall we form a conception of what extends beyond the ages? What were His operations before that creation whereof we can conceive? How great the grace which He conferred on creation? What the power exercised by Him over the ages to come? He existed; He pre-existed; He co-existed with the Father and the Son before the ages. It follows that, even if you can conceive of anything beyond the ages, you will find the Spirit yet further above and beyond. And if you think of the creation, the powers of the heavens were established by the Spirit, the establishment being understood to refer to disability to fall away from good. For it is from the Spirit that the powers derive their close relationship to God, their inability to change to evil, and their continuance in blessedness. Is it Christ's advent? The Spirit is forerunner. Is there the incarnate presence? The Spirit is inseparable. Working of miracles, and gifts of healing are through the Holy Spirit. Demons were driven out by the Spirit of God. The devil was brought to naught by the presence of the Spirit. Remission of sins was by the gift of the Spirit, for 'ye were washed, ye were sanctified, . . . in the name of the Lord Jesus Christ, and in the holy Spirit of our God.' There is close relationship with God through the Spirit, for 'God hath sent forth the Spirit of His Son into your hearts, crying Abba, Father.' The resurrection from the dead is effected by the operation of the Spirit, for 'Thou sendest forth thy spirit, they are created; and Thou renewest the face of the earth.' If here creation may be taken to mean the bringing of the departed to life again, how mighty is not the operation of the Spirit, Who is to us the dispenser of the life

that follows on the resurrection, and attunes our souls to the spiritual life beyond? Or if here by creation is meant the change to a better condition of those who in this life have fallen into sin, (for it is so understood according to the usage of Scripture, as in the words of Paul 'if any man be in Christ he is a new creature'), the renewal which takes place in this life, and the transmutation from our earthly and sensuous life to the heavenly conversation which takes place in us through the Spirit, then our souls are exalted to the highest pitch of admiration. With these thoughts before us are we to be afraid of going beyond due bounds in the extravagance of the honour we pay? Shall we not rather fear lest, even though we seem to give Him the highest names which the thoughts of man can conceive or man's tongue utter, we let our thoughts about Him fall too low?"

71. Both citations from Basil, On the Holy Spirit 19.48, NPNF^2 8:30.

72. To be more precise: "Lately when praying with the people, and using the full doxology to God the Father in both forms, at one time "with the Son together with the Holy Ghost," and at another "through the Son in the Holy Ghost," I was attacked by some of those present on the ground that I was introducing novel and at the same time mutually contradictory terms." On the Holy Spirit 1.3, in NPNF^2 8:3. A sustained attack "Against those who assert that the Spirit ought not to be glorified" is ch. 19.

73. Athanasius, Letters to Serapion [1.15–33], 1.19–20, in Athanasius, trans. and ed. Khaled Anatolios (London: Routledge, 2004), 218.

74. Gregory of Nazianzus, Oration 41 On Pentecost 14, NPNF^2 7:384.

75. Gregory of Nyssa, On the Holy Spirit, NPNF^2 5:321.

76. For a helpful discussion, see J. N. D. Kelly, Early Christian Doctrines, rev. ed. (New York: Harper & Bros., 1960), 258–63; and Robert Letham, The Holy Trinity: In Scripture, History, Theology, and Worship (Phillipsburg, NJ: P&R Publishing, 2004), 148–66.

77. Cyril of Jerusalem, Catechetical Lectures 4.16, NPNF^2 7:23.

78. The scholarly opinion is that the catechetical orations were preached around the mid-fourth century, hence a few decades prior to Constantinople.

79. Athanasius, Letters to Serapion on the Holy Spirit 1.20, in Anatolios, trans. and ed., Athanasius, 220. For the Spirit's role in the Trinity in Athanasian theology, see Letham, Holy Trinity, 141–44.

80. E.g., Athanasius, Letters to Serapion 1.28, in Anatolios, trans. and ed.,

Athanasius, 227. A strong defense of the unity of the Trinity and the Spirit's role therein can also be found in Gregory of Nyssa, *On 'Not Three Gods'*, NPNF[2] 5:334.

81. Gregory of Nazianzus, *On The Holy Spirit*, #4, in NPNF[2] 7:318–19.

82. Ibid., #14, NPNF[2] 7:322.

83. Athanasius, *Letters to Serapion* 1.21, in Anatolios, trans. and ed., *Athanasius*, 220–21.

84. Kelly, *Early Christian Doctrines*, 257. The following references to Athanasius are provided by Kelly from Athanasius, *Letters to Serapion* 1.21; 1.22–27; 1.2; 1.20; 3.7; 1.25; 3.2, respectively.

85. Ephrem the Syrian, *Eighty Rhythms upon the Faith, against the Disputers* 18.1, in J. B. Morris, ed., *Selected Works of S. Ephrem the Syrian* (Oxford: John Henry Parker/London: F. and J. Rivington, 1847), 165–66, available at https://archive.org/details/selectedworksse01ephrgoog. Also known as Ephrem (or Ephraem or, as named by Pope Benedict XV in 1920, a "Doctor of the Church"), Ephraim is the leading Syrian spiritual writer.

86. Ephrem the Syrian, *Eighty Rhythms upon the Faith* 73.1; Morris, ed., *Selected Works of S. Ephrem the Syrian*, 339.

87. Gregory of Nazianzus, *On The Holy Spirit*, #10, NPNF[2] 7:321.

88. Basil, *On the Holy Spirit* 21.52, NPNF[2] 8:33–34.

89. Ibid., 18.46, NPNF[2] 8:28–29. For a strong defense of the full equality of the Spirit in the Trinity, see also Gregory of Nyssa, *On the Holy Spirit*, NPNF[2] 5.315–28.

90. Basil, *Letter 105*, NPNF[2] 8:186.

91. Basil, *On the Holy Spirit* 15.36, NPNF[2] 8:22.

92. Ambrose, *On the Holy Spirit* 1.16.176–79, NPNF[2] 10:113–14.

93. Ambrose, *On the Duties of the Clergy* 3.18.102–3, NPNF[2] 10:84.

94. Ambrose, *On the Holy Spirit*, Preface 1.2–3, NPNF[2] 10:93.

95. Ibid., 1.8.99, NPNF[2] 10:106.

96. Ibid., 1.9.100–107, NPNF[2] 10:106–7. Behind this particular reasoning is an extensive allegorical explanation related to oil and anointment as types of the Spirit.

97. Hilary of Poitiers, *On the Trinity* 8.21–23, NPNF[2] 9:143–44.

98. Ibid., 2.1, NPNF[2] 9:52.

99. Ambrose, *On the Holy Spirit* 1.5.62–64, *NPNF*[2] 10:101–2.

100. Ibid., 1.10, *NPNF*[2] 10:108.

101. Hilary of Poitiers, *On the Trinity* 2.3, *NPNF*[2] 9:52.

102. Augustine, *On the Trinity* 5.11.12, *NPNF*[1] 3:93.

103. Augustine, *Tractates on John 105*, *NPNF*[1] 7:396.

104. Augustine, *On the Trinity* 15.17.31, *NPNF*[1] 3:216–17. While Augustine's way of supporting the designation of the Spirit as love is somewhat complex here, the main point is clear: that as love the Spirit is what unites Father and Son.

105. Ibid., 15.19.35, *NPNF*[1] 3:219.

106. Ibid., 15.19.33, *NPNF*[1] 3:217.

107. Ibid., 15.18.32, *NPNF*[1] 3:217.

108. Hilary of Poitiers, *On the Trinity* 2.31–32, *NPNF*[2] 9:60–61.

109. Ambrose, *On The Holy Spirit*, 1.7, *NPNF*[2] 10:104: "The Holy Spirit is not a creature, seeing that He is infinite . . ." (beginning of the epigraph).

110. Ambrose, *On The Holy Spirit*, 1.2.30, *NPNF*[2] 10:97.

111. Ibid., 2.1, *NPNF*[2] 10:117 (beginning of the epigraph)

112. Ibid., 1.3, *NPNF*[2] 10:98.

113. Ibid.

114. Augustine, *On the Trinity*, the preamble to chap. 6 in book 1, in *NPNF*[1] 1:21; see also, e.g., 1.2.4, *NPNF*[1] 1:19.

115. Ibid., 1.4.7, *NPNF*[1] 3:20.

116. Augustine, *Letter 169 to Bishop Evodius*, *NPNF*[1] 1:540.

117. See, e.g., Hilary of Poitiers, *On the Trinity* 2.26–27, *NPNF*[2] 9:59.

118. Ambrose, *On the Holy Spirit* 3.1.1, *NPNF*[2] 10:135.

119. Ambrose, *On the Holy Spirit* 1.3.40, *NPNF*[2] 10:98.

120. This section draws directly from Kärkkäinen, *Holy Spirit*, 27–28.

121. *NPNF*[2] 14:3.

122. *NPNF*[2] 14:163.

123. I was inspired by Donald Thorsen, *Explorations in Christian Theology* (Grand Rapids: Baker Academic, 2010), ch. 19: "The Works of the Spirit."

4

Medieval Contributions and Clarifications

Orientation

While early Christian theologians carefully worked out definitive solutions to trinitarian problems, and while these yielded ecumenical creedal statements, still it is not quite accurate to say that the Christian understanding of the Trinity was now final and conclusive, written in stone. Theologians of the subsequent medieval period (c. 500–1500) built on early Christian orientations and, in a few cases, introduced elements that were distinctively novel. One theologically and ecumenically critical development in the doctrine of the Holy Spirit with weighty implications for the Trinity belongs to this time period, namely, the so-called *filioque* debate, which has to do with the derivation of the Spirit in the Trinity. Yet even this debate's roots go back to the time of Augustine and other Latin Fathers.

The purpose of this chapter is to continue the narrative of the doctrine and spirituality of the Holy Trinity with the focus on medieval contributions. Our survey of this millennium-long era falls into the following major segments. First, as a fitting continuation to the previous chapters' focus on Spirit's role in the Trinity, a survey of medieval mystics' and spiritual mothers and fathers' trinitarian experiences both in the Christian East and West will follow. That section once again reminds us that unlike, say, mathematical or logical truths, spiritual truths such as the Trinity are just that, namely *spiritual* in the sense that they are both cognitive and discursive. That said, the experiences, visions, and charisms witnessed to by these Christians would not have been conceived of, or interpreted as trinitarian, without this background: the NT's intuitive trinitarian structure in terms of God appearing as Father, Son, and Spirit, and the early church's doctrinal definitions.

As stated in the introduction, if there is any constructive element or novelty to this trinitarian primer, it is the continuous insistence on the need to consult both scriptural-doctrinal sources and the spiritual-mystical experiences of the church. If we don't, we are not doing justice to the way the doctrine of the Trinity developed. (Unfortunately, in this short guide we are not able to account properly for the third foundational source of the doctrine of God, namely prayer, liturgy, and sacraments.)

Second, this chapter will offer a brief consideration of the church-dividing issue related to the derivation of the Spirit in the Trinity, called the *filioque* debate. Next, the third section of this chapter will focus on doctrinal affirmations and contributions by some leading theologians, particularly the Latin church's "Angelic Doctor" Thomas Aquinas and the Greek church's first—and last!—"systematic" teacher, John of Damascus. Finally, before moving to Reformation and modern trinitarian materials, the rise of the so-called social trinitarianism—with focus on relationality and communion—will be considered.

Mystical Experience and Visions

Apophatic Mysticism in the East

As already established, a defining difference in orientation and method between the theological visions of the Christian East and West is the distinction between apophatic and kataphatic theologies.[1] The former, typical of the East, is much less drawn to clearly defined, "positive" descriptions of divine mysteries and instead approaches the mystical divine realities and symbols through "negative," indirect, suggestive terms. Spiritual vision and discernment is as important—or even more so—than intellectual acumen and shrewdness. In the words of Symeon the New Theologian—one of the three in the Greek church to be named the "theologian" (alongside St. John the Apostle and Gregory of Nazianzus), "the things that are sealed up and closed, unseen and unknown by all men, are opened up by the Holy Spirit alone."[2] True and authentic knowledge of God, in the spirit of humble prayer and repentance, requires a combined spiritual and intellectual catharsis, "a purification of the mind that rids us of all false ideas about God."[3] Vladimir Lossky, a late-twentieth-century authority on Eastern theology, describes the process of "ascending" to God with these words:

> The negative way of the knowledge of God is an ascendant undertaking of the mind that progressively eliminates all positive attributes of the object it wishes to attain, in order to culminate finally in a kind of apprehension by supreme ignorance of Him who cannot be an object of knowledge. We can say that it is an intellectual experience of the mind's failure when confronted with something beyond the conceivable.[4]

Rather than an isolated doctrine to be merely believed, in Eastern Christianity the Trinity is present everywhere, so to speak. Just think of the Eastern doctrine of the Spirit; it is conceived in trinitarian manner through the lens of a profound Spirit Christology, that is, whatever Christ does, the Spirit is there and vice versa. To be linked with the resurrection life of the incarnated and crucified Christ, human beings are united through the Spirit in the eternal life of the Father. Consider this highly trinitarian account from Maximus the Confessor highlighting the salvific meaning of Christ's incarnation:

> In becoming incarnate, the Word of God teaches us the mystical knowledge of God because he shows us in himself the Father and the Holy Spirit. For the full Father and the full Holy Spirit are essentially and completely in the full Son, even the incarnate Son, without being themselves incarnate. Rather, the Father gives approval and the Spirit cooperates in the incarnation with the Son who . . . gives adoption by giving through the Spirit a supernatural birth from on high in grace.[5]

Not only mystical and apophatic, the Eastern trinitarian vision is also authentically communal and cosmic in orientation. This correlates with the idea of the human person having been created in the image of God as the "mini-cosmos" and of the church patterned in the image of the triune God. In one of his most unique—even astonishing—statements, Maximus names the Spirit as the kingdom of God: "[T]he kingdom of God the Father who subsists essentially is the Holy Spirit. Indeed, what Matthew here [in The Lord's Prayer] calls kingdom another evangelist elsewhere calls Holy Spirit: 'May your Holy Spirit come and purify us.'"[6] This insight is related to the cosmic presence of the Spirit in the created order, particularly in all intelligent beings. What is remarkable about Maximus's teaching is that it links together the Spirit's presence in nature as the principle of life, the Spirit's work as the basis for distinctively human life, including intelligence and morality, as well as the Spirit's deifying work. What an astonishingly wide and deep trinitarian vision is shown in this lengthy citation:

> The Holy Spirit is not absent from any created being, especially not from one which in any way participates in intelligence. For being God and God's Spirit, He embraces in unity the spiritual knowledge of all created things, providentially permeating all things with His power, and vivifying their inner essences in

accordance with their nature. In this way he makes men aware of things done sinfully against the law of nature, and renders them capable of choosing principles which are true and in conformity with nature. . . . The Holy Spirit is present unconditionally in all things, in that He embraces all things, provides for all, and vivifies the natural seeds within them. He is present in a specific way in all who are under the Law, in that He shows them where they have broken the commandments and enlightens them about the promise given concerning Christ. In all who are Christians He is present also in yet another way in that He makes them sons of God. But in none is He fully present as the author of wisdom except in those who have understanding, and who by their holy way of life have made themselves fit to receive His indwelling and deifying presence.[7]

Some of the best-known early mystical writings from the East are the works of Pseudo-Dionysius the Areopagite, from the fifth or sixth century.[8] In a typical Neoplatonic fashion,[9] Pseudo-Dionysius conceived of the world as a hierarchical structure in which all things come from God and lead back to God. God stands on top of everything and the whole universe is related in an orderly way to God. This God is covered by an unapproachable mystery.[10] The vision of the triune God in Areopagite's *Mystical Theology* is breathtaking. He doesn't spare words in trying to convey it to us:

Trinity, which exceedeth all Being, Deity, and Goodness! Thou that instructeth Christians in Thy heavenly wisdom! Guide us to that topmost height of mystic lore which exceedeth light and more than exceedeth knowledge, where the simple, absolute, and unchangeable mysteries of heavenly Truth lie hidden in the dazzling obscurity of the secret Silence, outshining all brilliance with the intensity of their darkness, and surcharging our blinded intellects with the utterly impalpable and invisible fairness of glories which exceed all beauty! . . . For, by the unceasing and absolute renunciation of thyself and all things, thou shalt in pureness cast all things aside, and be released from all, and so shalt be led upwards to the Ray of that divine Darkness which exceedeth all existence.[11]

A leading medieval Greek theologian—as much as he was also a prayer warrior and spiritual mystic—is the fourteenth-century Gregory of Palamas,[12] whose theology of God's "energies" as distinct from "essence" established itself as a pan-Orthodox teaching.[13] "This distinction is that between the essence of God, or His nature, properly co-called, which is inaccessible, unknowable, and incommunicable; and the energies or divine operations, forces proper to and inseparable from God's essence, in which He goes forth from Himself, manifests, communicates, and gives Himself."[14] Gregory's distinction in a major way helped the East to avoid any notion of pantheism in its robust teaching on the union in deification (*theosis*) between the triune God and humanity. While real, human participation in God relates to the divine energies, never to the unknown, mysterious essence.

We already established that the mystical (and at times, apophatic) approach to the theology of God is not limited to the East. In the medieval West, it appears in the works of theologians such as John Scotus Erigena and Nicholas of Cusa, as well as the Western mystical tradition of the fourteenth and fifteenth centuries, including Meister Eckhart and Thomas à Kempis.[15]

The Western Mystical Orientation

The Irish-born John Scotus Erigena (or Eriugena) of the ninth century represents the so-called Carolingian Renaissance, an intellectual revival accompanied by fresh theological work after a period of relative silence. It was characterized by the return to the classical sources, including (as in Erigena's case) familiarity with Greek sources as well.[16] The following typical prayer reflects this mystical tradition:

> O Thou who art the everlasting Essence of things beyond space and time and yet within them; Thou who transcendest yet pervadest all things, manifest Thyself unto us, feeling after Thee, seeking Thee in the shades of ignorance. Stretch forth Thy hand to help us, who cannot without Thee come to Thee; and reveal

Thyself unto us, who seek nothing beside Thee; through Jesus Christ our Lord. Amen.[17]

Similar to his Eastern counterparts, under the influence of Neoplatonism (as conveyed particularly through Pseudo-Dionysius), Erigena emphasized the transcendence and incomprehensibility of God. "God is above all being. He is wholly unknowable and can neither be perceived nor conceived. We can know that he is but not what he is. . . . When we declare that God is omnipotent, omniscient, and the like, we are only trying to say in figurative language that he is greater than can be said or thought."[18] Not only apophatic, but remarkably "panentheistic," to use a modern nomenclature—that is, God and world are brought close to each other but not equated as in pantheism—Erigena's focus was on God's immanence: the "divine nature embraces everything; apart from God or outside of him there is nothing. He is Being unlimited and undifferentiated; the world is Being circumscribed and divided. . . ."[19]

Widely considered the most significant apocalyptic prophet of the Middle Ages in the Christian West, the twelfth-century Italian monk Joachim of Fiore was a man of visions and spiritual experiences *par excellence.* Famously, he divided history into three periods, that of the Father, of the Son, and finally of the Spirit. The era of the Spirit was the endtime apocalyptic pouring out of the Spirit—and, according to Fiore, was started with none other than St. Benedictine! Consider Joachim's profound trinitarian experience on a Pentecost Sunday:

> In the meantime, when I had entered the church to pray to Almighty God before the holy altar, there came upon me an uncertainty concerning belief in the Trinity as though it were hard to understand. . . . When that happened, I prayed with all my might. I was very frightened and was moved to call on the Holy Spirit whose feast day it was to deign to show me the holy mystery of the Trinity. The Lord has promised us that the whole understanding of truth is to be found in the Trinity. I repeated this and began to pray the psalms to complete the number I had intended. Without delay at this moment the shape of a ten-stringed psaltery appeared in my mind.[20]

Before delving into the doctrinal considerations and developments among some Eastern and Western medieval masters, let us take up briefly the question of the *filioque*, a church-dividing debate at the turn of the second millennium.

Filioque and the East/West Split

In this section[21] I look at how and why the *filioque* debate evolved and what was at stake; following that there is a brief consideration of its contemporary (to us) implications.

As mentioned, the term *filioque* (Latin: "and from the Son") refers to the addition by Latin Christianity to the Nicene-Constantinopolitan Creed of 381 concerning the dual procession of the Spirit both from the Son and the Father. The original form of the Creed said that the Holy Spirit "proceeds from the Father." While some of the historical details are debated,[22] it is clear that in the first major breach of the Christian church in 1054 the *filioque* clause played a major role along with political, ecclesiastical, and cultural issues.

Why was this word added in the first place? There are several reasons, both biblical and historical. Undoubtedly, the NT itself is ambiguous about the procession of the Spirit. On the one hand, the Johannine Jesus says that he himself will send the Spirit (John 16:7) or that he will send the Spirit (called *Parakletos* here) who proceeds from the Father (15:26). On the other hand, Jesus prays to the Father in order for him to send the Spirit (14:16), and promises that the Father will send the Spirit in Jesus's name (14:26). On top of these scriptural reasons, it is to be noted that the Augustinian idea of the Spirit as shared love, followed by other Latin writers, contributed to the rise of the idea of the procession of the Spirit both from the Father and Son. Why? Because for the Spirit to be a "bond," it is possible (though that was not Augustine's view) to conceive the Spirit in nonpersonal terms and, whether that is the case or not, in terms of having a "beginning" or "source" in both Father and Son. There is also the possibility that the addition also served a function in opposing Arianism. Mentioning the

Son alongside the Father as the origin of the Spirit could have been seen as a way to defend consubstantiality.[23]

It is important to our discussion to note that from its first appearance in the creeds and Latin church's liturgical language, the Christian East has vehemently opposed this addition.[24] The reasons for the opposition are many and varied, some more solid while others overstatements. What is indisputable is that the Westerners launched this addition unilaterally, without consultation with the East.[25] Similarly, it is true that, more often than not, the subordination of the Spirit to Jesus has plagued the Christian West with theological corollaries in ecclesiology, the doctrine of salvation, and elsewhere.[26] Less credible (at least to me) is the claim that it also compromises the monarchy of the Father as the source of divinity.[27] Even if some of these and related objections from the East may be in need of qualification, the Eastern critique of the *filioque* is important both ecumenically and theologically. It deserves a full hearing.[28] The West acted wrongly in unilaterally fixing the ecumenically binding creed. At the same time, it can be argued that *filioque* is not heretical—as the Eastern criticism too often implies—but that it is ecumenically and theologically unacceptable and therefore should be removed. This is the growing consensus of both Protestant and Roman Catholic theologians.[29] An alternative to *filioque* that reads "from the Father through the Son" would be also acceptable to the Christian East.[30]

What follows is a consideration of the continuing affirmations of the patristic doctrinal and creedal-confessional traditions among some leading Eastern and Western medieval teachers. We will begin with John of Damascus of the East and thereafter move to Thomas Aquinas and some other Latin theologians.

Medieval Teachers East and West

John of Damascus

We have seen that the conventional alleged categorical juxtaposition between the unity-driven approach to God among the Latin theologians and threeness-driven approach among the Greek-speakers is a gross oversimplification. Yet, there is some truth to the claim that there are differences of emphasis in the two trinitarian traditions. Whereas the followers of St. Augustine all the way to Aquinas and those following in his footsteps began to move toward an emphasis on the oneness, at times leading to a fairly thin account of plurality, John of Damascus's reestablishment of the Alexandrian-Cappadocian Fathers' relational orientation helped the East preserve a more dynamic relation between one and many in the Godhead. Careful attention to the way John orders the discussion of the doctrine of God in the first book of his *The Orthodox Faith*[31] shows this. In keeping with Christian tradition—and evident in later Western works such as Aquinas's first part of his *Summa Theologiae*—oneness is affirmed first.[32] That, however, is done briefly (linked with the Eastern stress on incomprehensibility), before John launches into the details of the doctrine of the Trinity.[33]

Having reminded the reader of God's incomprehensibility in the very beginning of *Orthodox Faith*,[34] John reminds us that the "proof" for God's existence can be found both in the Scripture and the "knowledge . . . implanted in us by nature,"[35] whereas the *"Proof that God is one and not many"* can only be had in the last instance by the scriptural witness.[36] Immediately after this brief orientation to the existence and oneness of God, the Damascene begins his consideration of the plurality in God by first introducing the Father–Son relationship with the employment of the metaphor of the Word. In keeping with tradition, both the Son's distinction from the Father and his preexistence and eternity are affirmed:[37]

So then this one and only God is not Wordless. And possessing the Word, He will have it not as without a subsistence, nor as having had a beginning, nor as destined to cease to be. For there never was a time when God was not Word: but He ever possesses His own Word, begotten of Himself, not, as our word is, without a subsistence and dissolving into air, but having a subsistence in Him and life and perfection, not proceeding out of Himself but ever existing within Himself.

And lest the mere biunity were affirmed, the Spirit is introduced immediately following the Word. Whereas the affirmations about the deity of the Spirit are similar to those of the Son—and of course in keeping with tradition—the form of the argumentation is somewhat novel and complex:

Moreover the Word must also possess Spirit. For in fact even our word is not destitute of spirit; but in our case the spirit is something different from our essence. For there is an attraction and movement of the air which is drawn in and poured forth that the body may be sustained. And it is this which in the moment of utterance becomes the articulate word, revealing in itself the force of the word. But in the case of the divine nature, which is simple and uncompound, we must confess in all piety that there exists a Spirit of God, for the Word is not more imperfect than our own word. Now we cannot, in piety, consider the Spirit to be something foreign that gains admission into God from without, as is the case with compound natures like us. Nay, just as, when we heard of the Word of God, we considered it to be not without subsistence . . . but as being essentially subsisting, endowed with free volition, and energy, and omnipotence: so also, when we have learnt about the Spirit of God, we contemplate it as the companion of the Word and the revealer of His energy, and not as mere breath without subsistence. . . . [W]e must contemplate it as an essential power, existing in its own proper and peculiar subsistence, proceeding from the Father and resting in the Word, and shewing forth the Word, neither capable of disjunction from God in Whom it exists, and the Word Whose companion it is, nor poured forth to vanish into nothingness, but being in subsistence in the likeness of the Word, endowed with life, free volition, independent movement, energy . . . having no beginning and no end.

For never was the Father at any time lacking in the Word, nor the Word in the Spirit.[38]

Now, after these careful deliberations, John of Damascus is ready to give a detailed and comprehensive account of the Holy Trinity at large. Echoing the approach of the Scholastics of the Latin West, he begins that summative statement by listing a large number of attributes and features of the "One God," such as that God himself has "no beginning and God is imperishable and immortal, everlasting, infinite, uncircumscribed, boundless, of infinite power, simple, uncompound, incorporeal," and so forth. God is also the "fountain of goodness and justice, the light of the mind . . . ," creator, sustainer, "master and lord and king over all, with an endless and immortal kingdom." Interestingly, again, there is a need to affirm that in God there is "one essence, one divinity, one power, one will, one energy, one beginning, one authority, one dominion, one sovereignty." Concerning the Father, John employs the argument of Athanasius according to which "He could not have received the name Father apart from the Son: for if He were without the Son, He could not be the Father." The relational nature of the fatherhood also proves the preexistence of the Son, or else a change was introduced to the status of the Father (that is, had he even been without the Son, one could not speak of the Father). Hence, in agreement with the teaching of the "holy catholic and apostolic Church," John affirms "the existence at once of a Father: and of His Only-begotten Son, born of Him without time and flux and passion, in a manner incomprehensible and perceived by the God of the universe alone." Having already affirmed the full deity of the Spirit, the following concluding statement authoritatively summarizes the core of the shared trinitarian doctrine of the yet undivided church:

So then . . . the three absolutely divine subsistences of the Holy Godhead agree: for they exist as one in essence and uncreate. But with the second signification it is quite otherwise. For the Father alone is ingenerate, no other subsistence having given Him being. And the Son alone is generate, for He was begotten of the Father's essence without beginning and without time. And only the Holy Spirit proceedeth from the Father's essence, not having been generated but simply proceeding. For this is the doctrine of Holy Scripture.

As if wanting to conclusively brush away all doubts of the equal status of the Holy Spirit in the Trinity, the Damascene continues strongly affirming the third article of the Constantinopolitan Creed and adding a number of attributes and qualifications applying to the Son as well: "Likewise we believe also in one Holy Spirit, the Lord and Giver of Life: Who proceedeth from the Father and resteth in the Son: the object of equal adoration and glorification with the Father and Son, since He is co-essential and co-eternal: the Spirit of God, direct, authoritative, the fountain of wisdom, and life, and holiness. . . ."[39]

In keeping with the Eastern church's venerated tradition, John adds one more essential caveat, namely the primacy of the Father in the Trinity. Although there is no difference with regard to the equality of deity, there is the Greek theologians' idea of the Father as the "source" of Son and Spirit: "All then that the Son and the Spirit have is from the Father, even their very being: and unless the Father is, neither the Son nor the Spirit is. And unless the Father possesses a certain attribute, neither the Son nor the Spirit possesses it: and through the Father, that is, because of the Father's existence, the Son and the Spirit exist, and through the Father, that is, because of the Father having the qualities, the Son and the Spirit have all their qualities."[40]

Thomas Aquinas

Thomas Aquinas, Anselm of Canterbury, Peter Abelard, Bonaventure, the Venerable Bede, and some other theological masters of the high medieval era are typically counted among the Scholastics or the "schoolmen." Intellectually brilliant and rationally capable, these teachers of the church helped further define the contours of the Christian doctrine of God. The rise of modern universities and theology's place therein as the "queen of sciences" greatly contributed to the sophistication of the theological enterprise.[41] In this enterprise, the medieval masters were engaged in helping introduce Aristotelian, Arabic (Islamic), and Jewish philosophies to the universities and through educated leaders to the church.

Lest a one-sided, overly intellectual picture emerge, it is important to remember that the Scholastics were no strangers to spiritual experiences and mystical visions. Just think of Bonaventure as an example. A great theologian and a mystic at the one and the same time, his insight into God as self-diffusive love, linked with the ancient trinitarian principle of *perichoresis* (the mutual indwelling of Father, Son, and Spirit), could only be expressed in mystical spiritual terms:

> . . . then you can see
> that through the highest communicability of the good, there must be a Trinity of the Father and the Son and the Holy Spirit. From supreme goodness, it is necessary that there be in the Persons supreme communicability; from supreme communicability, supreme consubstantiality; from supreme consubstantiality, supreme configurability; and from these supreme coequality and hence supreme coeternity; finally, from all of the above, supreme mutual intimacy, by which one is necessarily in the other by supreme interpenetration and one acts with the other in absolute lack of division of the substance, power and operation of the most blessed Trinity itself.[42]

From Anselm of Canterbury we have learned the rule of *fides quarens intellectum* (literally: "faith seeking understanding"): "For I do not seek to understand that I may believe, but I believe in order to understand."[43] Building on Augustine and the whole of Christian tradition, Anselm reminded us that Christian doctrines are true because they are divinely revealed and that the Christian must accept them on the authority of the church. Yet, at the same time, Anselm insisted on the rational nature of the church's beliefs; therefore, doctrines could—and should—be proven with the help of intellectual faculties.

Among the schoolmen, the most luminous is, of course, the Angelic Doctor, St. Thomas of Aquinas.[44] With regard to the trinitarian doctrine, he sought to both ratify the Augustinian heritage and help clarify some key issues. Following the Bishop of Hippo, Thomas begins with the unity of God and then discusses triunity. In the first part of his magisterial *Summa Theologiae*, Aquinas devotes nearly thirty "questions" (read: chapters) to the unity and thereafter about half as many on threeness.[45] It is easy to see that, in comparison to John of Damascus, the discussion of the unity of God occupies a much more central place in Aquinas.

The beginning point for Aquinas's theology of the Trinity has to do with consideration of the nature of relations of origins as the basis of threeness.[46] There are four such relations, namely fatherhood and sonship as well as procession and spiration.[47] The significant and lasting contribution of Aquinas is that the relations rising out of the divine processions must be real.[48] This means that these relations (such as Father–Son) are identical with the divine essence.[49] There are distinctions, however, since relations as defined by Aquinas refer to relative oppositions. In other words, while fatherhood and sonship are identical with divine nature, they also imply real distinctions: one is Father, the other is Son.[50]

Based on the clarification of the relations of origins above, the Son's proceeding is generation that is defined as the "procession of the Word in God." Employing the (then) common Aristotelian potentiality-actuality template (the former denoting a yet-to-be-achieved state or condition, the latter denoting the completion), Aquinas surmises this generation (procession) is from a perfect nature of Father to that of the Son[51]—in other words, this is "likeness in the nature of the same species."[52] Whereas the Son's generation as the Word is linked with intelligence, that of the Spirit has to do with (divine) will and love—a somewhat complex and ambiguous argumentation by the Angelic Doctor.[53] Much clearer is Thomas's claim, following Augustine, that the Holy Spirit proceeds from both the Father and the Son and is their mutual love.[54] Similarly, Augustinian is the teaching that "the Father and the Son love each other and us, by the Holy Ghost, or by Love proceeding."[55]

In addition to advancing significantly the meaning of the relations in the divine nature, yet another of Thomas's lasting contributions has to do with the concept of "person." Building on Boethius's earlier classic definition from the fifth century, according to which *person* is "[t]he individual substance of a rational creature,"[56] Aquinas argued that all individual beings with a rational nature are called persons, and God belongs to that category. Since the word *person* refers to something most perfect in the world, it is appropriate to apply it to God, even though, of course, only analogically. Importantly, he also links the discussion of divine persons to relations and affirms their compatibility.[57]

Now, having established the number of persons as "three" in God as opposed to another number,[58] Aquinas draws the following important conclusion of their equality in status. Citing affirmatively Athanasius's statement that "the three persons are co-eternal and co-equal to one another" (and building on Aristotle's logical conclusion, as well as Boethius's theological point), Aquinas states:

> We must needs admit equality among the divine persons. For, according to the Philosopher (Metaph. x, text 15, 16, 17), equality signifies the negation of greater or less. Now we cannot admit anything greater or less in the divine persons; for as Boethius says (De Trin. i): "They must needs admit a difference [namely, of Godhead] who speak of either increase or decrease, as the Arians do, who sunder the Trinity by distinguishing degrees as of numbers, thus involving a plurality." Now the reason of this is that unequal things cannot have the same quantity. But quantity, in God, is nothing else than His essence. Wherefore it follows, that if there were any inequality in the divine persons, they would not have the same essence; and thus the three persons would not be one God; which is impossible. We must therefore admit equality among the divine persons.[59]

Finally and, in terms of mutual relationality, very importantly, Aquinas robustly affirms that Father and Son are in each other—and with full legitimacy we may extend that to the Spirit, whose equal sharing in the divine nature and status has been affirmed without any doubt. Writes Thomas: "The Father is in the Son by His essence, forasmuch as the Father is His own essence and communicates His essence to the Son not by any change on His part. Hence it follows that as the Father's essence is in the Son, the Father Himself is in the Son; likewise, since the Son is His own essence, it follows that He Himself is in the Father in Whom is His essence."[60] Appropriately, the Jesuit Gerald O'Collins summarizes the legacy of the Angelic Doctor:

> There is one divine nature, substance, or essence. There are two processions . . . , the generation of the Son and the spiration/breathing of the Spirit. There are three persons . . . or subjects. There are four (subsistent) relations . . . : paternity, filiation, active spiration, and passive spiration. . . . Thomas along with other medieval theologians endorsed the radical, loving interconnectedness (*circumincessio*) of the three divine persons, something better expressed in Greek as their *perichoresis*, or reciprocal presence and interpenetration. Their innermost life is infinitely close relationship with one another in the utter reciprocity of love.[61]

"Social Trinitarianism"

Above was mentioned the changing understandings of the term *person*, which has played a role in the shaping of trinitarian traditions.[62] After the patristic period, intellectual and individualistic tones began to emerge and take over, as illustrated in Boethius's definition of the person as "an individual substance of rational nature."[63] This kind of an "account of *person* highlighted the individuality and rationality of the reality that is the center of action and attribution. It had nothing as such to say about the freedom, history and interrelatedness of persons, let alone about the way *person* functions analogically."[64] Reason and intelligence becomes the way to define even the nature of God. But that is far from the biblical idea of love and, thus, relationality.

Christian tradition could have taken a lesson from its own resources on the way toward a more balanced understanding of what the term *person* means. An important biblical way of speaking of God has to do with *koinonia* language, that is, communion between Father, Son, and Spirit, as well as between the triune God and the people of God. Often linked with the Holy Spirit, *koinonia* relates to all trinitarian members: "May the grace of the Lord Jesus Christ, and the love of God, and the fellowship [*koinonia*] of the Holy Spirit be with you all" (2 Cor 13:14).

Communion speaks of relationality. That was, of course, a typical feature among the Cappadocians. Theirs was the emphasis on three distinct persons (*hypostaseis*) and their plurality in unity, on the one hand, and on the other hand, mutuality and *perichoresis*.[65] Nor was the idea of relationality any stranger to the Latin Fathers. Particularly important was the role it played in Augustine's theology, as noted above. His focus on love as a key category in itself leans toward communion and relationality.

The Augustinian lead was picked up and significantly recast by the medieval developer of social trinitarianism, Richard of St. Victor, in his highly acclaimed *De Trinitate* (never fully translated into modern English).[66] Tutored by Hugh of St. Victor, a spiritual and mystical theologian, Richard was drawn to the importance of love as the defining metaphor for speaking of Trinity. In arguing for the plurality of persons in God, Richard's point of departure is God as supreme goodness (*summum bonum*), which includes love. Love that is higher than self-love is oriented toward another, the one who receives the love. Love given and received is mutual love. That logic, as compelling as it is, would only lead to biunity, namely lover and beloved. How to move toward threeness? Richard adds that for the perfect love yet another person is needed. Why? Having just two to share love still implies some kind of selfishness in that the one who loves may expect a return. But in case there are three, that expectation is not necessarily there, as one is loved for love's sake. [67] In summary form: "[P]erfect love is always directed toward what is distinct from and in some sense outside the self. Self-love is imperfect love. God's love must be perfect *and* not in any way dependent upon the creation. Thus, God's love must be other-directed within God himself. This is why there must be at least two persons (incommunicable existents) within God: the lover and the beloved."[68] Theologically put, there is a "'movement' from self-love (the Father) to mutual love (the Father and Son) to shared love (the Father, Son, and Holy Spirit)."[69]

There is, of course, a serious logical challenge to Richard's thinking, routinely noticed by commentators, namely, "Why stop with three persons?" Wouldn't four or twenty or two hundred be an illustration of even higher love? Of course that would! But it would also be to miss the limited and profound point of the importance of perfect love Richard wanted to highlight in the trinitarian God. Based on the biblical texts highlighting God's nature as love, his goal was to elucidate the necessity of relationality and plurality in the one God.

Although the incipient "social trinitarianism" evident in many patristic traditions and among some later teachers of the church such as Richard bears an important similarity to what is a widespread trend in contemporary theology, namely social analogy or the social Trinity, those two are in no way to be equated. When the distinction between medieval and our times is kept in mind, the following definition by Thomas Thompson is spot-on: social trinitarianism is a view in which God "is conceived of *most fundamentally* neither as one divine person . . . nor as three persons in some weak, highly equivocal sense, whose individuation is finally dubious . . . ; rather, God is conceived of quite unequivocally as three divine persons who coexist as one God in a unity sublimely unique, but best likened to that of a family, or a community, or a society—for example, the church."[70]

After this review of medieval testimonies, experiences, and doctrinal clarifications of the trinity both in the Christian and East, the following chapter takes a look at the theological developments in the Reformation era and in modernity. The reason that discussion is shorter and less detailed than the patristic and medieval is due to the simple fact that topics other than Trinity began to take upper hand. Particularly the Reformation divines simply took the traditional doctrine of God as authoritative and did not add much that was new.

Notes

1. This section draws directly from Veli-Matti Kärkkäinen, *The Holy Spirit: A Guide to Christian Theology* (Louisville: Westminster John Knox, 2009), 31–39; and an anthology of texts in Kärkkäinen, *Holy Spirit and Salvation: The Sources of Christian Theology* (Louisville: Westminster John Knox, 2010), chs. 4 and 5.

2. Symeon, *Symeon the New Theologian, the Discourses*, trans. C. J. deCatanzaro (Mahwah, NJ: Paulist, 1980), 24.4, p. 264.

3. Daniel B. Clendenin, *Eastern Orthodox Christianity: A Western Perspective* (Grand Rapids: Baker, 1994), 56.

4. Vladimir Lossky, *In the Image and Likeness of God*, ed. John H. Erickson and Thomas E. Bird (Crestwood, NY: St. Vladimir's Seminary Press, 1974), 13.

5. Maximus the Confessor, *Commentary on the Our Father* 1–2, in *Maximus Confessor: Selected Writings*, trans. and notes by George C. Berthold, The Classics of Western Spirituality (Mahwah, NJ: Paulist, 1985), 103.

6. Maximus the Confessor, *Commentary on the Our Father* 4, in ibid., 106.

7. Maximus the Confessor, *First Century on Various Texts* 72–73, in *The Philokalia: The Complete Text*, vol. 2, compiled by St. Nikodimos of the Holy Mountain and St. Makarios of Corinth, trans. and ed. G. E. H. Palmer, Philip Sherrard, Kallistos Ware, with the assistance of the Holy Transfiguration Monastery, et al. (London: Faber and Faber, 1979), 180–81.

8. Acts 17:34 mentions that Dionysius, a member of the Areopagus, was baptized by St. Paul in the aftermath of the apostle's famous speech at Mars Hills, the Areopagus, in Athens. For a highly useful discussion of Dionysius and some other leading Eastern mystics/theologians, see Vladimir Lossky, *The Mystical Theology of the Eastern Church* (Crestwood,

NY: St. Vladimir's Seminary Press, 1976); ch. 2 is titled appropriately: "The Divine Darkness"!

9. Ibid., 29–32, issues a warning not to categorize the Areopagite too uncritically as a Neoplatonist even if he shares its influences.

10. See Justo L. González, *A History of Christian Thought*, vol. 2, *From Augustine to the Eve of the Reformation* (Nashville: Abingdon, 1971), 91–94.

11. Dionysius the Areopagite, *Mystical Theology* 1, in *Dionysius the Areopagite: On the Divine Names and the Mystical Theology*, ed. Edwin Clarence (London: SPCK, 1920), 192–93; also available at http://www.ccel.org.

12. A basic introduction is John Meyendorff, *St. Gregory Palamas and Orthodox Spirituality* (Crestwood, NY: St. Vladimir's Seminary Press, 1974).

13. An authoritative exposition is Lossky, *Mystical Theology of the Eastern Church*, ch. 4.

14. Ibid., 70.

15. For some aspects of these theologies, see John W. Cooper, *Panentheism: The Other God of the Philosophers—from Plato to the Present* (Grand Rapids: Baker Academic, 2006), ch. 2 particularly. For an easy access to selected original texts of these theologians, see William Madges, *God and the World: Christian Texts in Perspective* (Maryknoll, NY: Orbis, 1999).

16. A helpful introduction to the Carolingian era is offered by González, *History of Christian Thought*, vol. 2, ch. 4.

17. Erigena's prayer in *Prayers of the Middle Ages: Light from a Thousand Years*, ed. J. Manning Potts (Nashville: Upper Room, 1908), 38, also available at http://www.ccel.org.

18. As paraphrased in Edmund J. Fortman, ed., *The Theology of God: Commentary* (New York: Bruce, 1968), 153–54.

19. As paraphrased in ibid., 154, on the basis of John Scotus Erigena, *De divisone naturae* [On the Division of Nature], 1.12; 3.17. That said, to consider Erigena's theology "pantheist" (as Fortman implies, 154) is a category mistake.

20. Joachim of Fiore, *Ten Stringed Psalter*, Preface, quoted in *Apocalyptic Spirituality: Treatises and Letters of Lactantius, Adso of Montier-en-Der, Joachim of Fiore, the Franciscan Spirituals, Savonarola*, trans. Bernard McGinn (Mahwah, NJ: Paulist, 1979), 99.

21. This section draws directly from Veli-Matti Kärkkäinen, *The Trinity: Global Perspectives* (Louisville: Westminster John Knox, 2007), 56–59; and Kärkkäinen, *Holy Spirit*, 30.

22. The standard view is that this addition was first accepted by the Council of Toledo in 589 and ratified by the 816(?) Aachen Synod. It was incorporated in later creeds such as that of the Fourth Lateran Council in 1215 and the Council of Lyons in 1274.

23. Against the standard view, Richard Haugh surmises that the addition happened just by way of transposition without any conscious theological reason. Richard S Haugh, *Photius and the Carolingians: The Trinitarian Controversy* (Belmont, MA: Norland, 1975), 160–61.

24. An important early critic was the ninth-century patriarch of Constantinople Photius. See his *On the Mystagogy of the Holy Spirit*, various eds. and trans. (Astoria, NY: Studion Publications, 1983); a particularly useful discussion in this volume is that of Michael Azkourl, "Introduction," 3–27 (trans. James Graves).

25. For a highly useful contemporary ecumenical discussion from an Orthodox perspective, see Theodore Stylianopoulos, "The Filioque: Dogma, Theologoumenon or Error?" in *Spirit of Truth: Ecumenical Perspectives on the Holy Spirit*, ed. Theodore G. Stylianopoulos and S. Mark Heim (Brookline, MA: Holy Cross Orthodox Press, 1986), 25–58.

26. Vladimir Lossky has most dramatically articulated the charge of "Christomonism" against Western theology. According to him, Christianity in the West is seen as unilaterally referring to Christ, the Spirit being an addition to the church, to its ministries and sacraments. Lossky, "The Procession of the Holy Spirit in Orthodox Trinitarian Doctrine," in *In the Image and Likeness of God*, ed. John H. Erickson and Thomas E. Bird (Crestwood, NY: St. Vladimir's Seminary Press, 1985), ch. 4, available also as a separate essay at http://jbburnett.com/resources/lossky/lossky_img4-process-filioq.pdf.

27. This charge becomes more understandable in light of the established view of the East, discussed above, that the Father is the "source" (*arche*) of the divinity. In defense, see, e.g., Kallistos Ware, *The Orthodox Church* (New York: Penguin Books, 1993), 210–14.

28. For an important discussion by a Baptist theologian, see Nick Needham, "The Filioque Clause: East or West?" *Scottish Bulletin of Evangelical Theology* 15 (1997): 142–62.

29. So, e.g., Wolfhart Pannenberg, *Systematic Theology*, vol. 1, trans.

Geoffrey Bromiley (Grand Rapids: Eerdmans, 1991), 319. For a helpful discussion, see Lukas Vischer, ed., *Spirit of God, Spirit of Christ: Ecumenical Reflections on the Filioque Controversy* (London: SPCK/ Geneva: WCC, 1981). Only a tiny majority of contemporary Western theologians support the addition. The best-known advocate of *filioque* was Karl Barth, who feared that dismissing it would mean ignoring the biblical insistence on the Spirit being the Spirit of the Son. See Karl Barth, *Church Dogmatics*, ed. G. W. Bromiley and T. F. Torrance (Edinburgh: T&T Clark, 1956), I/1:480.

30. Boris Bobrinskoy, *The Mystery of the Trinity: Trinitarian Experience and Vision in the Biblical and Patristic Tradition*, trans. Anthony P. Gythiel (Crestwood, NY: St. Vladimir's Seminary Press, 1999), 302–3.

31. The full title of this work in *NPNF*[2] series (vol. 9) is: *An Exact Exposition of the Orthodox Faith.*

32. Pannenberg's (*Systematic Theology*, 1:289) comment is spot-on in this regard: "If we look at the basic structure of his [John of Damascus's] argument, we are forced to say that there, as in Gregory of Nyssa, we can see a trace of the derivation of the Trinitarian distinctions from the divine unity, i.e., from the divine spirituality ([*The Orthodox* Faith] 1.6–7). . . ."

33. The judgment of Robert Letham, in his *The Holy Trinity: In Scripture, History, Theology, and Worship* (Phillipsburg, NJ: P&R Publishing, 2004), 237, about a dramatic difference between John and Aquinas is an overstatement. However, where Letham is right is that already in the first part of his work, the Damascene speaks of the distinctions of trinitarian persons and their perichoretic relations.

34. "*No one hath seen God at any time; the Only-begotten Son, which is in the bosom of the Father, He hath declared Him.* The Deity, therefore, is ineffable and incomprehensible. *For no one knoweth the Father, save the Son, nor the Son, save the Father.* And the Holy Spirit, too, so knows the things of God as the spirit of the man knows the things that are in him. Moreover, after the first and blessed nature no one, not of men only, but even of supramundane powers, and the Cherubim, I say, and Seraphim themselves, has ever known God, save he to whom He revealed Himself." John of Damascus, *Exposition of the Orthodox Faith* 1.1, in *NPNF*[2] 9:1b (note that pagination in this *NPNF* volume restarts from the beginning of this work of John; hence, each page number is followed by "b" [as in 1b], to distinguish it from pagination

beginning from the first work in the volume, in which case the normal formatting is used).

35. Ibid., 1.3, *NPNF*[2] 9:2b.

36. Ibid., 1.5, *NPNF*[2] 9:4b. Interestingly, John adds that there is also a rational argument in defense of the unity—employing the form of an argumentation that could easily be presented by Latin teachers as well: "The Deity is perfect, and without blemish in goodness, and wisdom, and power, without beginning, without end, everlasting, uncircumscribed, and in short, perfect in all things. Should we say, then, that there are many Gods, we must recognise difference among the many. For if there is no difference among them, they are one rather than many. But if there is difference among them, what becomes of the perfectness? For that which comes short of perfection, whether it be in goodness, or power, or wisdom, or time, or place, could not be God. But it is this very identity in all respects that shews that the Deity is one and not many" (ibid.).

37. Ibid., 1.6, *NPNF*[2] 9:4b–5b.

38. Ibid., 1.7, *NPNF*[2] 9:5b.

39. All citations after the previous footnote are from ibid., 1.8, *NPNF*[2] 9:6b–9b.

40. Ibid., 1.8, *NPNF*[2] 9:9b–10b.

41. For the Scholasticism of Aquinas and others, see González, *History of Christian Thought*, vol. 2, ch. 8.

42. Bonaventure, *The Soul's Journey into God*, 6.2, in Bonaventure, *The Soul's Journey into God; The Tree of Life; The Life of St. Francis*, trans. and ed. Ewert Cousins (Mahwah, NJ: Paulist, 1978), 104.

43. Anselm of Canterbury, *Proslogium*, ch. 1, in *Proslogium; Monologium; An Appendix in Behalf of the Fool by Gaunilon; and Cur Deus Homo*, trans. Sidney Norton Deane (1926 [1903]), 7, available at http://www.ccel.org.

44. For a highly useful overview of Aquinas (and his Dominican School), see González, *History of Christian Thought*, 2:258–79.

45. The version used here is in St. Thomas Aquinas, *Summa Theologica*, trans. Fathers of the English Dominican Province (Benziger Bros. edition, 1947), available at http://www.ccel.org (hereafter abbreviated as ST). Following an established custom, the passages indicated therein are marked as follows: 1.28.4 = part 1, question 28, article 4.

Similar to Augustine, Aquinas's contributions to the doctrine of the Trinity can, of course, be found in more than one major work. One important treatment can be found in his *Summa contra Gentiles* bk. 4.1–26 (available in English in various translations, e.g., under the title *Contra Gentiles: On the Truth of the Catholic Faith*, various trans., ed. Joseph Kenny, O.P. [New York: Hanover House, 1955–57], at http://dhspriory.org/thomas/ContraGentiles.htm). There, his approach is apologetic in nature as it is written with Muslims, Jews, and some heretical opinions in view. As is appropriate, Thomas discusses the unity of God therein already in book 1.

46. In the epigraph to ST 1.27 (and so throughout), Aquinas states that "the divine Persons are distinguished from each other according to the relations of origin."

47. Aquinas, ST 1.28.4.

48. Ibid., 1.28.1. Being real means that they are not "accidental." In line with Aristotelian-medieval ontology, "accident" is something that is not permanent or essential to the nature of the thing.

49. Ibid., 1.28.2: "Thus it is manifest that relation really existing in God is really the same as His essence. . . ."

50. Ibid., 1.28.3: "The idea of relation, however, necessarily means regard of one to another, according as one is relatively opposed to another. So as in God there is a real relation, there must also be a real opposition. The very nature of relative opposition includes distinction. Hence, there must be real distinction in God, not, indeed, according to that which is absolute—namely, essence, wherein there is supreme unity and simplicity—but according to that which is relative." A very helpful brief exposition can be found in William J. La Due, *The Trinity Guide to the Trinity* (Harrisburg, PA: Trinity Press International, 2003), 71–72.

51. Aquinas, ST 1.27.2. A further resource in argumentation has to do with intellect (and will), attributes the Scholastics considered to represent perfection, particularly in relation to divine nature.

52. In David Coffey, *Deus Trinitas: The Doctrine of the Triune God* (New York: Oxford University Press, 1999), 29.

53. Aquinas, ST 1.27.3, 4.

54. Ibid., 1.36.3: "Therefore, because the Son receives from the Father that the Holy Ghost proceeds from Him, it can be said that the Father spirates the Holy Ghost through the Son, or that the Holy Ghost

proceeds from the Father through the Son, which has the same meaning." Following Augustine, he further establishes that the Father and Son are "one principle of the Holy Ghost," ibid., 1.36.4.

55. Ibid., 1.37.2.

56. Boethius, *A Treatise Against Eutyches and Nestorius*, III, in Boethius, *Theological Tractates and the Consolation of Philosophy*, trans. Hugh Fraser Stewart and Edward Kennard Rand, The Loeb Classical Library, n.d., 86; at http://www.ccel.org.

57. Aquinas, ST 1.29, is devoted to the discussion of "person."

58. Ibid., 1.30.2.

59. Ibid., 1.42.1.

60. Ibid., 1.42.5.

61. Gerald O'Collins, *The Tripersonal God: Understanding and Interpreting the Trinity* (Mahwah, NJ: Paulist, 1999), 146–47.

62. This section draws directly from Kärkkäinen, *Trinity*, 59–64.

63. Boethius, *Against Eutyches and Nestorius* 3.

64. O'Collins, *Tripersonal God*, 143.

65. See, further, Cornelius Plantinga Jr., "Gregory of Nyssa and the Social Analogy of the Trinity," *The Thomist* 50, no. 3 (1986): 325–52.

66. See the important discussion of the influence of Richard on contemporary theology in Gary D. Badcock, "Richard of St. Victor," in *The Dictionary of Historical Theology*, ed. Trevor A. Hart (Grand Rapids: Eerdmans, 2000), 488–89.

67. Richard of St. Victor, *Book Three of Trinity* 3.2–3, 14–15, in *Richard of St. Victor, The Book of the Patriarchs; The Mystical Ark; Book Three of the Trinity*, Classics of Western Spirituality, ed. Grover A. Zinn (New York: Paulist, 1979), 374–76, 387–89.

68. See, further, Roger E. Olson and Christopher A. Hall, *The Trinity*, Guides to Theology (Grand Rapids: Eerdmans, 2002), 58–60.

69. O'Collins, *Tripersonal God*, 137–38; see also 143–44.

70. Thomas Robert Thompson, "Trinitarianism Today: Doctrinal Renaissance, Ethical Relevance, Social Redolence," *Calvin Theological Journal* 32, no. 1 (April 1997): 29–30.

5

Reformation and Modern Perspectives

The Reformers and Their Heirs

Turning to the "Divine Economy"

The first part of this chapter will concentrate on the Reformation. This section will be short and highly selective, as it focuses mostly on the magisterial reformers, Martin Luther and John Calvin, with some attention to Catholic reformers and their mystically-doctrinally oriented views. Then we'll look briefly at the post-Reformation "Protestant Scholastics," and finally at the trinitarian contributions of the post-Reformation "Heart-Religion," a spiritually and practically oriented revival.

As already mentioned, with some generalization it can be said that during the patristic era the main contours and doctrinal convictions about the Trinity were established. And thanks to the medieval masters and mystics, these trinitarian conceptions were further clarified and experiences of the triune God deepened. So, what role did trinitarian reflection play during the Reformation era? By and large, it is fair to say that for the reformers and their followers, in the forefront was "God-for-us"; in other words, what were the implications of trinitarian faith for Christian life and spirituality? Instead of focusing on the *doctrinal* clarifications concerning the Trinity, themes related to scriptural authority, Scripture's relation to church tradition, justification, faith, sacraments, and church acquired new urgency. The doctrine of the Trinity was highly valued but there was also often the feeling that basic work on it was already finished and new constructive efforts were neither needed nor appropriate. Take Calvin, for instance: despite his humanist learning and disciplined doctrinal competence, the Genevan reformer only rarely delved into the Scholastic-type sophisticated distinctions; rather, he highlighted the implications of the doctrines of election, providence, and salvation.[1] As Young-Ho Chun writes, "Anyone acquainted with the scholastic treatises on the Trinity, especially that of Thomas Aquinas, would be struck by the departure from their style. Rather than making a logically rigorous argument for a particular doctrine, for instance, asking how the one God can also be three persons, Calvin presents a biblically based exposition that largely avoids philosophical terminologies, even though he did not reject traditional terms such as *ousia, hypostasis, essentia, substantia,* and *homoousios.*"[2] Indeed, Philipp Melanchthon, Luther's right-hand (and author of significant portions of Lutheran confessional texts), surmised, "there is no reason why we should labor so much on exalted topics such as 'God,' 'The Unity and Trinity of God' . . . and the 'Manner of Incarnation.'. . . What, I ask you, did the Scholastics accomplish during the many ages they were examining only these points alone?"[3]

The "economy of salvation" and spiritualist orientation were also the hallmarks of the Catholic reformers and the wide and rich group of post-Reformation revival movements. Only among the so-called Protestant Scholastics, representatives of a highly analytical and doctrine-oriented Protestant "orthodoxy" of the post-Reformation era, did the return to philosophical and, at times, abstract distinctions take place.

In the following, a brief survey of these various Reformation and post-Reformation interpretations and experiences of God will be presented, beginning with the "magisterial" reformers, Luther and Calvin, and their heirs (as distinct from "radical" reformers, that is, Anabaptists and others).

Luther's Crucified God

Martin Luther is best known, alongside the doctrine of the justification by faith, for his famous distinction between the "theology of glory" and "theology of the cross." In contrast to the theology of glory, which is based on human values and human perception of the world and God, the theology of the cross discerns God in the midst of suffering, shame, and even death. The true theologian, the theologian of the cross, sees things as they truly are and is able to identify God's love and mercy even when God employs God's "left hand" to punish and strike us as a preparation for the work of the "right hand" that lifts us up and saves.[4]

Closely related to the theology of the cross is Luther's profound appreciation of true love.[5] An Augustinian friar by his training and former affiliation, the Wittenberg reformer's early programmatic work, *Heidelberg Disputation* (1518), makes an important distinction between two kinds of love, namely divine and human love. Whereas human love is always basically selfish and looks for its own good, God's love seeks those who are not worthy in themselves to be loved and donates itself to the recipient.[6] On the basis of this profound vision of divine love, Luther shapes his trinitarian theology with the idea of God as self-giving love, an idea that goes back to Bernard of Clairvaux, Richard of Saint Victor, and others. Just think of the following profound description of the trinitarian God as Gift himself:

> These are the three persons and one God, who has given himself to us all wholly and completely, with all that he is and has. The Father gives himself to us, with heaven and earth and all the creatures, in order that they may serve us and benefit us. But this

gift has become obscured and useless through Adam's fall. There-fore the Son himself subsequently gave himself and bestowed all his works, sufferings, wisdom, and righteousness, and reconciled us to the Father, in order that restored to life and righteous-ness, we might also know and have the Father and his gifts. But because this grace would benefit no one if it remained so pro-foundly hidden and could not come to us, the Holy Spirit comes and gives himself to us also, wholly and completely.[7]

In keeping with the economic approach to the doctrine of God, Luther's delightful exposition of the work of creation based on Genesis 1:2 is deeply trinitarian. He explains:

Indeed, it is the great consensus of the church that the mystery of the Trinity is set forth here. The Father creates heaven and earth out of nothing through the Son, whom Moses calls the Word. Over these the Holy Spirit broods. As a hen broods her eggs, keep-ing them warm in order to hatch her chicks, and, as it were, to bring them to life through heat, so Scripture says that the Holy Spirit brooded, as it were, on the waters to bring to life those sub-stances which were to be quickened and adorned. For it is the office of the Holy Spirit to make alive.[8]

Calvin's "Latin Trinity"

Luther's younger Reformed colleague of Geneva, John Calvin, opens his magnum opus, the *Institutes of the Christian Religion* (which underwent several extensive revisions before taking its final form in 1559) by asserting that true knowledge consists of two parts: knowledge of God and knowledge of self.[9] In keeping with Aquinas and much of Christian tradition, Calvin—more so than Luther—affirmed robustly the "natural" knowledge of God on the basis of creation and world government.[10] Within every human person there exists a "natural instinct, some sense of Deity."[11]

Along with Luther and other reformers, Calvin, of course, also robustly affirmed the Trinity.[12] He titles the trinitarian discussion in the *Institutes* in a programmatic manner: "The Unity of the Divine Essence in Three Persons Taught, in Scripture, From the Foundation of the World."[13] This given title is an indication of "the difference from Aquinas. Rather than making a rigorous argument in syllogistic terms, based on the premise of the unity of the divine essence, and asking how the one God can also be three persons, Calvin presents a biblical based exposition in straightforward language that largely avoids philosophical terminology. It is the Trinity in plain Latin. Moreover, his discussion is largely concerned with the deity of the Son and the Holy Spirit, treated in order."[14] That said, Calvin was concerned about heretical views, both ancient and contemporary, and wished to correct them. He also harshly critiqued Jewish attacks against the Trinity.[15]

An important summative statement, interestingly quoting Gregory of Nazianzus, shows Calvin's deep anchoring in the patristic orthodoxy:

> [T]he Scriptures demonstrate that there is some distinction between the Father and the Word, the Word and the Spirit; but the magnitude of the mystery reminds us of the great reverence and soberness which ought to be employed in discussing it. It seems to me, that nothing can be more admirable than the words of Gregory Nanzianzen . . . : 'I cannot think of the unity without being irradiated by the Trinity: I cannot distinguish between the Trinity without being carried up to the unity.' Therefore, let us beware of imagining such a Trinity of persons as will distract our thoughts, instead of bringing them instantly back to the unity. The words Father, Son, and Holy Spirit, certainly indicate a real distinction, not allowing us to suppose that they are merely epithets by which God is variously designated from his works. Still they indicate distinction only, not division.[16]

Following the Latin tradition, Calvin affirms the principle of the *filioque* and the order of primacy in the Trinity, that is, "the Father being considered first, next the Son from him, and then the Spirit from both."[17] Lest this be understood in a manner undermining the full deity of the Spirit, Calvin adds this important statement: "Thus, too, the Spirit is called God absolutely by Christ himself. For nothing prevents us from holding that he is the entire spiritual essence of God, in which are comprehended Father, Son, and Spirit. This is plain from Scripture. For as God is there called a Spirit, so the Holy Spirit also, in so far as he is a hypostasis of the whole essence, is said to be both of God and from God."[18]

Having considered some leading Protestant reformers with regard to their trinitarian teaching, it is fitting to turn now to another major group of reformers, namely those on the Roman Catholic side. Similar to their medieval predecessors, Catholic reformers were also drawn to mystical visions of God.

Catholic Mystical Impulses

Luther's contemporary, the founder of the Society of Jesus, Ignatius of Loyola, was not only a missionary catalyst, profound thinker, and prolific author, but also a visionary mystic. Trinitarian spirituality shines forth brightly in his *Spiritual Exercises* and other manuals. Not only did he believe in the Trinity, he also loved the triune God. Just consider this autobiographical description:

> [W]hile I was preparing the altar and vesting, words came to me "Eternal Father, confirm me! Eternal Son, confirm me. Eternal Holy Spirit, confirm me. Holy Trinity, confirm me. My One and Only God, confirm me." I said this many times, with great vehemence, devotion, and tears; and I felt it very deeply. . . . When I had finished Mass and unvested, during my prayer at the altar there was so much sobbing and effusion of tears, all terminating in the love of the Holy Trinity, that I seemed to have no desire to leave. For I was feeling so much love and so much spiritual sweetness.—Then several times near the fire I experienced interior love for the Holy Trinity and impulses to weep. Later . . . whenever I remembered the Holy Trinity I felt an intense love and sometimes motions toward weeping. All these visitations terminated in the Name and Essence of the Holy Trinity.[19]

Named as the "Mystical Doctor," John of the Cross, the spiritual master of the Carmelite Order, helped bring about a spiritual renewal in the aftermath of the Reformation. Not unlike the mystics of the Eastern church, for John union with the triune God was the ultimate goal:

> And one need not marvel that God may bestow such elevated and extraordinary gifts on the souls whom He chooses to favor. If we consider that He is God, and that He bestows them as God with infinite love and goodness, it will not seem unreasonable to us; for He said that *on him who loved Him would come the Father, Son, and Holy Spirit, and They would make their abode in him* which had to be by making the person live and dwell in the Father, Son, and Holy Spirit in the life of God, as the soul would have us understand. . . .[20]

Toward Modernity

As we bring the first part of this chapter to a closure, it is proper to mention that the history of the trinitarian experiences and doctrines before modernity does not come to an end here. We could continue with a consideration of at least two separate groupings of post-Reformation movements. First, there is the rich and variegated group of "Religion of the Heart" revival and renewal movements, from Puritanism to Pietism to Methodism to Quakers, among others. Although not focused on doctrinal work but, rather, a spiritual renewal, more often than not some biblically based practical trinitarian insights emerged among these movements, and their spirituality at times exhibited profound trinitarian features. We think, for instance, of the Englishman John Owens's great work, *Of Communion with God the Father, Son and Holy Ghost*, a fine devotional work, written in a homiletical style and rich in "practical" teaching on the Trinity.[21]

The other set of movements in the aftermath of the Reformation not treated here is what's often called Protestant Scholasticism or Protestant Orthodoxy. These terms refer to seventeenth- and eighteenth-century Lutheran[22] and Reformed[23] theologians who took pains in formulating Christian doctrines in a most meticulous and articulated way. Unlike the revivalists, their main energies were devoted to making fine-tuned, at times highly abstract, doctrinal distinctions. That said, it is also true that these latter-day Scholastics devoted more time to the consideration of the divine essence than trinitarian doctrine *per se*.[24]

The second part of this chapter will very briefly touch on the complicated and contested status of the doctrine of the Trinity in modern theology up until its fervent rediscovery in contemporary theology after the mid-twentieth century. The first topic to be discussed here has to do with the continuing spread of anti- and non-trinitarian movements.

The Rise of Anti-Trinitarianism

A fitting place to begin the brief consideration of the status of the doctrine of the Trinity in modernity is to take notice of the reemergence of anti- and non-trinitarian movements. Their roots go back deeply into the Reformation period. Famously—or, to be more precise, infamously—one of the powerful early advocates of anti-trinitarianism, namely Michael Servetus (with various renderings of the name), a highly educated genius, stirred up so big a controversy that during Calvin's time he was executed as a heretic in Geneva.[25]

A useful way to classify the forms of anti-trinitarianism is to speak of "biblical" and "rational" versions.[26] Servetus can be counted under biblical anti-trinitarianism as he "was absolutely committed to the authority of Scripture, but regarded the doctrine of the Trinity to be a later distortion of biblical truth, rooted in Greek philosophy rather than in the Scriptures."[27] Among other errors, Servetus's unorthodox Christology, with its rejection of the creedal attribution of deity to Jesus, led to a denial of Trinity as it was understood in any classical manner.[28]

As famous as Servetus became, particularly at the end of his life, the most influential anti-trinitarian advocate during Reformation times was undoubtedly Faustus Socinus, whose legacy lived on in the Minor Reformed Church of Poland.[29] Its Racovian Catechism is a landmark of the movement's biblically based opposition to the doctrine of the Trinity. The Catechism clearly and unambiguously argues for the oneness of God without any plurality. All in all, Socinianist anti-trinitarianism, similarly to that of Servetus, claims to be based on the Bible. On these grounds, Jesus's deity is not affirmed but, rather, his humanity. This is to safeguard the unity and oneness of God; therein, a close family resemblance to modalist monarchianism can be discerned.[30]

The biblically based opposition to the creedal confession of the trinitarian doctrine continued here and there until and beyond the eighteenth century, represented by such well-known figures as Samuel Clarke and his *The Scripture Doctrine of the Trinity* (1712). It claims to investigate "all the texts in the New Testament related to that doctrine."[31] Interestingly, Clarke, and a number of others blamed for not committing themselves to the creedal trinitarian orthodoxy, were charged not for monarchianism but, rather, Arianism.[32]

Among the rational anti-trinitarianists, we find a number of different varieties, beginning with the Deism of John Toland and others. His *Christianity Not Mysterious* (1669)—with the telling subtitle: *A Treatise Shewing, That There is Nothing in the GOSPEL Contrary to REASON, Nor ABOVE it: And That No Christian Doctrine can be properly call'd A MYSTERY*—could not find any place whatsoever for a doctrine as "anti-natural" as the Trinity. Nor was there any doctrine of divine revelation left in the traditional sense of the word, nor a doctrine of Jesus's deity. Significantly, by the time John Tindall published his *Christianity as Old as the Creation: or, The Gospel a Republication of the Religion of Nature* (1731), he did not see it necessary anymore to oppose the doctrine of the Trinity, for the simple reason that he felt the battle against it was already won.[33]

To the distinguished and influential group of rationalist attacks against the Trinity belongs, of course, the whole Enlightenment project, heralded by Immanuel Kant and others. John Locke's manifesto *The Reasonableness of Christianity* (1695) is a particularly sustained effort to simply leave behind the classical doctrine of the Trinity and classical Christology.[34]

S. R. Holmes summarizes neatly the essence of rational anti-trinitarianism: "[It] begins with, and rapidly simply assumes, the claim that the received Trinitarian doctrine is incoherent; it further claims that there is a natural theology that teaches monotheism and that this natural theology is what is important in matters of belief."[35]

In the most persistent form of anti-trinitarianism, namely Unitarianism, the biblical and rational forms are integrated with each other. A self-designated contemporary (to us) confession of faith by the American-based Unitarian Universalist denomination states this:

> Most Unitarian Universalist Christians believe in God, but not the traditional God-as-Trinity that most Christian churches promote. The UU Christian God is all-loving, as our Universalist forbears taught, and a unity, as our Unitarian forebears taught. This God is too big to be contained in one person, one book, one tradition, or one time in history. To UU Christians, Jesus is an inspiration and his teachings are profound—he possesses a divine spark that is born in all of us, and can be cultivated our whole lives long.[36]

Modern Ambiguity and Argument

The Doctrine in Decline

As discussed above, one of the effects of the Enlightenment was a serious reconsideration of all major Christian doctrines, not least the Trinity. As a result, waves of anti-trinitarianism continued to flourish. The waning of the doctrine of the Trinity also had to do with the rise of biblical and dogmatic criticism. Whereas for older Protestant theology the Bible offered proofs of the Trinity, the biblical criticism of the Enlightenment destroyed that approach.[37] Apart from the Trinity's highly dubious nature as an intellectual conundrum, its sheer value and usefulness was harshly contested among the Enlightenment-driven intelligentsia. Although himself not anti-religious *per se*, the oft-cited words of Immanuel Kant express clearly the common sentiment: "The doctrine of the Trinity, taken literally, has *no practical relevance at all*, even if we think we understand it; and it is even more clearly irrelevant if we realize that it transcends all our concepts. Whether we are to worship three or ten persons in the Deity makes no difference."[38]

Of course, the church still stuck firmly to that cherished Christian confession and a number of attempts to reestablish the Trinity's central status in Christian teaching and spirituality took place simultaneously. Consider here the great contributions of the leading American theologian of the eighteenth century, the Congregationalist Jonathan Edwards,[39] and the nineteenth-century defender of Fundamentalist Reformed orthodoxy, Charles Hodge of Princeton.[40]

Inevitably, the parting of the ways during the modern era between two kinds of theologians and scholars deepened and widened, namely anti-trinitarians and conservatives. Outside of theological circles, some important attempts were made to reconceive the Trinity based on sources and materials other than the Bible and Christian tradition. Among them, the most ambitious is undoubtedly the Idealist philosopher G. W. F. Hegel's reconstruction, to be briefly introduced below.[41] Regarding Christian theology itself, new waves of constructive and creative approaches to the Trinity took place on a larger scale beginning in the mid-twentieth century.

Schleiermacher's Trinity

Friedrich Schleiermacher's *The Christian Faith* is routinely hailed as the textbook example of the utter marginalization of the doctrine of the Trinity among the modern theologians. In that over eight hundred-page-long monumental work, the "Father" of modern Protestant theology devoted a little more than ten pages to the topic, discussing it under "Conclusion."[42] Although the role and status of the Trinity in Schleiermacher's ingenious and complicated theological system is more complex than that,[43] there is no denying that a dramatic shift had occurred with regard to the doctrine's placement in dogmatics and the space and role devoted to it.

For Schleiermacher, the driving force was ~~human~~ experience most widely and inclusively understood. In order to understand Schleiermacher's locating of religion (and religiosity) in human experience and "feelings," we have to bear in mind that the German term translated as "feeling" (*das Gefühl*) is far broader and more complex than the English term. It denotes a primal, nonrational awareness of religious intuitions beneath and beyond all human experiences of the world.[44] This is what he named the "feeling of absolute dependence" (or, strangely, "piety").[45] Having established the primacy and foundational role of that "feeling" in religion, Schleiermacher reinterpreted all traditional doctrines, including Christology and Trinity, in light of this template. In other words, he ruled out metaphysical definitions of older doctrines, including God and Trinity, and considered doctrinal formulations as expressions of "piety." It is difficult to say what, indeed, was the content of his theology of God—other than that it does not follow tradition in many respects. For example, he was asserting that the "attributes" of God are not any kind of literal statements but rather merely expressions of human experience.[46]

No wonder, he surmised, that particularly the sophisticated and abstract trinitarian formulae of creeds and the rest of tradition could not possibly stem from the religious consciousness.[47] At the end of his *Christian Faith*, Schleiermacher notes:

> We have only to do with the God-consciousness given in our self-consciousness along with our consciousness of the world; hence, we have no formula for the being of God in Himself as distinct from the being of God in the world, and should not have to borrow any such formula from speculation, and so prove ourselves disloyal to the character of the discipline [theology] at which we are working.[48]

What about Christology and its relation to Trinity? For Schleiermacher, Christ possesses the highest and absolute God-consciousness. He explains that here is the key to "The Divine Trinity," "the doctrine of the union of the Divine Essence with human nature, both in the personality of Christ and in the common Spirit of the Church."[49] The important corollary is that this "trinitarian" doctrine is linked not only to the person of Christ but also to the church, following the earlier guiding principle set forth in *The Christian Faith*: "The Holy Spirit is the union of the Divine Essence with human nature in the form of the common Spirit animating the life in common of believers."[50] As said, it is very difficult to say with any accuracy what exactly is the content of Schleiermacher's doctrine of God and Trinity—particularly when he makes it clear in his program that the talk about "two-nature" Christology of the creedal tradition cannot of course be taken literally anymore, even in relation to human "piety."

If the nineteenth-century Schleiermacher sought to find a place for the Trinity through the lens of his radically reconceived *theological* framework, his contemporary, the leading Idealist thinker of the former century, G. W. F. Hegel, employed highly creative *philosophical* resources.

Hegel's Trinity

With philosophical colleagues such as J. G. Fichte and (the early) F. W. J. von Schelling, Georg W. Friedrich Hegel represents the so-called Idealist tradition in which, distinct from materialism, the spirit[ual] is considered to be the primary and ultimate reality. Therein, this German Idealist joins the long and venerated tradition of human thinking beginning from Plato and continuing throughout history.[51] In radical distinction to Immanuel Kant, Hegel refused to set the limits of knowledge and rational inquiry within knowledge based on sense-experience. Instead, Hegel believed that human knowledge can penetrate into transcendence and thus to the area of the metaphysical. Not only that, Hegel went further as he "saw reality not primarily as something that reason has to grasp, but rather as the unfolding of the very principle of rationality in the universe—what he called the Spirit. Not only is reality logical, but logic is reality." Furthermore, it is "a dynamic logic, one that moves through a dialectic, always seeking new and fuller truth."[52]

All of this takes us to the grand vision of this Idealist philosopher, which posits an integral connection between the structure of thought and the structure of reality: the unfolding of the history of the world (including nature) is but the process of the Spirit, ultimately the Spirit becoming conscious of itself, which leads to final union. On this basis, Hegel had come to the conclusion that incarnation, the idea of divine–human union, was a necessary idea and could be justified rationally.[53]

This leads to his distinctive doctrine of God. There is no doubt that in a real sense, the term (Absolute) "Spirit" is equivalent to the Divine in Hegel's thought. However, it is not a transcendent creator of the world as in classical theology. Rather, the Divine, the Spirit, is the reality or force permeating everything in the world. In some real sense, this God/Divine is also in the becoming. In his *Lectures on the Philosophy of Religion*, Hegel brings to culmination his "trinitarian" vision as part of the reflection on religion. In the Godhead, there are three moments of divine reality, something similar to the Christian doctrine of the Trinity. "Eternal" or "Essential Being," "the idea of God of and in itself," is something similar to the Father or immanent Trinity; "Representation" or "the form of appearance, that of particularization, of being for others" echoes the Christian idea of the incarnate Son; and finally, the "form of return from appearance to itself" resembles the Holy Spirit, which manifests itself in community and its cult. Thus, in Hegel's world-embracing system, the final goal of all historical development and the process of the Spirit is God returning to himself in humanity. This takes place in the religious life in which humanity comes to know God as God knows himself. This is the final reconciliation within reality.[54]

What, if anything, is distinctive about the Christian religion and the Christian doctrine of God? Hegel responds in his idiosyncratic and complex manner: "This is the *consummate religion*, the religion that is the being of spirit for itself, the religion in which religion has become objective to itself. . . . It is *religion* that has become objective to itself—religion as the consciousness of God, or the self-consciousness of God as the return of consciousness into itself."[55]

With the dawn of the twentieth century, for a few decades nothing spectacular emerged in the doctrine of the Trinity. The frontiers between traditionalists and modern revisionists, briefly outlined above, stayed fairly intact. Only with the rise of powerful movements such as Karl Barth's neo-orthodoxy, by the mid-twentieth century or so, did a whole new enthusiasm begin to grow both in Protestant and Roman Catholic circles, and more quietly within Eastern Orthodox theology, whose contributions until then remained almost unknown in the Christian West. That is the story of the trinitarian renaissance started in the latter part of the twentieth century and still going on into the third millennium. That will be briefly outlined next in the last chapter of this primer.

Notes

1. See Gerald L. Bray, *The Doctrine of God*, Contours of Christian Theology (Downers Grove, IL: InterVarsity, 1993), 105; see also 199–201 for the differences between the reformers' approach to God and that of their predecessors.

2. Young-Ho Chun, "The Trinity in the Protestant Reformation: Continuity Within Discontinuity," in *The Cambridge Companion to Trinity*, ed. Peter C. Phan (New York: Cambridge University Press, 2011), 136.

3. Philipp Melanchthon, *Loci Communes Theologici* (1521), in *Melanchthon and Bucer*, ed. and rev. Wilhelm Pauck, trans. Lowell J. Satre (Philadelphia: Westminster, 1969), 21 (the citation is in "Dedicatory Letter," a kind of introduction).

4. According to Luther, only that person "deserves to be called a theologian . . . who comprehends the visible and manifest things of God seen through suffering and the cross." Martin Luther, *Heidelberg Disputation # 20*, in *Career of the Reformer I*, vol. 31 in *Luther's Works*, ed. Harold J. Grimm and Helmut T. Lehmann (Philadelphia: Fortress

Press, 1957), 40. For a helpful guide, see Alister E. McGrath, *Luther's Theology of the Cross* (Oxford: Oxford University Press, 1985).

5. An authoritative exposition is Tuomo Mannermaa, *Two Kinds of Love: Martin Luther's Religious World*, trans. Kirsi I. Stjerna (Minneapolis: Fortress Press, 2010).

6. "The love of God does not find, but creates, that which is pleasing to it. . . . Rather than seeking its own good, the love of God flows forth and bestows good." Luther, *Heidelberg Disputation* # 28, in *Career of the Reformer I*,31:57.

7. Martin Luther, *Word and Sacrament III*, vol. 37 in *Luther's Works*, ed. Robert H. Fischer (Philaelphia: Fortress Press, 1961), 366. In his *Large Catechism*, Luther teaches: God . . . created us . . . to redeem and sanctify us. Moreover, having bestowed upon us everything in heaven and on earth, he has given us his Son and his Holy Spirit, through whom he brings us to himself. . . . [W]e could never come to recognize the Father's favor and grace were it not for the Lord Christ, who is a mirror of the Father's heart. Apart from him we see nothing but an angry and terrible Judge. But neither could we know anything of Christ, had it not been revealed by the Holy Spirit." "Large Catechism," Creed, III, 64–65, in *The Book of Concord: The Confessions of the Evangelical Lutheran Church,* trans. and ed. Theodore G. Tappert with Jaroslav Pelikan, Robert H. Fischer, and Arthur C. Peipkorn (Philadelphia: Fortress Press, 1959), 419.

8. Martin Luther, *Lectures on Genesis: Chapters 1-5*, vol. 1 in *Luther's Works*, ed. Jaroslav Pelikan (St. Louis: Concordia, 1958), 9.

9. John Calvin, *Institutes of the Christian Religion,* trans. Henry Beveridge, 1.1.1, available at http://www.ccel.org (hereafter, *Institutes*). The chapter title (for 1.1) is "The Knowledge of God and of Ourselves Mutually Connected. . . ."

10. The chapter title for Calvin, *Institutes* 1.5: "The Knowledge of God Conspicuous in the Creation, and Continual Government of the World."

11. Ibid., 1.3.1.

12. For details of Calvin's approach to the Trinity, see Robert Letham, *The Holy Trinity: In Scripture, History, Theology, and Worship* (Phillipsburg, NJ: P& R Publishing, 2004), 252–68.

13. The heading in Calvin, *Institutes*, 1.13.

14. Letham, *Holy Trinity*, 252. That said, we should not think that an

intellectual rigor and a detailed consideration of trinitarian problems were absent in Calvin. Just consider this passage: "When the Apostle calls the Son of God 'the express image of his person,' (Heb 1:3), he undoubtedly does assign to the Father some subsistence in which he differs from the Son. For to hold with some interpreters that the term is equivalent to essence (as if Christ represented the substance of the Father like the impression of a seal upon wax), were not only harsh but absurd. For the essence of God being simple and undivided, and contained in himself entire, in full perfection, without partition or diminution, it is improper, nay, ridiculous, to call it his express image (χαρακτερ). But because the Father, though distinguished by his own peculiar properties, has expressed himself wholly in the Son, he is said with perfect reason to have rendered his person (hypostasis) manifest in him. And this aptly accords with what is immediately added—viz. that he is 'the brightness of his glory.'" Calvin, *Institutes*, 1.13.2.

15. See ibid., 1.13.9, 10.

16. Ibid., 1.13.17.

17. Ibid., 1.13.18.

18. Ibid., 1.13.20.

19. Ignatius of Loyola, *Spiritual Diary* # 48, 63, 109–10, in Ignatius of Loyola, *Ignatius of Loyola: Spiritual Exercises and Selected Works*, ed. George E. Ganss, S.J., et al. (Mahwah, NJ: Paulist, 1991), 244–45, 253.

20. John of the Cross, *The Living Flame of Love*, Versions A and B, trans. with introduction and commentary by Jane Ackerman (Binghamton, NY: Medieval & Renaissance Texts & Studies, 1995), Prologue, 70.

21. John Owens, *Of Communion with God the Father, Son and Holy Ghost* (repr. Edinburgh: Banner of Truth Trust, 1965); available at http://www.ccel.org.

22. The standard—and most accessible—English source for Lutheran Scholastic theologies is the compendium by Heinrich Schmid, *The Doctrinal Theology of the Evangelical Lutheran Church*, 3d ed., rev. and trans. C. A. Hay and H. E. Jacobs (Minneapolis: Augsburg, 1899); available at http://www.ccel.org.

23. The standard—and most accessible—English source for Reformed Scholastic theologies is the compendium by Heinrich Heppe, *Reformed Dogmatics: Set Out and Illustrated from the Sources*, rev. and ed. E. Bizer,

trans. G. T. Thomson (London: Allen & Unwin, 1950; reprint ed.: Eugene, OR: Wipf & Stock, 2007).

24. An invaluable contribution to our understanding of post-Reformation theologies is the work of the American theologian Richard Muller. See his four-volume *Post-Reformation Reformed Dogmatics* (Grand Rapids: Baker Academic, 2003).

25. Historians still debate the role of Calvin—or lack thereof—in the process leading up to the killing of Servetus (the same can be said of Martin Bucer and some other Reformation leaders). For a reliable detailed account of the event, see Bruce Gordon, *Calvin* (New Haven: Yale University Press, 2009), 217–32; useful also is Eric Kayayan, "The Case of Michael Servetus," *Mid-American Journal of Theology* 8 (1992): 117–46.

26. I am following here closely the highly useful account in ch. 8 of Stephen R. Holmes, *The Quest for the Trinity: The Doctrine of God in Scripture, History, and Modernity* (Downers Grove, IL: InterVarsity, 2012).

27. Ibid., 170. Servetus's main writings, namely *On the Errors of the Trinity* and *Dialogues on the Trinity*, are handily accessible as *The Two Treatises of Servetus on the Trinity*, trans. Earl Morse Wilbur (Cambridge: Harvard University Press, 1932), available at http://www.teleiosministries.com/pdfs/Doctrines_of_Men/errors_trinity_servetus.pdf.

28. His key christological orientation comes to the fore in the very beginning statement of *On the Errors of the Trinity*: "Any discussion of the Trinity should start with the man. That Yahshua, surnamed Christ, was not a hypostasis but a human being is taught both by the early Fathers and in the Scriptures, taken in their literal sense, and is indicated by the miracles that he wrought. He, and not the Word is also the miraculously born Son of Yahweh in fleshly form, as the Scriptures teach—not a hypostasis, but an actual Son. He is an elohim, sharing Yahweh's divinity in full; and the theory of a *communicatio idiomatum* is a confusing sophistical quibble. This does not imply two Yahwehs, but only a double use of the term elohim, as is clear from the Hebrew use of the term. Christ, being one with Yahweh his Father, equal in power, came down from heaven and assumed flesh as a man. In short, all the Scriptures speak of Christ as a man." *The Two Treatises of Servetus on the Trinity*, Bk. 1, p. 3. For a useful source, see Jerome Friedman, *Michael Servetus: A Case Study in Total Heresy* (Geneva: Libraire Droz S.A., 1978).

29. Although more recent works can be found, I still consult and find useful the classic modern study, David Munroe Cory, *Faustus Socinus* (Boston: Beacon, 1932; repr.: Eugene, OR: Wipf & Stock, 2009). A quick overview of the trinitarian views can be found in chs. 12 and 13, on the doctrine of God and Christology, respectively. Part 1 also contains useful information about the Polish Brethren Church, its history and teachings.

30. In agreement with Holmes, *Quest for the Trinity*, 171 with references to other sources.

31. From the title page of Samuel Clarke, *The Scripture Doctrine of the Trinity* (London, 1712), available at https://archive.org/details/scripturedoctrin00clar.

32. For details, see Holmes, *Quest for the Trinity*, 173–75.

33. For details of Toland, Tindal, and others, see Holmes, *Quest for the Trinity*, 176–79 particularly.

34. See, further, Roger E. Olson and Christopher A. Hall, *The Trinity*, Guides to Theology (Grand Rapids: Eerdmans, 2002), 81–83.

35. Holmes, *Quest for the Trinity*, 180.

36. "Christian Unitarian Universalists," Christian Universalist Association website at http://www.uua.org/beliefs/who-we-are/beliefs/christianity.

37. See, further, Wolfhart Pannenberg, *Systematic Theology*, vol. 1, trans. Geoffrey Bromiley (Grand Rapids: Eerdmans, 1991), 301–2.

38. Immanuel Kant, *The Conflict of the Faculties*, trans. and introduced by Mary J. Gregor (New York: Abaris Books, 1979), 65, 67 (emphasis in the original). Accessed 2/27/2017 at https://www.scribd.com/document/171424223/Immanuel-Kant-The-Conflict-of-the-Faculties. The reason this citation with no breaks is to be found in two separate pages has to do with the format of the book: it contains both German original and English translation consecutively.

39. For a brief, useful consideration, see Olson and Hall, *The Trinity*, 87–90.

40. For a brief, useful consideration, see Holmes, *Quest for the Trinity*, 190–91.

41. For a fine exposition and assessment, see Stanley J. Grenz, *Rediscovering the Triune God: The Trinity in Contemporary Theology* (Louisville: Westminster John Knox, 2004), 24–32. Hegel, of course, made a major effort to develop the Trinity from his idea of the

Absolute Spirit. For Pannenberg's incisive dialogue with and critique of Hegel and other Idealists such as Lessing, who attempted to derive Trinity from self-consciousness, see Pannenberg, *Systematic Theology*, 1:292–98.

42. Friedrich Schleiermacher, *The Christian Faith*, ed. H. R. Mackintosh and J. S. Stewart, 2d ed. (London/New York: T&T Clark, 1999), §170–72, pp. 738–51. Claude Welch claims that the reason for the dismissal was that for the Father of Modern Theology, Trinity was nothing more than an "unnecessary and unwarranted addition to the faith." Claude Welch, *In This Name: The Doctrine of the Trinity in Contemporary Theology* (New York: Charles Scribner's Sons, 1952), 5.

43. For a balanced and critical reassessment of the doctrine of the Trinity in Schleiermacher, see Grenz, *Rediscovering the Triune God*, 17–24.

44. In Schleiermacher's technical and idiosyncratic manner, religion has to do with "the immediate consciousness of the universal being of all finite things in and through the infinite, of all temporary things in and through the eternal." Friedrich Schleiermacher, *On Religion: Addresses in Response to Its Cultural Critics*, trans. Terrence N. Tice (Richmond: John Knox, 1969), 36, cited in Stanley J. Grenz and Roger E. Olson, *Twentieth-Century Theology: God and the World in a Transitional Age* (Downers Grove, IL: InterVarsity, 1992), 44; for an accessible account of Schleiermacher's theology, including the doctrine of God, see 39–51.

45. For his own classic exposition, see Schleiermacher, *The Christian Faith*, §4, pp. 12–18 particularly.

46. "All attributes which we ascribe to God are to be taken as denoting something special in God, but only something special in the manner in which the feeling of absolute dependence is to be related to Him." Schleiermacher, *The Christian Faith*, §50.1, p. 194.

47. Ibid., §170.1, pp. 738–39; see further Olson and Hall, *The Trinity*, 91–92.

48. Ibid., §172.1, p. 748.

49. Ibid., §170.1, p. 738.

50. Ibid., §123.1, p. 569.

51. A highly useful primer is Paul Redding, "Georg Wilhelm Friedrich Hegel," in *The Stanford Encyclopedia of Philosophy*, Fall 2015 edition, ed. Edward N. Zalta, available at http://plato.stanford.edu/archives/fall2015/entries/hegel/.

52. Justo L. González, *A History of Christian Thought*, vol. 3: *From the Protestant Reformation to the Twentieth Century* (Nashville: Abingdon, 1975), 315–17, at 315; for Hegel's philosophy and views of religion, see the highly useful account in Grenz and Olson, *Twentieth-Century Theology*, 31–39.

53. See, further, in Alister E. McGrath, *The Making of Modern German Christology, 1750–1990*, 2d ed. (Grand Rapids: Zondervan, 1994), 50–55.

54. Phrases in citations in this paragraph are from Hegel, *Lectures on the Philosophy of Religion* (1824), in *G. W. F. Hegel: Theologian of the Spirit*, The Making of Modern Theology, ed. Peter C. Hodgson (Minneapolis: Fortress Press, 1997), 220 (emphases deleted). Alongside Grenz and Olson, *Twentieth-Century Theology*, 36–37, consult also Edmund J. Fortman, ed., *The Theology of God: Commentary* (New York: Bruce, 1968), 281–82; a more technical explanation is offered in Stanley J. Grenz, *Social God and the Relational Self: A Trinitarian Theology of the Imago Dei* (Louisville: Westminster John Knox, 2001), 26–29.

55. G. W. F. Hegel, "The Consummate Religion: The Lectures of 1824," in *Lectures on the Philosophy of Religion*, vol. 3: *The Consummate Religion*, ed. Peter C. Hodgson (Berkeley: University of California Press, 1988 [1985]), 163–64.

6

___

Contemporary Trinitarianism and Its Prospects

Continuing Relevance in the Third Millennium?

The opening sentences of *The Trinity and the Kingdom*, by the world-class systematic theologian Jürgen Moltmann, pose a timely question to us: "What do we think of when we hear the name of the triune God? What ideas do we associate with the Trinity? What do we experience in the fellowship of the Father, the Son and the Holy Spirit?"[1] Before hastening to respond to this rhetorical question, listen to the way this German Reformed thinker on the Trinity continues to probe us: "Why are most Christians in the West, whether they be Catholics or Protestants, really only 'monotheists' where the experience and practice of their faith is concerned? Whether God is one or triune evidently makes as little difference to the doctrine of faith as it does to ethics?"[2] Moltmann is, of course, not the only one to raise such questions at the turn of the third millennium. Often cited is the astonishing observation by another trinitarian giant of contemporary times from the same country, the late Roman Catholic Karl Rahner: "We must be willing to admit that, should the doctrine of the Trinity have to be dropped as false, the major part of religious literature could well remain virtually unchanged."[3] Similar kinds of comments from other contemporary theologians across denominational and geographical borders can be registered.[4]

Against this commonly perceived trinitarian anemia, whether it is totally accurate or not, there is also an unprecedented vibrancy and creativity in the wider ecumenical investigation into the Trinity, so much so that it is not mistaken to speak of the "the rebirth of Trinitarian theology . . . as one of the most far-reaching theological developments of the century."[5] That said, one should probably not join this statement with a half-truth voiced in all almost current textbooks and inquiries into the Trinity, namely that, after the formative work done on the Trinity by the end of the patristic era, trinitarian theology fell into a kind of dormancy. Were that charge against much of Christian theological history true, it would mean that for the most part the church and theology operated as if the Trinity were not an essential part of spirituality, mission, and thinking! That is, of course, a gross overstatement. Even if—particularly among the lay faithful—the doctrine's "practical" meaning might have remained blurred at times, the trinitarian structure of faith, prayer, salvation history, liturgy, and Christian life has been a constant presence.

In sum: as we celebrate the continuing vibrancy of trinitarian inquiry, including its practical implications, let us not naïvely cast a shadow of omission on much of our own religious history.[6] It is also true that defending the intelligibility and homiletical-pedagogical mandate of making such inquiry (at least somewhat) understandable to the faithful is a continuing challenge to the church and academia. Undoubtedly, it is true that

> [t]his doctrine in many ways presents strange paradoxes. It is very widely held. It is not simply the special view of a particular

denomination or sect. It is part of the faith of the universal church. Yet it is a widely disputed doctrine, which has provoked discussion throughout all the centuries of the church's existence. It is held by many with great vehemence and vigor. These advocates are certain they believe the doctrine, and consider it crucial to the Christian faith. Yet many are unsure of the exact meaning of their belief. It was the very first doctrine dealt with systematically by the church, yet it it still one of the most misunderstood and disputed doctrines.[7]

We do well to remember the long and winding road of the evolution of the *doctrine* of the Trinity. That is what we have registered over and over again in our survey. Leonard Hodgson's observation is noteworthy: "Christianity began as a Trinitarian religion with a Unitarian theology. The question at issue in the age of the Fathers was whether the religion should transform the theology or the theology stifle the religion."[8] Religion—or, to be more precise, salvation history as revealed in the Scriptures—came to shape theology, and rightly so.

A substantial challenge—and asset—to the establishment of the continuing relevance of the doctrine of the Trinity has to do with learning the proper "grammar." A major difficulty with the theology of God has simply to do with the limitations of human language. Indeed, it tests the meaningfulness and propriety of a common, logical communication.[9] Of course, already Augustine observed this difficulty: "Yet, when the question is asked, What three? human language labors altogether under great poverty of speech. The answer, however, is given, three 'persons,' not that it might be [completely] spoken, but that it might not be left [wholly] unspoken."[10] The challenge to those who teach and preach about the Trinity is thus immense: "There has to be a way of presenting it that will not hide these riches but bring them out in an adequate manner."[11]

Theologians should beware of not making an already complicated doctrine even more obscure—and preachers, too! The key is to learn the proper grammar. No one has expressed it more appropriately than the Roman Catholic Brazilian liberationist, Leonardo Boff:

> Every science has its technical terms for expressing exactly what it wants to say. Theology has a mass of key words to express what is thought in faith. Words are more important in theology than in any other science, since no one can see or experience God empirically, as the realities of the world are experienced. Technical terms in theology established the consensus reached after many trials, errors and insights through generation after generation of Christian thinkers.[12]

One will not lose one's salvation for the lack of understanding the trinitarian canons and nuances, but the saved ones should excel in understanding more properly the little we can of God who, after all, is mystery. In that sense, and only in that sense, the advice from Philipp Melanchthon is sound: "We adore the mysteries of the Godhead. That is better than to investigate them."[13] Knowing *about* the doctrine of the Trinity is not the same as knowing the triune God. As Moltmann reminds us, for the church fathers, knowing meant "knowing in *wonder*. By knowing or perceiving one participates in the life of the other."[14] This is doxological knowledge, knowing God by way of worshiping the triune God, Father, Son, and Spirit. This is the true trinitarian grammar!

Those who have learned the trinitarian grammar and seek to get closer to God may also hope to get some insight into the doctrine's practical implications. Although one should resist the uncritical tendency to only "believe what works," it is exciting that in recent years a number of studies have emerged that relate the Trinity to various key topics in Christian life, community, and the wider world. Just consider areas and themes as diverse as these: from the critique of sexism and affirmation of equality,[15] to ecclesiology[16] and mission,[17] to pastoral theology and ministry,[18] to political theology[19] and economy.[20] Even movements such as American process theology, often considered to be oblivious of to the concept of the Trinity, is showing interest in the topic.[21] And think about postmodern approaches to theology: with all their suspicions toward tradition, they have also found affinity with some of the key claims of this doctrine.[22] Perhaps most astonishingly—and as an indication of the continuing creative force present in contemporary theology—even interfaith studies have turned to Trinity as a major asset, whether it relates to Christianity's relation to Buddhism,[23] or Islam,[24] or Hinduism,[25] or Confucianism,[26] as well as to various aspects of the theology of religions in general.[27] This is in keeping with the claim that the Trinity is the most distinctive feature of Christian faith. At the same time, being a relational and dynamic concept, it can also help Christians relate to the religious Other.[28]

Today's Trinitarian Renaissance

Twentieth-Century Foundations

Although the task of this primer is to seek to provide a solid and trustworthy account of the *history* of the doctrine of the Trinity, it would not be advisable to make a complete stop at the door of the twentieth century. A brief mapping out of key orientations, leading themes, and promises, as well as challenges, will wrap up the book, and so help the student of the history of theology to consider the evolution of the theology of the Trinity both from the perspective of the past and through some current interests.[29] The following brief survey of the latest developments will identify key theological players and their principal contributions. Hopefully, it gives the reader an opportunity to reflect on the continuities and discontinuities between the past and present.

Basically, all current trinitarian surveys identify the groundbreaking significance of three European theologians who have helped set the stage for much work to follow. They are the late Swiss Reformed Karl Barth, the late German Catholic Karl Rahner, and the Greek Orthodox John Zizioulas. Let us look at them in that order.

Karl Barth located his doctrine of the Trinity, fittingly named "revelational trinitarianism,"[30] in the context of the doctrine of revelation at the beginning of his massive multi-volume *Church Dogmatics.*[31] Barth's simple formula of revelation puts it this way: "*God* reveals Himself. He reveals Himself *through Himself.* He reveals *Himself.*"[32] This simply means that God's self-revelation is the "root of the doctrine of the Trinity."[33] Or to put it another way: God is the Revealer, Revelation, and Revealedness.[34] No wonder, then, that the Trinity not only occupies a prominent place in his dogmatic presentation, but also serves as its structuring principle. As Alar Laats summarizes it:

> The modes of being of God "evolve" from one another in the same way as the three different moments of the one event of revelation. The Son proceeds from the Father as revelation proceeds from the revealer and the Holy Spirit proceeds from the Son, and therefore also from the Father, as the revealedness proceeds from revelation and through that from the revealer. . . . And the unity of the Trinity is the unity of the single event of revelation.[35]

In keeping with tradition—and differing from the emphases of some contemporary theologians such as Moltmann (to be discussed below)—Barth also seeks to defend the absolute freedom of God in the revelation and work of salvation. Technically put, this means that the "immanent" Trinity (the way the Father, Son and, Spirit exist in their eternal, mutual, loving relationship) and "economic" Trinity (the way this triune God relates to the world as Creator, Provider, and Consummator) should not be conflated but, rather, carefully distinguished. Barth says that God "remains free, in operating, in giving Himself. On this freedom of His rests the distinction between the essence as such and His essence as the Operator, the Self-manifesting."[36] In other words, there is a close correspondence between the immanent and economic Trinity but no identity, lest divine freedom and mystery be compromised.

The reference to the immanent and economic Trinity brings to our attention to the Catholic Karl, namely Rahner.[37] Among a number of lasting contributions to the twentieth-century doctrine of God, he is best known for what, in hindsight, is named as "Rahner's Rule."[38] It goes like this: *"The 'economic' Trinity is the 'immanent' Trinity and the 'immanent' Trinity is the 'economic' Trinity."*[39] What does this mean? Simply that, rather than seeking to inquire into abstract terms about the "inner," hidden life of the triune God to which we humans hardly have any access (immanent Trinity), we should instead turn to the knowledge of Father, Son, and Spirit as provided in revelation and the "economy" of salvation (that is, what God is doing in the world as Creator, Sustainer, and Sanctifier). What can be known of God on this basis ("economic Trinity") is a reliable guide to how God is in God's own life ("immanent Trinity"), and vice versa.[40]

To put this rule in other words: God is in himself the same God we meet in salvation history. Since God is faithful, we may fully trust that the way God appears to us in his dealings with us is the way God exists in his own inner life. At the same time, we have to remember that we humans should not pretend to know too much about God. It is, rather, that however little we may gather on the basis of the economic Trinity, this can be considered reliable. The Lutheran commentator Ted Peters helpfully explains:

> Rahner proposes this rule in order to advance the thesis that it is God as one or another of the divine persons who relates to the world; it is not God as the unity of the divine being. The way we experience God is through God's saving activity within history—through the economy of salvation—and here we know God as the redeeming word in Christ and as uniting love in the Spirit. We do not know God in general. We experience God first in the economy of salvation, and Rahner believes we can trust this experience. In the economy of salvation, God is communicating the Godself. God is actually internally just the way we experience the divine in relation to us, namely, as Father, Son, and Spirit.[41]

Turning to revelation and the economy of salvation would save theology, so Rahner underlined, from the danger of abstract speculations about the Trinity, an unfortunate hallmark of much of (particularly Western) tradition.

The third formative voice is the Greek Orthodox John Zizioulas who, alongside the British Bishop Kallistos (born Timothy Ware) and the late Russian-born American Vladimir Lossky, is the best-known contemporary spokesperson in the West for Eastern Orthodox tradition. Standing in the long and venerable apophatic tradition, Lossky reminds us that in the "negative" way of the East, the knowledge of God is not really knowledge but, rather, total ignorance. Rather than intellectual knowledge, it is a mystical ecstasy.[42] That, however, does not mean that therefore God is inaccessible to us; God is present to us in his "energies" (a doctrine derived from the Palamite) rather than in his inaccessible essence. Furthermore, the contemporary Orthodox trinitarian theology[43] also follows the tradition of the East in affirming the monarchy, the primacy of the Father, though not in a way that would compromise relationality and the full deity of any of the three. This is to ensure a "personal" (based on the person of the Father) origin of the Trinity, against what the Orthodox see as the fallacy of the West, namely the impersonal divine essence as the source.[44] Yet another leading theme for Lossky is the insistence on the simultaneous and equal coexistence of one nature and three persons, in a mutual relationship. In other words, Lossky does not want to go with either of the typical textbook opinions, namely that Eastern theology's starting point is threeness and Western tradition's unity; rather, he wants to have them both—and at the same time![45] As mentioned already, Eastern Orthodox theology also opposes vehemently any notion of the *filioque*. Therein, the emphasis is put on the mutual rather than subordinate role of the Spirit in the Trinity:

The Son and the Spirit thus appear, throughout the Gospel, as two divine persons sent into the world, the former to quicken our personal liberty, the latter to unite Itself with our nature and regenerate it. These two persons each have their proper relation to the Father (generation and procession); they also have between them a relationship of reciprocity. . . . The Spirit leads us, through the Son, to the Father, where we discover the unity of the three. The Father . . . reveals Himself through the Son in the Spirit. Here is affirmed a process, an order from which issues that of the three names: Father, Son and Holy Spirit.[46]

Affirming these foundational Greek Church's trinitarian tenets, Zizioulas's most distinctive contribution has to do with his widely acknowledged trinitarian communion approach.[47] This is best illustrated in the book title of his celebrated collection of essays, *Being as Communion*, with its telling subtitle, *Studies in Personhood and the Church* (ET 1985). The book's main claim is that there is no true personal being without communion, relationality; nothing exists as an "individual" in itself. Even God exists in communion, as eternal communion of Father, Son, and Spirit: "The being of God could be known only through personal relationships and personal love. Being means life, and life means *communion*."[48] According to Zizioulas, in the Trinity the three persons of the Godhead interrelate with one another. They share an intratrinitarian love relationship. With this same love, the triune God relates to human beings and the world embracing them in a mutual *koinōnia*. Zizioulas's basic argument can be summarized like this, with his own words:

From the fact that a human being is a member of the Church, he becomes an "image of God," he exists as God Himself exists, he takes on God's "way of being." This way of being . . . is a way of *relationship* with the world, with other people and with God, an event of *communion*, and that is why it cannot be realized as the achievement of an *individual*, but only as an *ecclesial* fact.[49]

In rehabilitating communion and relationality as the ontologically foundational concept about God and thus true personhood, Zizioulas simply claims to stand on the shoulders of the Cappadocians. (The fact that historical experts have detected some serious problems in his claim for an exact continuity with the Cappadocians' line should not cast a shadow on the significance of the Greek bishop's trinitarian proposal. After all, it stands on a broad historical trajectory, most ably developed during the patristic era by the Greek theologians). Zizioulas's communion ontology and doctrine of the Trinity have been immensely influential for the doctrine of God during the last decades and continue to shape the landscape. Several theologians, such as Jürgen Moltmann, Wolfhart Pannenberg, the liberationist Leonardo Boff, and the late Catholic feminist Catherine Mowry LaCugna, built on the communion idea.

The next part of this selective survey of twentieth-century contributions to the developing trinitarian doctrine will focus on two leading European Protestant theologians, the late Lutheran Wolfhart Pannenberg and the Reformed Jürgen Moltmann, who is still actively doing academic writing at this time. Their approaches to the doctrine of the Trinity, while engaging widely the tradition, also illustrate new and novel "turns" in contemporary trinitarian discourse. The section following that will highlight more briefly the work of two Roman Catholics, the American feminist Elizabeth Johnson and Brazilian liberationist Leonardo Boff. Their views of the Trinity fall under the nomenclature "contextual."

Pannenberg and Moltmann

The title Pannenberg gives to the first chapter of the first volume of his *Systematic Theology* reveals the basic agenda of all of his theology: "The Truth of Christian Doctrine as the Theme of Systematic Theology."[50] Against all forces of modernity and postmodernism, Pannenberg boldly sets up a coherent, logical presentation of Christian doctrine in defense of truth. That theological argumentation is based from the beginning to the end on a trinitarian vision of the Christian God.[51] An important move in his treatment of the doctrine of the Trinity has to do with the order of discussion; indeed, he completely revises the traditional way. While it is customary to treat the unity of God prior to the Trinity—as became the established norm already in Thomas Aquinas and the Scholastics—Pannenberg first provides a detailed discussion of threeness (in chapter 5 of the first volume of his *Systematic Theology*) before considering the unity (ch. 6). In other words, the threeness of God is the basis for talking about the Christian God. Why so? Because, in keeping with Barth, Pannenberg surmises that the Christian theology of God is based on the coming of the Son of the Father in the power of the Spirit, as narrated in the biblical revelation.

For the most part, Pannenberg follows Rahner's rule. He looks at how the three trinitarian persons appear and relate to one another in the event of revelation in the life and message of Jesus. Important here is Jesus's announcement of the nearness of the rule of God. Jesus taught us to know God as Father. Jesus's self-distinction (though not differentiation) from, and humble service to, the Father establish his sonship. The Spirit is introduced by virtue of his involvement in God's presence in the work of Jesus and in the fellowship of the Son with the Father. Ultimately, the deity of the Spirit came to be established because of the Spirit's role as the medium of fellowship, otherwise "the Christian doctrine of the deity of the Spirit would be a purely external addition to the confession of the relation of the Son to the deity of the Father."[52]

Based on these foundational considerations, Pannenberg considers carefully the meaning of "The Reciprocal Self-distinction of Father, Son, and Spirit as the Concrete Form of Trinitarian Relations."[53] Applying Hegel's concept of self-distinction, which means that by giving oneself to one's counterpart one gains one's identity from the other, Pannenberg maintains that the Father is "dependent" on the Son for his identity and that the Son and the Spirit are "dependent" on the Father and each other for theirs. For example, by distinguishing himself from the Father (and yet subordinating himself to the service of the coming of God's kingdom), Jesus not only gains his status as Son but also establishes the Father's deity. Furthermore, as the result of Jesus's self-humiliation (Phil 2:5–11), the Father hands over the kingdom to the Son, and at the end the Son hands it back to the Father (1 Cor 15:24), thus making room for the eternal lordship of the Father.[54]

Differently from tradition, which assigns the Father the status of being without origin, Pannenberg argues for a genuine
mutuality, which Peters appropriately coined as the principle
of "dependent divinity."[55] While the relations between the
Father and Son are irreversible (the Father is not begotten by
the Son), the Father's fatherhood is dependent on the Son.
Employing biblical passages that speak of the "transfer" of ultimate authority, the rule of the kingdom of God (without which
the Father could not be God) from the Father to the Son and
finally in the eschatological consummation back to the Father
(Matt 28:18; 1 Cor 15:24–29; Phil 2:9–11), the mutual dependency and relationality is being established. He summarizes:

> In the handing over of lordship from the Father to the Son, and
> its handing back from the Son to the Father, we see *a mutuality in
> their relationship* that we do not see in the begetting. By handing
> over lordship to the Son the Father makes his kingship *dependent*
> on whether the Son glorifies him and fulfils his lordship by ful-
> filling his mission. The self-distinction of the Father from the Son
> is not just that he begets the Son but that he hands over all things
> to him, so that his kingdom and his own deity are now *dependent*
> upon the Son. The rule of kingdom of the Father is not so exter-
> nal to his deity that he might be God without his kingdom.[56]

Having firmly established the threeness, what about unity?
Indeed—somewhat ironically, in light of Christian tradition
that (both in the East and West) took for granted the unity and
worked hard to establish threeness and relationality—the task
of ensuring oneness has become *the* major challenge in contemporary theology. It has led many to abandon all notions of
"substance" and "essence" and, like Moltmann, to refer to the
concept of *perichoresis*, a mutual indwelling of three persons,
as the seat of unity. What is Pannenberg's choice? Here again,
he seeks to hold on to the best of the tradition and yet, at the
same time, to propose his own innovative suggestion. The way
he deals with unity can briefly be put this way: Agreeing with
tradition that the concept of "essence" is needed to affirm the
unity of the three persons, Pannenberg also revises this concept radically in order to move beyond the now-disputed sub-

stance ontology of the past. He conceives "the divine essence as the epitome of the personal relations among Father, Son, and Spirit. . . . This requires a concept of essence that is not external to the category of relations."[57]

Above it was mentioned that in the Christian East the primacy of the Father is a basic tenet of trinitarian doctrine—and in that sense a notion of "hierarchy" enters the Trinity. While theologians such as Moltmann uncompromisingly oppose any such notion, Pannenberg interestingly speaks of the monarchy of the Father but not exactly in the same way as Greek theology. Pannenberg's innovation is this: although the Father possesses monarchy, he does not do that "alone," that is, apart from dependency on the Son and the Spirit:

> The monarchy of the Father is God's absolute lordship. The Son serves it, and so does the glorifying of the Father and the Son by the Spirit. But the monarchy of the Father is mediated by the Son, who prepares the way for it by winning form for it in the life of creatures, and also by the Spirit, who enables creatures to honor God as their Creator by letting them share in the relation of the Son to the Father. *This is the action of the one God* by the Father, Son, and Spirit as it may be seen in light of the eschatological consummation of the kingdom of God in the world. Only herein is the one God the acting God as even before he is already the living God in the fellowship of Father, Son, and Spirit.[58]

An important aspect of Pannenberg's trinitarian development is a most cautious way of negotiating the economic–immanent distinction. On the one hand, alongside the majority of contemporary theologians, he critiques tradition for keeping them too distant from each other, resulting at times in a somewhat distanced and nonengaged God in relation to the world.[59] On the other hand, he rejects the other extreme, the kind of panentheistic intimate way of connecting them, as do Moltmann and others, because that may lead to the compromising of absolute divine freedom and mystery. Indeed, he fears that "the equation of the two means the absorption of the immanent Trinity in the economic Trinity." If so, the result would be highly concerning: "This steals from the Trinity of the salvation history all sense and significance. For this Trinity has sense and significance only if God is the same in salvation history as he is from eternity"[60]

Pannenberg's German Reformed counterpart, Jürgen Moltmann, has developed an innovative approach to the Trinity that has stirred up much discussion, debate, and also a critical following.[61] Similar to Pannenberg and against tradition's point of departure in God as one ("substance" or "subject"), Moltmann advocates the understanding of God as "triunity, the three-in-one."[62] Trinity means nothing less than "the Christianization of the concept of God."[63] He calls this a "social doctrine of the Trinity." Rather than focusing on one divine substance, it focuses on "relationships and communities," reflecting the general turn from "subject" to relationality.[64] To put it another way: Moltmann places himself in the forefront of "social trinitarianism," that is, the vision of God focused on Father, Son, and Spirit as the divine community. Whether historically valid or not, these trinitarian advocates often appeal to the Cappadocians in the East and the Victorines in the West as the historical pedigree.

Known also as the "theologian of hope," a persistent theme in Moltmann's theology in general and the doctrine of God in particular has to do with suffering. The title of one of his first major treatises, *The Crucified God*, set the tone for his constructive and creative theological program. Under its telling subtitle, *The Cross of Christ as the Foundation and Criticism of Christian Theology*,[65] Moltmann, a former POW during WWII, targeted sharp criticism against what classical theology had come to name as divine impassibility, the view according to which it is impossible for God to suffer.[66] He continued that same critique in his subsequent work, titled *The Trinity and the Kingdom of God: The Doctrine of God*, by raising the rhetorical question: "How can Christian faith understand Christ's passion as being the revelation of God, if the deity cannot suffer?"[67] Indeed, he surmises: "[A] God who cannot suffer is poorer than any man. For a God who is incapable of suffering is a being who cannot be involved. Suffering and injustice do not affect him. . . . But the one who cannot suffer cannot love either. So he is also a loveless being."[68]

Working from this point of departure, Moltmann follows Pannenberg (and Rahner) in taking the coming of Christ as the beginning point of the doctrine of the Trinity. But he does it in his own novel way. More precisely, "the cross of the Son stands from eternity in the center of the Trinity."[69] That is so because the event of the cross—particularly the cry of dereliction—represents "a deep division in God himself, in so far as God abandoned God and contradicted himself, and at the same time a unity in God, in so far as God was at one with God and corresponded to himself."[70] For Moltmann, the words of Psalm 22, "My God, my God, why have you forsaken me?" on the lips of the dying Jesus express ultimate suffering and anguish of the innocent victim. At the same time, this cry also relates to the deep pain of the Father who deserts his Son: "The grief of the Father here is just as important as the death of the Son."[71] Thereby God "accepts and adopts it [suffering] himself, making it part of his own eternal life."[72]

This relational, passion-driven orientation has everything to do with Moltmann's way of negotiating the God–world relationship, another question at the heart of the contemporary doctrine of God. Fittingly called "trinitarian panentheism,"[73] it brings God and world into a close, intimate relationship. Moltmann's creative way of constructing a trinitarian doctrine of creation illustrates this well. Contending that the world was created because of God's love,[74] in critical judgment of Barth's insistence on divine freedom that assumed that God could have decided not to create the world had he so wished, Moltmann believes creation "out of freedom" means creation "out of love." God's freedom is the freedom of love.[75] On the basis of this reasoning, he concludes:

> Creation is a fruit of God's longing for "his Other" and for that Other's free response to the divine love. That is why the idea of the world is inherent in the nature of God himself from eternity. . . . And if God's eternal being is love, then the divine love is also more blessed in giving than in receiving. God cannot find

bliss in eternal self-love if selflessness is part of love's very nature. God is in all eternity self-communicating love.[76]

Now, two important theological questions emerge, namely "What is the way Moltmann establishes the unity of the triune God?" and "What about the relationship between the economic and immanent Trinity?" It is here that Moltmann again reveals his highly creative and constructive thinking and is not afraid to test the limits of conventional orthodoxy. Since these two questions relate deeply to each other, it is best to handle them together. Again, taking his point of departure from the center of his trinitarian doctrine, namely the cross, Moltmann puts it unambiguously: "In order to grasp the death of the Son in its significance for God himself, I found myself bound to surrender the traditional distinction between the immanent and the economic Trinity, according to which the cross comes to stand only in the economy of salvation, but not within the immanent Trinity."[77] Furthermore, Moltmann argues not only that the economic Trinity reveals the immanent Trinity but that it has a retroactive effect on the immanent Trinity: "The pain of the cross determines the inner life of the triune God from eternity to eternity," similar to the responsive love in glorification through the Spirit.[78]

Alongside a great number of contemporary theologians (including Pannenberg), Moltmann is understandably critical of the tradition's ways of establishing the unity of God either based on the unity of the divine substance or on one divine subject.[79] Rather, he finds useful the dynamic ancient concept of *perichoresis*, the mutual indwelling of trinitarian persons in each other, "the unitedness, the at-oneness of the three Persons with one another, or: the unitedness, at-oneness of the triune God." This unity, he states, "must be perceived in the *perichoresis* of the divine Persons."[80] But that unity can ultimately be conceived *eschatologically*, in the final reconciliation between the economic and immanent Trinity. Hence, Moltmann states succinctly: "The unity of the Father, the Son and the Spirit is then the eschatological question about the consummation of the trinitarian history of God."[81] It is here that both the quest for the final establishment of unity and the uniting of the economic and immanent Trinity come together. Summarizes Moltmann: "The economic Trinity completes and perfects itself to immanent Trinity when the history and experience of salvation are completed and perfected. When everything is 'in God' and 'God is in all,' then the economic Trinity is raised into and transcended in the immanent Trinity."[82] Rightly, Pannenberg concludes that Moltmann thus "link[s] the consummation of salvation history in eschatology with the consummation of the trinitarian life of God in itself."[83]

Yet another novel move in Moltmann's theological program at large, and trinitarian theology in particular, is its liberationist and sociopolitical emphasis. While technically only few would take a white German academician living in his wealthy homeland as a typical liberationist, he sees a proper theology of God as a powerful instrument of social criticism. Critical of all notions of hierarchy or monarchy in the Trinity, he rejects the absolute use of power even with regard to God. Using somewhat idiosyncratic (and even confusing terminology), he opines that Christian "monotheism," a doctrine of God without a proper social trinitarianism, necessarily leads to patriarchy and hierarchy.[84] That happens both in the church and wider society. In its stead, he advocates a concept of the triune God that leads to an equal fellowship of men and women.[85] Whereas the non-trinitarian "monotheism" supports domination and abuse of power, an authentic trinitarianism supports equality, belonging, and flourishing. For him, the Trinity is not a hierarchical entity but, rather, a fellowship of persons: "We understand the scriptures as the testimony to the history of the Trinity's relations of fellowship, which are open to men and women, and open to the world."[86] God's kingdom is about the fatherly and motherly compassion rather than about domination and subjection.[87]

This view, of course, carries over to the nature of the church community. In his trinitarian ecclesiology (the doctrine of the church), Moltmann develops a vision of the church as a fellowship of men and women in equality patterned after an equalitarian Trinity.[88] That kind of church cherishes the biblical vision of John 17:20, in which "the unity of the Christian community is a trinitarian unity. It corresponds to the indwelling of the Father in the Son, and to the Son in the Father. It participates in the divine triunity, since the community of believers is not only fellowship with God, but in God too."[89]

This vision of inclusion, equality, and communion resonates deeply with many strands of contextual theologies. The following section presents briefly two leading representatives of trinitarian doctrines in that genre, one feminist, the other Latin American liberationist.

Feminist and Liberation Approaches

Speaking of "feminist" theology as an umbrella concept embracing all theologies done by and from the perspective of women is no longer acceptable. Instead, one should identify a number of different female theologies. The most common forms in the English-speaking parlance are the following: feminist (white/Caucasian), womanist (African American/black), Latina and/or *Mujerista* (Hispanic), Asian American, as well as African, Asian, and Latin American womens' theologies, among others. While they are all united in the central task of liberation, making womens' voices and concerns heard among theologians,[90] they also display different methods and represent differing agendas around the same leading liberative goal. Although women's experiences are hardly uniform across the diverse cultural spectrums, some common features include marginalization, subordination, denial of access, and lack of worth. Patterns of domination and submission vary dramatically. Relationality, community, and belonging are highly cherished female values (and, of course, not uncommon among many men either). In light of these widely shared female experiences, it can be safely said that what unites most of these different female approaches to theology and the doctrine of God is the conviction that masculine and male-driven talk about God is both in need of radical correction and that it could be redeemed to serve equality and justice between women and men.[91]

The way we talk about God matters—and matters a lot! Many female theologians suspect that the whole project of person-ification of God as *Father* is a form of patriarchy that makes mechanisms for the oppression of women appear justified and that in itself it fosters male dominance. Even though only a few female scholars would argue that by necessity the symbol of divine fatherhood leads to the misuse of power for violence, rape, and war, such unfortunate examples throughout history are not hard to find. In order to remedy the limited and poten-tially oppressive way of addressing God, a number of female theologians have turned to the analysis of theological language as *metaphor* to open up, correct, and balance traditional reli-gious talk. Making a distinction between "conceptual" (that is, propositional) and metaphorical language,[92] Sallie McFague, whose work explores the intersections of feminism, process theology, ecology, and economics, reminds us that traditional theology, with its focus on the former category, operates with literalist, patriarchal ways of naming God, and this leads to exclusivism and a distant and rigid conception of the God–world relationship. The turn to the metaphorical may serve as a corrective.

A related asset that many female theologians employ in search of inclusivity and equality with regard to God-talk is to revisit Christian tradition, including the biblical text. Eliz-abeth Johnson writes: "Feminist interpretation makes pierc-ingly clear that although egalitarian impulses are discernible in the Bible, the texts as such were written mostly by men and for men in a patriarchal cultural context and reflect this fact."[93] That is exactly the reason why the ways of addressing the gender issue in the Scriptures must be subjected to a self-critical assessment. How much of this is based on biblical reve-lation and how much on sociocultural and political conditions of the past? The way out is to highlight the metaphorical and symbolic nature of all God-talk, whether in the Bible or else-where in tradition. Johnson adds here a highly interesting caveat. In her search for complementary, corrective, and balanced ways of naming God, she suggests "SHE WHO IS" as an alternative and balancing name, building, of course, on the most profound self-revelation of God in the OT (Exod 3:14). After all, she reminds us "there is no name that we can comprehend that would satisfactorily designate the Holy One."[94]

Johnson identifies three different approaches to the task of naming the Christian God.[95] One of them, quite a favorite among the first generation of feminists, was to add feminine traits such as nurture and care to speak of God. That was to soften and make more inclusive the predominantly male and patriarchal intuition of God as Father. The second way is to speak of God in terms of the Spirit, which can be more easily cast in feminine terms. But even these tactics still maintain the duality of male–female in the Divinity. The third approach, favored by Johnson, is to seek equivalent but diverse images of God as male and female. "The mystery of God is properly understood as neither male nor female but transcends both in an unimaginable way."[96] As a result, the main target for her *She Who Is: The Mystery of God in Feminist Theological Discourse*, is "[n]ormative speech about God in metaphors that are exclusively, literally, and patriarchally male."[97] This is highly important for the simple reason that, in the estimation of this Catholic theologian, the ecclesial language in liturgy, prayer, and catechesis suggests that "God is male, or at least more like a man than a woman, or at least more fittingly addressed as male than as female."[98]

From the Christian tradition, Johnson finds useful metaphors to speak of the triune God, particularly the following three: Spirit-Sophia, Jesus-Sophia, and Mother-Sophia.[99] The term *sophia* of course refers to Wisdom, an important biblical figure usually depicted in female terms as evident in the Proverbs and elsewhere.[100] Let us take up few examples of the first category, in order to illustrate Johnson's metaphorical way of conceiving the theology of God. Speaking of God's transcendent creative presence and activity in the world with the help of Spirit "points to the livingness of God who creates, sustains, and guides all things and cannot be confined."[101] Obviously, Johnson notes, this kind of activity is close to the life of women as it relates to birth, healing, teaching, inspiration, and so forth.

> Whether hovering like a nesting mother bird over the egg of primordial chaos in the beginning (Gen 1:2), or sheltering those in difficulty under the protective shadows of her wings (Pss 17:8; 36:7: 57:1; 61:4; 91:1; Isa 31:5), or bearing the enslaved up on her great wings toward freedom (Exod 19:4; Deut 32:11–12), divine Spirit's activity is evoked with allusion to femaleness.[102]

When the resources of the inclusive and balanced trinitarian theology are utilized, these and similar complementary and balancing ways of addressing the Divine highlight values dear to women, that is, love, communion, relationality, belonging, and mutuality.[103] This approach links a panentheistic vision of the mutuality of God and world with the metaphor of friendship, which has a close affinity with women's experience of closeness and sharing.[104]

What about the "Father"? Another Catholic feminist, the late Catherine Mowry LaCugna, makes the important point that the term *father* is not a proper name as much as it is a *personal* way to identify God: "The total identification of God with Jesus the Son, even unto death on a cross, makes it impossible to think of God as the distant, omnipotent monarch who rules the world just as any patriarch rules over his family and possessions."[105] What is most distinctive about naming God as Father is that God is seen in relation, first to Son and Spirit, and then to the world. If relationality is the key—as the Cappadocians and others already intuited—then adopting new kinds of ways of addressing God based on the same principle sound justified, such as Mother–Daughter, Father–Daughter, Mother–Son, Lover–Beloved, and Friend–Friend.[106] Indeed, it is relationality—and thus intimacy, belonging, and mutuality—that is suggested in the biblical notion of Father.

The concerns and intuitions of feminists and other female theologians—a subcategory in the wider liberation theologies camp—finds a lot of commonality among Latin American liberationists from among whom I have selected the Brazilian Franciscan priest Leonardo Boff to highlight the distinctive feature of the doctrine of God. Among many theological contributions, Boff's *Trinity and Society* represents a mature and balanced doctrine of the Trinity written with a view toward its advocacy of liberation, equality, and dignity of all.[107] That said, the book in itself does not necessarily strike one as distinctively "contextual" or liberationist. Rather, it is a carefully drafted and tightly argued fairly classical trinitarian doctrine of God, based on the best of biblical, historical, and contemporary traditions. There is a wide and deep engagement of the long trinitarian tradition, including also the Eastern teachers.

Working from the center of classical trinitarian doctrine, Boff sets forth a powerful proposal for a view of the trinitarian God as a communion of equal persons. This social doctrine of the Trinity serves as a critique of oppressive models of communities, whether political, social, or ecclesiastical. Similar to Moltmann and female theologians, Boff is in search of a model of community patterned after the Trinity that would be inclusive and equalitarian. He also gleans from Rahner, Zizioulas, and many others.

Building on the ancient communion theology, Boff sets the tone for the consideration of the theology of God by titling the opening chapter of the *Trinity and Society* as "From the Solitude of One to the Communion of Three."[108] Following Zizioulas, Boff argues that "In the Beginning Is Communion,"[109] and, in the footsteps of Moltmann, he offers a critical reconstruction of the kind of monotheism that sees God as unrelated to the world and its suffering. God exists in a loving, mutual relationship. This kind of communion in the Godhead "can be seen as a model for any just, egalitarian (while respecting differences) social organization. On the basis of their faith in the triune God, Christians postulate a society that can be the image and likeness of the Trinity."[110]

One of Boff's important theological observations is that the way we imagine God may have unprecedented sociopolitical consequences. Highlighting several "disintegrated under-standings" of God that have advanced inequality, hierarchy, or anarchy in society, he diagnoses a truncated understanding of the Trinity. A one-sided focus on the Father may lead to authoritarian notions; a one-sided focus on the Son "without reference to the Father and union with the Spirit can lead to self-sufficiency and authoritarianism." Finally, focus on the Spirit alone may give rise to "anarchism and lack of con-cern."[111] Ultimately, the result may be "an a-Trinitarian monotheism."[112] As a remedy to these and related fallacies, Boff recommends communion theology, emphasizing the inner-trinitarian love and mutuality of Father, Son, and Spirit. It is based on the ancient principle of *perichoresis*:

> Speaking of God must always mean the Father, Son and Holy Spirit in the presence of one another, in total reciprocity, in immediacy of loving relationship, being one for another, by another, in another and with another. No divine Person exists alone for its own sake; they are always and eternally in relation-ship with one another: the father is Father because he has a Son; the Son is Son only because he has a Father; the Spirit is Spirit only because of the love in which the Father begets the Son and the Son gives back to the Father.[113]

In this perichoretic unity, "each [person of the Trinity] is itself, not the other, but so open to the other and in the other that they form one entity, i.e., they are God."[114]

That said, Boff is not naïvely using trinitarian theology for advancing earthly goals. Indeed, he exposes the dangers of an "utilitarian" perspective in which the Trinity's value is assessed on the basis of its liberationist impulse. Instead—and in keeping with what was said above of the nature of his trini-tarian study—the Franciscan wishes to start "from above," that is, from a cautious and humble inquiry into the life of the tri-une God as revealed in Holy Scriptures, spiritual traditions, prayer, and liturgies. Only thereafter, he reminds us, it is appropriate to reflect on developing a socially and politically relevant liberation program drawing from Trinity as the template of loving, equalitarian, and inclusive community. "Trinity is not something thought out to explain human problems. It is the revelation of God as God is, as Father, Son, and Holy Spirit."[115]

An aspect of liberation dear to Boff's heart is overcoming sexism. His trinitarian vision of God holds to a "trans-sexist theology of the maternal father and paternal mother." To advance such a vision of God, theology should not rely exclusively on male—nor even female—resources but employ both. This means that we can speak of the trinitarian God using the symbols of either father or mother or by a combination of them. Boff adds importantly that this is not contrary to the classical tradition; the Council of Toledo (675) spoke of the "Father's womb," in which the Son was conceived.[116]

Having now mapped out a number of key themes, discoveries, and debates in the latest phase of the development of the trinitarian doctrine, let us close this primer with a brief summing up of where the trinitarian reflection is currently and what might be its future directions for the sake of the third millennium.

Where We Are, and What's Next?

Notwithstanding the danger of oversimplifying a highly complex and multilayered set of interpretations of the trinitarian doctrine in contemporary global and ecumenical theology, it might be useful at the end to attempt a summary of some of the key features. To keep it concise, I will relate the statements to the materials covered above, understanding that often the names of the individual theologians are used also as templates:

- Following Barth, the rest of the contemporary theology of God has adopted the Trinity as the "first word" about the Christian God. With regard to Moltmann and other social trinitarians, as well as (somewhat differently) Pannenberg, this has meant that the threeness rather than unity has been adopted as the starting point of doing theology.

- Following Rahner, contemporary theology has chosen the "from-below" approach to the knowledge of God, that is, beginning from the economic rather than immanent Trinity. Barth already embraced this turn by locating the Trinity in the *prolegomena*, the doctrine of revelation. Moltmann and Pannenberg embodied the Rahnerian tactic by focusing on the coming and life of Jesus Christ as revealed in the NT. A corollary implication has been the connecting of the trinitarian doctrine with historical events, particularly salvation history and incarnation.

- Moltmann has helped many colleagues to pay a close attention to the implications of the Trinity for divine suffering and, by implication, for our own suffering.

- Zizioulas's revisiting of the patristic idea of relationality and *koinonia* has led to the rediscovery of communion theology, an idea incipient in the biblical notion of God as love. The implications of divine community for the ways human communities and personhood should be envisioned has inspired much practical reflection.

- The turn to "history" has made the negotiation of the relationship between the economic and immanent Trinity a focal issue and debate. Whereas Moltmann's trinitarian panentheism seeks to draw God as close to the world as possible and even envisions the blurring of the distinction at the end of the eschatological consummation, Pannenberg sides with tradition in keeping the economic and immanent distinct, albeit not separated.

- Due to the primacy of threeness—in a departure from tradition—the unity of God has become a major challenge for most contemporary trinitarian proposals. Pannenberg both supports tradition's way of speaking of the "essence" of God, although not in terms of substance or subject but, rather, relationally. Moltmann and other social trinitarians eschew any notion of essence and rather speak of some kind of perichoretic unity.

- The questions of liberation, inclusivity, and belonging have risen to a central place in Jürgen Moltmann, the feminist Elizabeth Johnson, the liberationist Leonardo Boff, and many others. While acknowledging that the doctrine of the Trinity is first and foremost about God and only derivatively about its potential for giving us advice on human issues, the practical implications have also been duly noted. [117]

Where next? It seems to me that alongside the continuing careful consideration of the nuances of the trinitarian tradition's details and the accuracy of interpretations,[118] the flourishing of fresh constructive proposals will continue. One of the many reasons is the growing ecumenical collaboration across the boundaries and increased mobility among theologians.

Important work will continue among theologians from the global South (Africa, Asia, and Latin America). A number of theologians have already made inroads into the construction of the doctrine of the Trinity employing distinctively African resources, including (but not limited to) the ancestry theme.[119] Similar work is being done increasingly among Asian theologians, many of whom are also dealing with the pertinent issues of a multifaith society.[120] From the Latin American context, a leading liberationist doctrine of God was already discussed briefly. Alongside Boff, a number of other liberationists have made contributions to the growing liberation tradition.[121]

Closely related to the work done in the global South is the increasing diversity of "contextual" theologies done both there and in the global North. These constructive proposals engage critically their own specific environment, culture, thought patterns, and religious heritage. This will undoubtedly continue enriching and challenging trinitarian reflection. No theology has ever been done in a vacuum. The more faithful we can be to our location, the better we are able to serve our people in their need to have the word incarnated in their own lives.

Beyond the Asian context, the challenges and opportunities coming from interfaith encounters and religious pluralisms will undoubtedly occupy the minds of many in the future.[122]

Perhaps somewhat surprisingly, some leading science and theology scholars have also recently shown growing interest in the intersection of the Trinity and what we know of the origins, workings, and destiny of our cosmos.[123]

In sum: with the rediscovery of the urgency and fruitfulness of trinitarian theology after the mid-twentieth century, the prospects for continuing renewal of this vibrant theme are positive. The third millennium started with a new flood of proposals, suggestions, and insights. How these will bear fruit takes us beyond the scope of this inquiry.

Notes

1. Jürgen Moltmann, *The Trinity and the Kingdom: The Doctrine of God*, trans. Margaret Kohl (Minneapolis: Fortress Press, 1993 [1981]), 1.

2. Ibid.

3. Karl Rahner, *The Trinity*, trans. Joseph Donceel (New York: Herder & Herder, 1970), 10–11.

4. See, e.g., the late Canadian Baptist Stanley J. Grenz, *Rediscovering the Triune God: The Trinity in Contemporary Theology* (Minneapolis: Fortress Press, 2004), ix; cf. the comment about "practical modalism" among ordinary Christians by the Reformed American Robert Letham, *The Holy Trinity: In Scripture, History, Theology, and Worship* (Phillipsburg, NJ: P&R Publishing, 2004), 5.

5. Grenz, *Rediscovering the Triune God*, ix.

6. For a useful list of reasons why this trinitarian renaissance has occurred, see the comprehensive reflection in Millard J. Erickson, *God in Three Persons: A Contemporary Interpretation of the Trinity* (Grand Rapids: Baker, 1995), 11–29.

7. Ibid., 11–12.

8. Leonard Hodgson, *The Doctrine of the Trinity*, Croall Lectures, 1942–1943 (New York: Charles Scribner's Sons, 1944), 103.

9. For a helpful discussion of logical ramifications of the doctrine of the Trinity, see Stephen T. Davis, *Logic and the Nature of God* (London/ Basingstoke: Macmillan, 1983), ch. 9.

10. Augustine, *On the Trinity*, 5.9.10, *NPNF*[1] 3:92.

11. Leonardo Boff, *Trinity and Society*, trans. Paul Burns (Eugene, OR: Wipf & Stock, 2005 [1988]), 111. Another Roman Catholic theologian, Gerald O'Collins, speaks of something that can be named as "trinitarian sense" among Christians; even when doctrinal formulations are still in the making, there is a need and inclination to think in terms of biblical salvation history that is trinitarian, speaking of Father, Son, and Spirit. Gerald O'Collins, *The Tripersonal God: Understanding and Interpreting the Trinity* (Mahwah, NJ: Paulist, 1999), 4–5.

12. Boff, *Trinity and Society*, 58.

13. Quoted in Moltmann, *The Trinity and the Kingdom*, 1.

14. Ibid., 9 (emphasis in the original).

15. Alvin F. Kimel, ed., *This Is My Name Forever: The Trinity and Gender Language for God* (Downers Grove, IL: InterVarsity, 2001).

16. Miroslav Volf, *After Our Likeness: The Church as the Image of the Trinity* (Grand Rapids: Eerdmans, 1998).

17. Lesslie Newbigin, *The Open Secret*, rev. ed. (Grand Rapids: Eerdmans, 1995).

18. Paul Fiddes, *Participating in God: A Pastoral Doctrine of the Trinity* (Louisville: Westminster John Knox, 2000).

19. Miroslav Volf, *Exclusion and Embrace: A Theological Exploration of Identity, Otherness, and Reconciliation* (Nashville: Abingdon, 1996).

20. M. Douglas Meeks, *God the Economist: The Doctrine of God and Political Economy* (Minneapolis: Fortress Press, 1989).

21. Joseph Bracken, *The Triune Symbol: Persons, Process, and Community* (Lanham, MD: University Press of America, 1985).

22. David S. Cunningham, "The Trinity," in *The Cambridge Companion to Postmodern Theology*, ed. Kevin J. Vanhoozer (Cambridge: Cambridge University Press, 2003), 186–202.

23. Roger Corless and Paul F. Knitter, eds., *Buddhist Emptiness and Christian Trinity: Essays and Explorations* (Mahwah, NJ: Paulist, 1990).

24. Risto Jukko, *Trinitarian Theology in Christian-Muslim Encounters: Theological Foundations of the Work of the French Roman Catholic Church's Secretariat for Relations with Islam* (Helsinki: Luther-Agricola-Society, 2001).

25. Raimundo Panikkar, *The Trinity and the Religious Experience of Man: Icon-*

Person-Mystery (Maryknoll, NY: Orbis/London: Darton, Longman & Todd, 1973),

26. Jung Young Lee, *The Trinity in Asian Perspective* (Nashville: Abingdon, 1996).

27. S. Mark Heim, *The Depth of the Riches: A Trinitarian Theology of Religious Ends* (Grand Rapids: Eerdmans, 2001); Gavin D'Costa, *The Meeting of Religions and the Trinity* (Maryknoll, NY: Orbis, 2000). For a critical dialogue with these and similar proposals, see Veli-Matti Kärkkäinen, *Trinity and Religious Pluralism: The Doctrine of the Trinity in Christian Theology of Religions* (Aldershot, Hampshire, UK: Ashgate, 2004).

28. See, further, Marjorie Hewitt Suchocki, *Divinity and Diversity: A Christian Affirmation of Religious Pluralism* (Nashville: Abingdon, 2003).

29. For a recent identification of patterns or "models," consult Stephen R. Holmes, *The Quest for the Trinity: The Doctrine of God in Scripture, History, and Modernity* (Downers Grove, IL: InterVarsity, 2012), ch. 1. See also the useful compendium of essays by four trinitarian scholars in Jason S. Sexton, ed., *Two Views on the Doctrine of the Trinity* (Grand Rapids: Zondervan, 2014).

30. Stanley J. Grenz, *The Social God and Relational Self: A Trinitarian Theology of the Imago Dei* (Louisville: Westminster John Knox, 2001), 34.

31. Karl Barth, *Church Dogmatics*, ed. Geoffrey William Bromiley and Thomas Forsyth Torrance, trans. G. W. Bromiley (Edinburgh: T&T Clark, 1956–1975) [hereafter: CD]. Indeed, *Church Dogmatics* comes in three parts and thirteen part-volumes, totaling almost ten thousand pages. Written until his death in 1968, the tome was not yet fully finished! For a detailed exposition and assessment of Barth's doctrine of the Trinity, see Kärkkäinen, *Trinity*, ch. 5; Grenz, *Rediscovering the Triune God*, 34–55.

32. Barth, CD I/1:296 (italics in text).

33. Subheading in Barth, CD I/1:304.

34. The epigraph to ibid., §8 (295), reads: "God's Word is God Himself in His revelation. For God reveals Himself as the Lord and according to Scripture this signifies for the concept of revelation that God Himself in unimpaired unity yet also in unimpaired distinction is Revealer, Revelation, and Revealedness."

35. Alar Laats, *Doctrines of the Trinity in Eastern and Western Theologies: A Study with Special Reference to K. Barth and V. Lossky* (Frankfurt am Main: Peter Lang, 1999), 25.

36. Barth, CD I/1:426.

37. For a detailed exposition and assessment, see Kärkkäinen, *Trinity*, ch. 6; Grenz, *Rediscovering the Triune God*, 55–71.

38. Ted Peters, *God as Trinity: Relationality and Temporality in Divine Life* (Louisville: Westminster John Knox, 1993), 96–103.

39. Rahner, *The Trinity*, 22 (italics in text).

40. For a reliable exposition, see Roger E. Olson and Christopher A. Hall, *The Trinity* (Grand Rapids: Eerdmans, 2002), 98.

41. Peters, *God as Trinity*, 96–97.

42. For an introduction to the Eastern mystical and apophatic approach, see Vladimir Lossky, *The Mystical Theology of the Eastern Church* (Crestwood, NY: St. Vladimir's Seminary Press, 1976), 7–22.

43. Ibid., ch. 3. For a helpful discussion of the trinitarian traditions in the East, see Boris Bobrinskoy, *The Mystery of the Trinity: Trinitarian Experience and Vision in the Biblical and Patristic Tradition*, trans. Anthony P. Gythiel (Crestwood, NY: St. Vladimir's Seminary Press, 1999).

44. Lossky, *Mystical Theology*, 58–59.

45. Ibid., 86–88.

46. Vladimir Lossky, *Orthodox Theology: An Introduction*, trans. Ian and Ihita Kesarcodi-Watson (Crestwood, NY: St. Vladimir's Seminary Press, 1978), 39, 48 respectively.

47. For a detailed exposition and assessment, see Kärkkäinen, *Trinity*, ch. 7; Grenz, *Rediscovering the Triune God*, 131–46.

48. John Zizioulas, *Being as Communion: Studies in Personhood and the Church*, trans. John Meyendorff (Crestwood, NY: St. Vladimir's Seminary Press, 1997 [1985]), 16 (italics in text).

49. Ibid., 15 (italics in text).

50. Wolfhart Pannenberg, *Systematic Theology*, vol. 1, trans. Geoffrey W. Bromiley (Grand Rapids: Eerdmans, 1991), 1. For a succinct discussion of Pannenberg's method in light of his overall theology, see Stanley J. Grenz, *Reason for Hope: The Systematic Theology of Wolfhart Pannenberg* (New York: Oxford University Press, 1990), ch. 1.

51. For a detailed exposition and assessment, see Kärkkäinen, *Trinity*, ch. 9; Grenz, *Rediscovering the Triune God*, 88–106.

52. Pannenberg, *Systematic Theology*, 1:268; so also 1:304–5.

53. Subheading in ibid., 1:308.

54. The detailed discussion can be found in ibid., 1:308–27 particularly.

55. Peters, *God as Trinity*, 135–42.

56. Pannenberg, *Systematic Theology*, 1:313 (emphases mine). The ideas of self-distinction and dependency among the three persons also leads Pannenberg to revise traditional terminology as it relates to the coming of the Son and the Spirit. Instead of the "generation" of the Son and the "procession" of the Spirit, Pannenberg uses terms that suggest self-distinction and mutuality such as "handing over," "giving back," "glorification," "(voluntary) submission," and so forth.

57. Ibid., 1:334–35, 366–67. As explained in Kärkkäinen, "The Trinitarian Doctrines of Jürgen Moltmann and Wolfhart Pannenberg in the Context of Contemporary Discussion," in *Cambridge Companion to Trinity*, ed. Peter C. Phan (Cambridge: Cambridge University Press, 2010), 233–34. Indeed, the way he ensures unity is way more complex than that, but the basic idea still holds; for details, see ibid., 233–35, and literature therein.

58. Pannenberg, *Systematic Theology*, 1:389 (emphases mine).

59. Ibid., 332–33.

60. Ibid., 331.

61. For a detailed exposition and assessment, see Kärkkäinen, *Trinity*, ch. 8; Grenz, *Rediscovering the Triune God*, 73–88.

62. Moltmann, *Trinity and the Kingdom*, 10–16, at 10.

63. Ibid., 132.

64. Ibid., 19.

65. Jürgen Moltmann, *The Crucified God: The Cross of Christ as the Foundation and Criticism of Christian Theology*, trans. R. A. Wilson and John Bowden (Minneapolis: Fortress Press, 1993 [1973]).

66. This doctrine is routinely linked with "immutability," that is, God is not able to change (because that would imply that in the future, there is a state that is "better" than what God is today—or that there might be a state which implies that today God is "worse" than in the days to come).

67. Moltmann, *Trinity and the Kingdom*, 21.

68. Moltmann, *Crucified God*, 222.

69. Moltmann, *Trinity and the Kingdom*, xvi; so also, e.g., 78.

70. Moltmann, *Crucified God*, 244.

71. Ibid., 243.

72. Moltmann, *Trinity and the Kingdom*, 119.

73. Also called "eschatological [trinitarian] panentheism." See Richard Bauckham, *The Theology of Jürgen Moltmann* (London: T&T Clark, 1995), 185–87, 242–44, among others; Grenz, *Rediscovering the Triune God*, 82–84.

74. See especially Jürgen Moltmann, *God in Creation: A New Theology of Creation and the Spirit of God*, trans. Margaret Kohl (Minneapolis: Fortress Press, 1993 [1985]), ch. 4.

75. Ibid., 75.

76. Moltmann, *Trinity and the Kingdom*, 106.

77. Ibid., 160.

78. Ibid., 161.

79. Ibid., 148–50.

80. Ibid., 150.

81. Ibid., 149.

82. Ibid., 161.

83. Pannenberg, *Systematic Theology*, 1:330.

84. "Monotheism is monarchism." Moltmann, *Trinity and the Kingdom*, 191.

85. Ibid., 164–65.

86. Ibid., 19; see also 17–18 and 191–92.

87. Ibid., 71.

88. This is developed in Moltmann, *The Church in the Power of the Spirit: A Contribution to Messianic Ecclesiology*, trans. Margaret Kohl (Minneapolis: Fortress Press, 1993).

89. Moltmann, *Trinity and the Kingdom*, 202.

90. "Even with all their diversity, feminist, womanist, and *mujerista* theologies have one thing in common: they make the liberation of women central to the theological task." Mary McClintock Fulkerson, "Feminist Theology," in *The Cambridge Companion to Postmodern Theology*, ed. Kevin J. Vanhoozer (Cambridge: Cambridge University Press, 2003), 109.

91. See the section "Destabilizing the Patriarchal Divinity," in Wonhee Anne Joh, *Heart of the Cross: A Postcolonial Christology* (Louisville: Westminster John Knox, 2006), 91–101.

92. Sallie McFague, *Models of God: Theology for an Ecological, Nuclear Age* (Philadelphia: Fortress Press, 1987), 31–36 and passim. See also her earlier programmatic *Metaphorical Theology: Models of God in Religious Language* (Philadelphia: Fortress Press, 1982).

93. Elizabeth A. Johnson, *She Who Is: The Mystery of God in Feminist Theological Discourse* (New York: Crossroad, 1995), 76.

94. Ibid., 241–43, at 241.

95. Ibid., 47–57.

96. Ibid., 55.

97. Ibid., 44.

98. Ibid., 5.

99. For a detailed exposition and assessment, see Kärkkäinen, *Trinity*, ch. 13; Grenz, *Rediscovering the Triune God*, 164–81.

100. Johnson, *She Who Is*, pt. 3.

101. Ibid., 83.

102. Ibid.

103. Ibid., 228–30.

104. Ibid., 233–36.

105. Catherine Mowry LaCugna, "Baptismal Formula, Feminist Objections, and Trinitarian Theology," *Journal of Ecumenical Studies* 26, no. 2 (Spring 1989): 243.

106. Ibid., 244–45.

107. For a detailed exposition and assessment, see Kärkkäinen, *Trinity*, ch. 19; Grenz, *Rediscovering the Triune God*, 118–31.

108. Boff, *Trinity and Society*, heading for "Introduction," 1.

109. Heading for ch. 1 in ibid.

110. Ibid., 11.

111. Ibid., 13–16, at 15.

112. Ibid., 20.

113. Ibid., 133.

114. Ibid., 32.

115. Ibid., 3.

116. Ibid., 120–21. For the feminine characteristics of each of the trinitarian persons, see 170–71 (Father), 182–83 (Son), and 196–98 (Spirit).

117. This list builds on and expands Kärkkäinen, "Trinitarian Doctrines of Jürgen Moltmann and Wolfhart Pannenberg," in Phan, ed., *Cambridge Companion to Trinity*, 412.

118. A promising new input in contemporary trinitarian theology comes from the analytic theology movement. For recent contributions, see Thomas H. McCall, *Which Trinity? Whose Monotheism? Philosophical and Systematic Theologians on the Metaphysics of Trinitarian Theology* (Grand Rapids: Eerdmans, 2010); William Hasker, *Metaphysics and the Tri-Personal God* (Oxford: Oxford University Press, 2013). One of the first monographs to appear in this genre is David Brown, *The Divine Trinity* (London: Duckworth, 1985).

119. For details, see Kärkkäinen, *Trinity*, chs. 24, 25, and 26, including rich bibliographic guidance.

120. For a detailed discussion, see ibid., chs. 21, 22, and 23, including rich bibliographic guidance.

121. For details, see ibid., chs. 18, 19, and 20, including rich bibliographic guidance.

122. Some of those contributions have been identified above in this chapter regarding Christianity's relation to Islam, Buddhism, Hinduism, and Confucianism.

123. See, e.g., John Polkinghorne, ed., *The Trinity and the Entangled World: Relationality in Physical Science and Theology* (Grand Rapids: Eerdmans, 2010).

Scripture Index

Subject Index